SMART,
SIMPLE
DESIGN

SMART, SIMPLE DESIGN

Using Variety Effectiveness to Reduce Total Cost and Maximize Customer Selection

G. D. Galsworth

omneo

AN IMPRINT OF OLIVER WIGHT PUBLICATIONS, INC.

85 ALLEN MARTIN DRIVE

ESSEX JUNCTION, VERMONT 05452

Copyright © 1994 by Gwendolyn D. Galsworth

Published by Oliver Wight Publications, Inc.

Oliver Wight Publications books may be purchased for educational,
business, or sales promotional use. For information, please call
or write: Special Sales Department, Oliver Wight Publications,
Inc., 85 Allen Martin Drive, Essex Junction, VT 05452.
Telephone: (800) 343-0625 or (802) 878-8161; FAX: (802) 878-3384.

Library of Congress Catalog Card Number: 93-061776

ISBN: 0-939246-62-7

Text design by Irving Perkins Associates

Printed on acid-free paper.

Manufactured in the United States of America.

2   4   6   8   10   9   7   5   3   1

To my dear Mother, Geraldine M. Galsworth,
source of inspiration, strength, and joy.
Thirty-nine years young has never looked more beautiful on anyone.

And to the Unity that is God,
Who makes all parts—however diverse and however various—One.

Acknowledgments

Smart, Simple Design is a book of two journeys—the first to discover the VEP methodology, the second to discover the book itself. In truth, the totality of these two streams of effort had many creators, those people who helped me find the principles, concepts, and techniques of the variety effectiveness approach, and those who assisted me with words, images, and form so the knowledge could be structured into a book and conveyed to you, the reader. People gave freely: information, clarification, verification, validation, extension, implication, illustration. And support. I know that I could not have done it without them. I want them to know that too.

First among these remarkable people is Dave Reis, president of United Electric Controls Company (UE) in Watertown, Massachusetts. His quiet leadership allowed VEP to take seed and take root at UE. I am also grateful for Dave's willingness to let me model some aspects of the book's prototype "struggling" company (Parts Unlimited Inc.) after UE, an organization of exceptional assets.

Another person at UE whose contribution was invaluable is Bruce Hamilton, VP of Operations. Bruce is a visionary. He saw the need for variety control and reduction as a distinct issue at UE and put out the call for my assistance. I had been working with UE for several years already and was continually amazed at the way the company kept shifting to improve. These shifts were invariably linked to specific methodologies the enterprise had learned, adapted, and applied: kanban, improvement teams, action centers, JIT, one-piece flow, work cells, suggestion systems, customer/supplier partnerships, and policy deployment through the X-Type Matrix. The company had established itself as a leader in best practices. It came as no surprise when UE won the 1990 National Shigeo Shingo Prize for Manufacturing Excellence.

Still it was not enough. Parts count was ballooning, and there was a complexity in the organization that defied efforts to define it, let alone unravel it. The old answers were not working, and the company's march toward manufacturing excellence seemed stalled. Bruce knew a new solution to the inventory problem had to be found, one that would allow the company: (1) to identify the problem more accurately, (2) to get to its true causes or triggers, (3) to eliminate or drastically reduce parts count, and (4) to make sure it didn't come back.

In 1991, Bruce's search led him to *Variety Reduction Program: A Production Strategy for Product Diversification* (Cambridge, Mass.: Productivity Press, 1988), a book written by Toshio Suzue and Akira Kohdate which provided a fresh perspective on parts inventory. Bruce organized a weekly lunchtime study group, charged with the mission: Understand the book; then implement it at UE. Volunteers began meeting. After about two months, the group had grasped the importance of the concept but was flagging in terms of application. As is the case with many books from Japan, the authors provided plenty of why-to but far less how-to. Bruce called me in. The journey of discovery was about to begin.*

Bruce, the study group, and I were quickly joined by many UE employees as a series of teams were formed around the central issues of runaway variety. The VEP methodology and *Smart, Simple Design* were born of that effort. My heartfelt appreciation to Bruce Hamilton for his discernment, and for his contribution to the policy chapter, conceptualization of the Early Victories Team, and coining of the term "variety effectiveness," infinitely more appealing language to sales and marketing than the earlier "variety reduction."

I also thank Bruce for asking Bonnie Rafuse (former UE Training Manager) to work on the VEP project with me. Committing to myriad tasks as only she can, Bonnie's involvement in early development days was invaluable. Her resourcefulness, thoroughness, and energy kept VEP's fledgling teams on track and supported. Bonnie also headed up the

* At the time, I was the director of business development and senior consultant at Productivity Inc. (sister company to Productivity Press) and saw in Bruce's request the possibility of creating a new practice area for Productivity clients. My deep appreciation goes to Norman Bodek, president of Productivity Inc. and Productivity Press, for his discerning support of the initial project and his continuing interest in VEP after I left the company some months later.

Education and Methods Team, contributed to content development, and coordinated the entire project. I thank you, Bonnie. You were a linchpin.

Another UE pro stepped in when Bonnie left the company for new opportunities—Patricia M. Wardwell. Pat is a star! She is sharp as a tack, politic, and widely experienced in manufacturing. Her pursuit of the truth (yes, there is truth in manufacturing) is relentless. For well over a year, we joined forces to continue surfacing the VEP methodology. Then the book took over. Through a blizzard of phone calls and faxes, at her UE desk and at her kitchen table, Pat scoured the pages and kept me on track. Especially during the final weeks of writing, when book deadlines and details were running my life, I "blessed" her name many times. Pat, thank you. And now, in Pat's "spare time," she trains and consults on VEP.

Maureen Hamilton also joined in the support of the project at the midpoint, and was often the only person who could find missing archives and elusive people (like her husband, Bruce). Her patience, competence, and good humor are legendary. If it could be done, found, or gotten, Maureen did. Thanks, Maureen, for the support and all those great laughs.

I am grateful to so many people at UE. Thanks to members of what became known as the "3-View Analysis" team: Arthur Barter, Levon Khatchadourian, Joe LePage, Aram Minassian, John Mondello, Berg Narjarian, Fernando Rego, Ed Velosa, and Gerry Yuskauskas, its fearless leader. And thanks to members of all the other VEP teams: Guy Alger, Gladys Appleby, Cindy Barter, Frank Barter, Tom Brennan, John Burke, Carlos Chaves, Bill Colby, Mike Contardo, Chris Cronin, Tony Cruz, Judy DeMartin, Mark DeNovellis, Dan Fleming, Jodie Glennon, Diana Hajian, Don Holm, Chris Jaffier, Don Jones, Joe Lyons, John Machado, George McGary, Maryrose Mix, Ryta Mullen, Al Nashawaty, Charlie O'Hearn, Manny Pereira, Paul Plant, Janet Raposo, Lee Sacco, Bob Sanders, Jim Silva, Joe Silva, Joan Sampson, Dave Smith, Terry Sousa, Hieu Tran, Bud Tucker, Dave Vaughan, Allan Waugh, Dave Williams, Pat Woods, and those whom I may have overlooked by name. Thanks also to Cheryl O'Connell, for her inventiveness and laser focus in leading control point reduction. And, finally, special thanks to that dynamic duo, Bob Rando, database maestro *par excellence*, and Barbara

Murphy, for their unwavering MIS assistance—tracking part counts, running sorts and quizzes, setting up attribute fields, and on and on. Thank you UE!

I can honestly say that this book would never have been written without Patricia E. Moody. Tricia is an astute manufacturing consultant, specializing in—just about everything. She is also editor of *Target* magazine. When I told her about VEP and my work at UE, she said point blank: "This is important—you need to write this book *so I can read it!*" Immediately, Tricia put me in touch with Oliver Wight Publishing and Jim Childs. The second journey began. But Tricia did more. She made her extraordinary creative gifts and writing expertise available to the manuscript, as well as her cogent insights into the world of business and profit. Tricia, I am deeply indebted to you for all you have done. Thank you.

John R. Clegg contributed immeasurably to the book through its art work and his computer sorcery. Imaginative, persistent, and immensely skilled, John is head of graphics for the Technology and Product Development Directorate at Arthur D. Little but still found time (on the weekends) to assist on the book. My thanks to you, John, for your beautiful work and to your wife, Jaimie and little Ian, for letting me steal so much of their time with you in the last weeks of the manuscript.

Business friends and associates helped with information and encouragement: Clark R. Shea and Stanley V. Mickens of Hamilton Standard; Stan Boliver, Connie Dyer, Karen Jones, and Chet Marchiwinski of Productivity Press and Productivity Inc., and their esteemed president, Norman Bodek; Joseph B. Pine II of Strategic Horizons; Geoffrey Boothroyd and Winston Knight of Boothroyd Dewhurst; William F. Hyde and Barry Levine of Brisch, Brin & Associates; R. Scott Leckie of International TechneGroup Inc.; Akira Kohdate and Toshio Suzue; A. Everett Instein; Nathan W. Young, Scott M. Whitehurst, and Ted Wozniak; Paul Turner of Marathon Products; Mark D. Bailey and Robert A. Williams of Hewlett-Packard; David M. Anderson of the University of California, Berkeley; Giorgio Merli, Paolo Mommo, and Roberto Mannanicci of Galgano & Associates (Milan); Daniel Verney; Camilla England of Inside Tracking Publishing; Sally Schwager of Charles E. Tuttle, Japan; Robert M. Williamson of Strategic Work Systems; Nicholas I. Vanderstoop of General Motors of Canada, Ltd.; Robert W. Hall of the Association of

Manufacturing Excellence; Brian Maskell of Brian Maskell and Associates; Beverly McCarthy of Ashford McCarthy Resources/QCI; James A. Johnson of Civacon; Manuel Tubino of C.O.R.F.O.-InTech Chile; Oscar Harasic of the Organization of American States; Kosroff Adanalian of Kosroff Jewelry; Jennifer Smith and Mona M. Ploesser of Oliver Wight Publishing, and Linda Ripinsky of Ripinsky & Company.

My heartfelt thanks go also to: my editor and publisher, Jim Childs, who masterfully found the right balance of distance and support to, in the first case, allow me to find the book, and in the second, finish it; J. Thomas Duffy for his untiring efforts in support of the manuscript, even as he furiously wrote his own screenplays; my brother, Gary L. Galsworth, for paying the bill on time—most of the time; my niece and nephew, Ondine Galsworth Atkinson and Dany Galsworth, whose lives are shining reminders to me of the beauty of expression.

Every writer knows that dealing with the technical portion of a book is only half the story. The other half is keeping one's spirit whole and body together. For their miraculous help in this, I am deeply grateful to: Dawn Bothie, Swami Chetanananda, Vivian Everett, Judy Harmony, Mataare, William Mueller, Margo Schmidt, David Sollars, and David Whyte.

And finally my eternal gratitude to Samual N. Bear, Anderson Merlin, and Philip Hylos for their creative encouragement, heartfelt support, and unwavering guidance. Truly, this book would never have been started or completed without them.

GWENDOLYN D. GALSWORTH
September 1994

CONTENTS

FOREWORD

by Bruce E. Hamilton

In 1987, when United Electric (UE) first began using the inventions of the Toyota Production System, we focused narrowly on our factory, seeking to eliminate waste from the production process. We were, as Shigeo Shingo put it, "constructively dissatisfied" with our production capability and determined to find a better way to manufacture. For the next three years, our success in reducing inventory and improving service was so great that it consumed our attention. As we examined and understood the huge waste from overproduction, for example, that had been created as we filled our stockrooms with large lots of partially completed product, we reduced lots from "nice round numbers" to the minimum order quantity. Then, as quick changeover techniques were employed, lot sizes were further reduced. Assemblies, previously produced in lots of 1,000 and then sorted for later use, were now triggered for production by a system that dictated that we build only what was needed, when it was needed, and in the smallest quantity determined by setup times.

All improvement could be measured by time saved: A reduction of the total elapsed time to fill a customer's order, a reduction in product development time to qualify a new supplier. Every invention we employed was directed to that end: Make the process go faster by eliminating waste. By 1990, our stockrooms had been eliminated and inventory had been reduced by 65 percent—many millions of dollars. Lead time dropped from months to days and perceived service was at an all-time high. Cellular production reduced flow distance from miles to feet and created a wholly new set of team and problem-solving skills required for production to work in a new way. For those of us in Production, this was an exciting time in our careers. We were changing the way things were done, and we were changing ourselves in the process.

Just when it seemed things couldn't get any better, they *didn't* get any better. Concepts such as kanban, cellular manufacturing, single-minute exchange of dies, and *poka-yoke* had produced huge early results, but now were considered the norm, the basis for daily production. And on that basis, improvement leveled off. Inventory dropped so far, and then stopped dropping; likewise with lead times. While the cycle of improvement is never-ending, the tools used in that improvement cycle tend over time to become maintenance tools rather than improvement tools. What further tools could we identify to break through the improvement plateau?

Once we had stripped away some of the grossest forms of waste in our business—large inventories, useless material handling and storage equipment, even excess buildings—we began to see a major new opportunity for improvement. There was a huge cost, both in time and money, for every part in our system that was *separate* from the functional cost of the part. In Production, we had learned how to identify waste in seven forms as taught by Toyota: Storage, transportation, overproduction, unnecessary processing, motion, defects, and waiting. In 1991, UE began working with Dr. Galsworth to establish a systematic method for identifying and eliminating an "eighth" waste—*unwarranted variety*.

Through the use of SMED (single-minute-exchange-of-dies), we reduced many lot sizes to one—but even for that one piece, we had to activate our entire production system. Now there appeared to be a means for reducing the variety costs associated with many parts by simply eliminating the part. This, in fact, we had addressed in a piecemeal fashion from the early days of our improvement process. However, in the absence of a clear method for measuring and identifying the trade-offs associated with variety—and more important, for *understanding* the root causes of variety—we seemed to be adding new variety at least at as great a rate as we were removing old variety. With thousands of parts and processes in our production system, the complexity of the problem dictated a new method for solution. This has evolved today into what Dr. Galsworth calls *variety effectiveness*.

Dr. Galsworth's book is the first thorough treatment of a method that can systematically identify the waste of needless variety. For older businesses especially, this book provides a blueprint for cutting back the mass of parts and processes resulting from years of product proliferation. But every business, established or start-up, can benefit from the methodology that extends the power of the Toyota Production System beyond production and into the design and development process. Most variety in part design, product structure, and process selection does not result from a customer's need, but from a series of internal policies and behaviors that needlessly complicate the production process. These include cost-accounting systems that actually *reward* part and process proliferation, engineering mores that eschew the use of previously developed designs, variety resulting from technology change, and inadequate design tools that actually make it easier for designers to develop a part from scratch than to search for an already-existing part. The customer is not in the equation.

The key benefit to designers in the method developed by Dr. Galsworth is that it supports broad selection for the customer while reducing variety in the product design in a manner transparent to the customer. By understanding which variety is negative, engineers and designers can contribute to profitability and service in a way that was not previously possible. VEP's simple but powerful techniques enable engineers to change the way they work, to work faster, and to develop products of exceptional selection that meet individual customer needs without adding layers of complication and cost to the production process. Dr. Galsworth's detailed process for improvement arms designers with a systematic method for identifying, classifying, and reducing unneeded variety.

For product marketers, the Variety Effectiveness Process® represents an alternative to the all-too-common process of product-line trimming and selection retrenchment. By minimizing the cost and time of new product development, VEP brings more new products to customers sooner. And it revitalizes old products through its dramatic cost-reduction potential.

For Production, the benefits are reduced part and process complexity, reduced equipment expense, reduced training expense, reduced material handling, improved turns, less stockouts, and fewer defects.

And for corporate management, there is the powerful message:

Corporate structure mirrors product structure. Simplify the first and the latter will follow. For United Electric, VEP has offered the opportunity for a second wave of improvement. I view variety effectiveness as an approaching revolution in the product development process. Its effects will touch all aspects of an organization's competitiveness and financial well-being. Dr. Galsworth's book is an excellent place to begin this process.

BRUCE E. HAMILTON
Vice President, Operations
United Electric Controls Company
Watertown, Massachusetts

Vice-Chairman
Shigeo Shingo Prize for Manufacturing Excellence

PART ONE

The Dilemma: The Need to De-Complicate

CHAPTER ONE

THE CONSUMING AGE

Relentless Pressures of a Voracious Marketplace

The management challenge of the 1990s is to reduce costs—and increase the perceived value of the product.

—ARTHUR L. KELLY,
PRIVATE INVESTOR AND DIRECTOR
OF DEERE, BMW, AND NALCO
CHEMICAL*

MARKETPLACE EXPLOSION

- Started in a garage in 1963, Nike Shoes sold only one kind of running shoe during its first four years of business. In 1967, a second shoe design was added. Nike now introduces an entirely new product line—over 300 styles—every six months.
- In the fourteen years between 1913 and 1927, an automobile bought from the Ford Motor Company meant only one thing: the Model-T. Today buyers can select a Ford from among literally dozens of models and hundreds of options.
- The opening of the Soviet bloc nations, China, and other modernizing Asian countries nearly quadrupled the world's available

* *Business Week*, "Stuck! How Companies Cope When They Can't Raise Prices," November 15, 1993, p. 148.

consumer market, with a potential increase in spending unparalleled in the annals of commerce. Motorola sold 8 million pagers in 1993 in China alone, up from 100,000 in 1990.

- High-tech products are hitting the market like hot cakes off the griddle, with life cycles collapsing faster than anyone can track. A short five years ago, you could count on a thirty-six-month product development cycle from concept to production. At this book's writing, eight months is more the norm—but products can come into *and* go out of the market in three months. Like fresh fruit, they have an increasingly short shelf life.

These are the realities of the market in the 1990s. More than at any previous time, the market is driven by the consumer's demand for choice. Customers are in the driver's seat, and they know it. They are voting with their pocketbooks in unprecedented numbers. And companies are scrambling to plug into them with expanded products. In 1990, 228,000 *new* retail products were introduced in the United States. The grocery stores and supermarkets of America now stock approximately 400,000 different items—brand names and generic. The marketplace is exploding.

The evolution of disposable diapers is a good case in point. Throwaway diapers, which made their debut in the early 1960s with a single universal one-size-fits-all product, now come in dozens of differentiated designs related to—well everything: fastening tapes, absorbency, softness, layer thinness, waist and leg bands, decorative designs, and special padding "where boys and girls need it most." These features are further segmented by gender, age, size, and packaging. Each of the three leading makers, Pampers, Luvs, and Huggies, carries nearly 50 product codes, with new competitors constantly making bids for Mom's dollars. Even horseshoes are proliferating, with over 600 different types, each with its own shape, width, and weight, and 50 kinds of nails. As vividly seen in the Nike and automobile examples above, even as product variations explode, product life cycles are collapsing.

Competing through new products has created a whole new set of rules. In the 1990s, winning today only means that you get a chance to play in the next round tomorrow. This is, however, not just a time of widening consumer choice—challenge enough for companies. The fact that the customer is king is the good news. The sobering news is that this is also a time of low pricing.

In the 1800s, *product availability* created the marketplace: If you could get it there, you could sell it. By the turn of the century, *price* or *affordability* defined the public's buying patterns, only to be replaced 20 years later by *choice* or *product differentiation*. In the 1970s, *quality* or *performance* surfaced as the principal consumer yardstick. Then, in the late eighties, quality linked up with *service* for the promise of total customer satisfaction. And that is just what consumers now want and often get—total availability, choice, quality, performance, *and* service. But there is more: They want these at ever-shrinking prices. The age of disinflation has arrived.

THE AGE OF DISINFLATION HAS ARRIVED!

Disinflation refers to a marketplace phenomenon driven by twin forces: rising product value and falling product prices. Formerly, a product's selling price was a function of cost plus an acceptable margin of profit. In the boom of the '50s and '60s, a business always had the option of absorbing its cost overruns and "improving" the bottom line by simply hiking up the price tag. Inflation—the name of that game—covered up many sins.

Those times have passed. After decades of marking up prices to cover inflationary rises in cost, manufacturers find themselves forced to reverse their customary pricing practices. In the face of disinflationary pressures, they must lower the price even as their costs and consumer demand soar.

Disinflation is an anomaly. A rush for products, *Business Week* reports, "normally generates pressures for higher, not lower, prices and produces higher, not lower, inflation. This time, however, the opposite is happening." Witness, the report continues, the plummeting prices in high-tech capital goods in the third quarter of 1993, which were ". . . an amazing 8.3% lower than a year earlier."* But these same falling prices produced a 20.8% rise in high-tech equipment sales for that same period. Bloody battles in the disk-drive sector reflect a similar phenomenon.

Traditional price setting (price = cost + profit) is dead. Instead companies, using a strategy known as price-targeting (also known as "design-to-price"), begin by setting a target price for a new model based on the customer's perspective, then back down into cost. The pressures to cut costs become extraordinary.

So the message is clear: Your opportunities in today's turbulent marketplace are truly unprecedented—*if* you can get and keep your costs down. Unfortunately, many organizations are blazing trails into this new competitive wilderness armed with weapons from the dark ages. Not only are they continually exposed to attacks from low-cost rivals, but their own business practices are making their survival, let alone their success, very iffy.

THE CHALLENGE

In the new world of disinflation, cost-cutting is, of course, essential. . . . The price a company charges is . . . the culmination of every decision it has made along the line. Without the cloak of inflation, all those decisions are directly exposed to the ruthless pressures of the marketplace.**

Disinflationary forces are setting a new cost-cutting agenda for even the most successful companies, a challenge made even more demanding due to high levels of product segmentation and international competition in the marketplace. Organizations that are leaders in product variety and

---

* *Business Week*, "Editorials: Welcome to the Age of Disinflation," November 15, 1993, p. 186.
  ** *Business Week*, November 15, 1993, p. 147.

product innovation stand to be the greatest losers. The very variety that won them markets during the last decade could sink them in this one. Many of these companies do not realize that they could become victims of their own growth.

The fact is: Even when design-to-price products create a consumer demand that makes a company's market presence unassailable outside the organization, the same products can create complication and confusion on the inside. Supporting an endless stream of varying products can trigger a chain of events within the enterprise that can burden its infrastructure to the breaking point.

To a large extent, this torrent of new products is the stepchild of widening capabilities in computer technology, at best a double-edged sword. One edge gives a company the ability to churn out new products in unprecedented number and variety, offering customers a selection and allowing the company entry into markets previously beyond reach. But the same computer revolution has released a flood of complexity. Leaps in product variety steadily and inexorably swell parts inventories and production processes, multiplying geometrically the myriad supplementary activities that support products—material handling; dies, tooling, fixtures, and their changeover and maintenance; management information systems (MIS) and drawings upkeep; and all the transactions (called *control points*) that underlie these. This buildup happens gradually, product by product and part by part, while the overall system makes a series of barely discernible micro-accommodations. The complication and congestion accumulate and the company begins to grind to a halt. It simply can't handle the detail.

THE SMART ORGANIZATION

Even when sales soar, the parallel expansion of organizational costs, complexity, and congestion can choke the infrastructure. Profits take a nosedive, and the company flounders.

The smart organization, by contrast, understands the dangers of unchecked variety proliferation and takes concrete steps to either prevent it or, if already in the throes, get it under control and then reduced.

THE ICEBERG EFFECT

Like an iceberg that has two-thirds of its mass underwater, most of the negative consequences of mushrooming variation are hidden from view (see Figure 1.1). Many companies that appear to thrive today may be on their way to a crash because they lack the know-why and know-how to prevent or control these disastrous effects. Whether they go belly-up quickly or sink slowly and painfully, it will be because, first of all, they misnamed the problem by calling it "deteriorating profits" or excess inventory; and secondly (but linked to the first), because the "solutions" to those conditions are not designed to address the real problem. Whatever salutary inroads may be made through the methods and strategies of lean production and continuous improvement (and they are considerable), these will not, after a certain point, help the company confront the problem *underneath* the production system. The problem is not the production system. It is not quality, service, or delivery. And it certainly is not the customer. The problem is the product itself.

Flawed assumptions about product cost and the effects of product variation on profit, complicated product structures, runaway part numbers, a computer classification system that obstructs engineers from easy access to existing part specifications—all conspire to make the rush for new products tantamount to corporate suicide for many maturing companies. Unfortunately, many young, up-and-coming enterprises may also be on their way to a shipwreck.

FIGURE 1.1. Danger! The Real Problem Remains Hidden

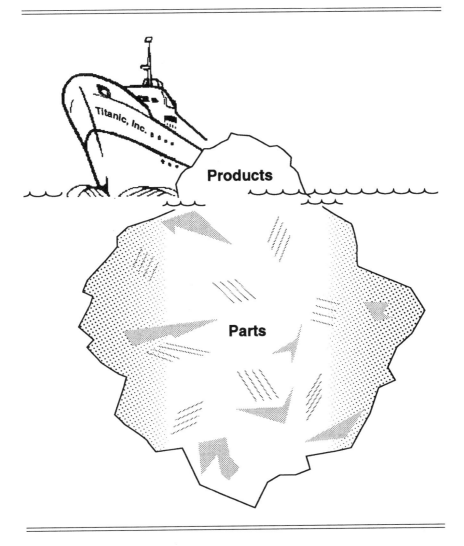

VARIETY EFFECTIVENESS

The purpose of this book is to inform organizations of the dangers of uncontrolled product proliferation, delineate its symptoms, spell out causes, and prescribe a cure. The cure is *VEP: The Variety Effectiveness Process*®—a systematic process for preventing or reducing unwarranted product and parts variation while offering maximum customer selection at a least-cost sum.

VEP is an innovative *systematic* approach that enables companies to find optimal levels both of parts inventory and the processes that support it. VEP deals directly with the front-end interface between marketing and product design. It works to de-complicate the organizational infrastructure and cut total costs while developing exceptional selection for customers.

The process includes a systematic assessment of the company's market offerings, the structure of its products, and the range of variation within each type of part in its parts inventory. In implementing VEP, a company can reduce its parts inventories by as much as 40 percent by modularizing and streamlining product structures and by eliminating or simplifying parts or making them multifunctional. As a direct result, the company also sees impressive reductions in the number of production processes, in associated tooling, fixturing, and dies, and in the paperwork and computer transactions that support all phases of the product development and production process.

Through specific step-by-step procedures and a series of hands-on tools, VEP helps companies find and eradicate the causes of unwarranted variety in engineering, marketing, MIS, purchasing, accounting and support, and operations. The bottom-line impact of the Variety Effectiveness Process for both mature and start-up manufacturers can be dramatic and can be achieved in a relatively short period of time.

VEP empowers companies so they're able to grapple with the real challenges and opportunities of the marketplace. In this period of exploding consumer demand and disinflationary pricing, VEP answers the central question of every organization: How can we continue to capture customers with products they delight in, at a *cost* low enough to set a *price* low enough to compete—*and* still make an acceptable profit and grow? This book answers that question.

The VEP process is very powerful. Even more powerful is the concept of *variety effectiveness.* That's what we really want companies to get. When they do, whether they adopt our improvement approach or invent one of their own, they will have recognized the danger, see it as it is embedded in their own organization—and want to do something about it. We believe awareness of this problem is the true power lever for change.

When an organization is aware of and operationalizes the principles and tools of variety effectiveness, it knows that simply introducing exciting new products—products that delight the customer—does not go far enough. New products and a commanding market share will not make your company more profitable *unless* the variety you offer in those products is *effective.*

Effective variety is the balance point between variety that adds value (we call this positive variety) and variety that adds cost (called negative variety). The first is customer-driven, the second is internally triggered. Effective variety is a continually shifting balance point, moving more and more toward the positive pole as the company lessens its load of negative variety and augment the positive kind.

The result is *smart, simple design. Smart* because it capitalizes on the best of the company's existing designs and parts, standardizing, modularizing, and integrating as much as possible, even as it maximizes customer selection. *Simple* because it confronts unneeded variation in products, parts, and production processes and systematically attacks policies and practices in Accounting, Purchasing, Design Engineering, Operations, and MIS (management information systems) that promote negative variety and eat away at profits. *Smart, simple design* is the answer to the question: How do we build profits in the face of widening customer demand for increasing product value at diminishing product prices?

ABOUT THIS BOOK—
CHAPTER BY CHAPTER

The goal of *Smart, Simple Design*, and the VEP method it presents, is to help you identify opportunities to simplify your company, dismantle the levels of complexity that have taken root there, and, once done, prevent their recurrence.

To do this, the book is in three parts. The first, "The Dilemma: The Need to De-Complicate," describes the origins of the problem and why it is important to do something about it. This chapter (1), "The Consuming Age: Relentless Pressures of a Voracious Marketplace," talks about the turbulence of the marketplace and the urgent need to cut costs. Chapter 2, "On the Horns of the Dilemma," looks at the symptoms of unwarranted variety and the fact that most current improvement strategies can have only a limited impact on it. The third chapter, "True Cost: Product Proliferation and the Bottom Line," discusses how traditional cost accounting can mask negative variety, and presents VEP's approach to this, including its *Tri-Cost Model* and *Parts Index*. In Chapter 4, "Triggers of the Variety Explosion," the focus shifts to formal and informal policies and practices that provoke negative variety. And in the fifth and final chapter in Part One, "Hot Products: The Power of Design," we suggest ways designers and engineers can build variety effectiveness into the products they create.

The second part of the book, "VEP: The Way to De-Complicate," explains the VEP methodology. In it, we describe VEP's systematic process for reducing parts inventory and present specific principles, tools, and procedures for minimizing negative variety. The first chapter in this section (Chapter 6, "De-Complicating the Organization: Where and How to Begin") outlines how to set up the organization for a successful VEP implementation—structuring VEP teams, assessing and upgrading parts classification systems, initiating policy review and revisions, and selecting a valid starting point for product line analysis. Chapter 7, "The Heart of VEP Analysis: The Six Tools," describes a set of six engineering tools that focus the VEP analysis on tangible, measurable improvements. These tools find their context in Chapter 8, "VEP Analysis: Finding and Reducing Negative Variety," where we share the approach called "3-View Analysis," VEP's step-by-step process for identifying and reducing negative variety in marketing, product structures, and part types. In the ninth and final chapter in this section, the analysis process is applied to the reduction of production processes and control points.

The third part of the book, "The Bottom Line," returns to the big picture—the challenge of organizational complexity and the power of variety effectiveness to transform it and make it profitable. This is the subject of Chapter 10, "Designing for the Bottom Line," the final chapter of the book.

MAXIMIZING YOUR SELECTION

Smart, Simple Design is structured with two different audiences in mind. Part One (Chapters 1 through 5) is especially for CEOs, CFOs, and VPs. The message to them is: Negative variety is killing your company. This first part of the book tells *why* change is needed. Part Two (Chapters 6 through 9) is meant to have special appeal to managers, middle managers, designers and engineers, operations managers, marketers, and finance people—people who see the big picture, deal with its effects every day, and are looking for ways they can impact it positively and pro-actively on an operational level. They want to know the *how* of the change that is needed because they are likely to be the ones to implement it.

Part Three, (Chapter 10) is the wrap, with important guidelines on implementation and reminders on the overall goal—increased profitability—and the dangers of ignoring the challenge of effective variety. It is a short chapter and a useful one. At the close of the book, you will find a Resource Section on VEP training, consulting and software support, and the VEP software package as well as a glossary of terms and an index.

Variety effectiveness is a vision of the change to come, and the VEP method is designed to facilitate that vision. In *Smart, Simple Design*, vision and method are joined to provide you with the insight you need to want to make the change, along with the tools and process you'll require to get on with it and begin to realize variety effectiveness in your organization. Our wish is to leave you not just with a sense of urgency about the problems hidden in product expansion but with the conviction, ability, and desire to do something about them.

CHAPTER TWO

ON THE HORNS OF THE DILEMMA

There is at least one point in the history of any company when you have to change dramatically to rise up to the next performance level. Miss the moment and you start to decline.

—ANDREW S. GROVE
CHAIRMAN OF INTEL

PARTS UNLIMITED INC.: STORY OF A COMPANY IN TROUBLE

Several years ago, I was asked to meet with the president of a medium-sized electronics company in the Midwest, which we will call Parts Unlimited Inc. (PUI). The purpose of the meeting was to analyze a troubling condition the company was experiencing—increasing revenues and plummeting profits. The VPs of Engineering, Marketing, and Operations, along with a number of company managers, were scheduled to attend as well.

Privately established in 1932, PUI entered the switch and control business with a single breakthrough product at a time when the market for such products was just beginning to expand. An instant hit, the new product became a nationally recognized brand name within two years. In the same two years, the work force tripled, as did the square footage of its facility. Annual sales climbed from $1.2 million in 1935 to $9 million in 1940. Since then PUI has remained an industry leader. Although the company now faces some competition from look-alike products, it still holds sway over an impressive 67 percent of market share.

Exponential Growth: Too Much of a Good Thing

It was in response to the military's need for new electronics-based products at the start of World War II that the company's product offerings exploded. Using its core products as base (at the time there were five), PUI engineers added more than 75 new models to the company catalog by the end of the war. In 1948, the company launched an aggressive product expansion strategy which, 15 years later, had created a total of 18 product lines and more than 200 models as well as hundreds of customer-specific options. Possible combinations numbered in the tens of thousands.

Ten years later, specific model numbers hovered near 400, and, by the late 1980s, partially as a result of the new market-in design efforts, that number had doubled again. Every year since, PUI customers have seen yet more new products. A few of these are highly innovative, pushing the industry to the next level. But many are derivatives, improvements, flankers, and extensions—reconfigurations of existing products, only slightly modified to respond to the company's ever-multiplying market niches.

As a result, PUI has earned a name for itself over the years as a customer-driven organization. Its quality is high, response time competitive, and prices attractive. The company is considered one of the hottest Just-in-Time (JIT) plants in the region and a model of value-adding manufacturing, cell design, kanban, Quality Function Deployment (QFD), and visual systems. It has won many awards for its improvement efforts and continues to search out breakthrough technologies in its never-ending quest for new and larger markets, lower costs, and greater profits.

Today PUI, still privately owned, offers more than 80 lines of products. Fifteen are the company's key money-makers, accounting for nearly 65 percent of the revenues. Another 20 contribute about 25 percent in yearly receipts. Demand for the remaining 45 is sporadic at best but, as yet, not so infrequent that any has been withdrawn. In addition, never wanting to disappoint an established client, the company has maintained a replacement policy for any part or product it offers—or has ever offered.

Visual Evidence of a Problem

Crossing the shop floor on my way to the 9:00 A.M. meeting, which is to take place in the Engineering Department, I pass through various operational areas. Stacks of point-of-use storage (POUS) bins overflow with thousands of small parts, and subassemblies line the racks on either side of the aisles. Shelves along the way are covered with tooling and fixtures, all neatly tagged, color-coded, and arranged. Small quantities of work-in-process (WIP) are stacked in orderly array in each work area.

I detour through a maze of desks where schedulers sit sifting through various Bills of Material (BOMs), preparing to get new orders rolling and stage the old ones. A dozen or more expediters are gearing up to handle the new schedule, the best ones of whom have thirty years with the company under their belt; they know how to work the system. As I turn down the hallway and head toward the conference room, I bump into Harvey Chasewaite, first-shift foreman and veteran of forty years at PUI; he's muttering to himself something about missing kits.

Finally I reach the Engineering Department and the meeting room. Piles of drawings and other documentation cover every available surface. Work in the department has a purposeful air. On entering the meeting room, I see Tom Vargas, PUI's president, at the head of the table surrounded by his direct reports. People are chatting in twos and threes as they wait for the session to begin. As I pass, I overhear Gary Scosberg, VP of Marketing, expressing doubts to the chief purchasing agent, Gerry Beryl, about the Engineering Department's ability to meet the new product introduction deadlines in time to coincide with the new marketing catalog scheduled to come out in five months. Scosberg's voice is good-humored but his face looks drawn and tired. "We're not talking rocket science here," he says. "We just want a few new features! Why can't people just design some simple extensions without leaving their personal creative paw prints all over them?"

Camilla Wardwell, VP of Operations, appears equally exasperated as she converses with Vargas, who seems intent on every word. I draw closer and hear her saying: "I know we can't just slash and burn our product line into manageability, Tom, but this customer-driven thing is getting out of hand. My expediters don't even know which of our products make real profit—and sometimes neither do I. If we introduce one more new product series this year, my staff will lynch me."

Dan Littel, Engineering VP and 30-year veteran of the company, is sharing a similar anxiety with the finance director, Maureen Gleason, recently promoted from the ranks of Purchasing: "We can't handle any more product, Maureen. Did we waste all that time and money on JIT?! I don't know exactly what caused it, but I *do* know that something is out of control and we are heading for a slide."

At the stroke of nine, Tom Vargas rises to his feet to begin the meeting. His opening sentence shocks the room into attention: "My company has become my own worst nightmare." After a long pause, he continues: "Our markets are turbulent, profits have been steadily declining for a decade, and we're looking at an eroding market share for the fifth year in a row. But our inventory continues to soar, up from $4 million three years ago to $5.6 million this year. In exactly the same period, our active parts count mushroomed from 9,454 to 13,156. That, ladies and gentlemen, is an average increase of 6.8 percent per year!

"We've been over these figures before. I have asked for and heard your plausible explanations: New products require new parts, to get more market share, we need to offer what—and whatever—our customers want, and they want things faster, so we need the inventory to cover. And, oh yes, our suppliers' lead times are horrendous.

"Well, I just met with Andie Randal and she gave me another piece of news: MIS anticipates that our inventory will hit $6 million by the end of year if our current rate continues. And Dan's group is predicting parts count will go up 20 percent if his engineers complete all the ECNs [engineering change notices] and development projects on their desks, as of today.

"Let's not kid ourselves. We all know that this is just the tip of the iceberg. There is something else out there. Walk around the shop floor. Spend some time in Drafting. Hang out in Purchasing for just a while. Talk to our sales guys and gals. Go to the machine shop. Listen. It's out there. This company is choking on its own chronic busyness. You can see it and you can feel it. And I want a name for it.

"My company has become my own worst nightmare. And I want to know what we're going to do about it! But first I want to know why! What went wrong?"

WHAT WENT WRONG?

From its earliest days, Parts Unlimited Inc. dedicated itself to providing its customers with anything and everything they wanted, and as a result, the company has been well-rewarded with a loyal and ever-widening customer base. Now, sixty years later, the company continues to dominate the market. Business remains brisk and revenues increase every year. But the company is in trouble.

Even though sales volume is up, profits are down. They haven't just leveled off. They are shrinking. For the first time in the history of PUI, break-even has become a critical issue. Despite the organization's considerable success in waste elimination, cycle-time reduction, and continuous improvement, costs are eating the company alive, and managers can see nothing but red on the horizon. There are many companies like PUI. After introducing a distinctive and popular new product, they grow by leaps and bounds during their early years. When competition rears its head, such companies often confront the problem by diversifying their product offerings. If the strategy works (and it often does, short-term), product expansion continues as these organizations pursue higher sales volume, greater revenues, new market share—and, of course, more profit.

But, like PUI, these same organizations sooner or later find themselves in the same puzzling "more revenues, less profit" conundrum, coupled with the operational gridlock Tom Vargas referred to as "chronic busyness." The search for the culprit and solutions begins anew. Often this is the point when cost-conscious companies launch inventory reduction initiatives. If company managers are well informed (and the vast majority of them are), they will select an array of the powerful and highly effective techniques clustered under the rubric of Just-in-Time, continuous improvement, or waste elimination.

Before examining the real source of the problem challenging PUI and companies like it, let's review the above-mentioned techniques to better understand the impressive and positive impact they can assert on a troubled enterprise—and their limitations.

The Improvement Revolution

In the late 1970s, companies began a transformation that spanned nearly two decades and is still ongoing. This transformation focused squarely on replacing antiquated operational approaches with dynamic new methods that improved quality and productivity performance, accelerated the flow of products and services to the customer, and helped companies become superior competitors. The key to the revolution was (and remains) ridding all systems of waste. *Waste* was the culprit, and waste reduction was the strategy for eradicating it.

In this approach, waste in a company is broadly described as *any activity that adds cost and not value to products or services*. A synonym for waste is the term "non-value-adding activity" (NVA) and its opposite is known as value-adding activity (VA); hence the term Value-Adding Management, or VAM.* Together, value-adding and non-value-adding activity make up the total of a company's endeavors (VA + NVA = Total Company Activity). But research shows that an average of 95 percent or more of this activity is *non*-value-adding, leaving only about 5 percent that adds value. Said another way, for every 100 hours of "work," 95 hours (on average) are spent in "doing things" that do *not* add value to the product or service, with only the remaining five hours spent on activity that *does* add value.

---

* The VAM approach is the brilliant distillation of the strategy underlying the Toyota Product System, as deduced by the Technical Transfer Council (TTC), a training and consulting firm based in Melbourne, Australia. The author came in contact with the VAM strategy in the mid-1980s when heading up the training and consulting group of Productivity Inc., which had formed a strategic alliance with TTC. The contribution of both TTC and Productivity Inc. to the following discussion is gratefully acknowledged.

The Seven Deadly Wastes of Production

Non-value-adding activities fall into seven broad categories of waste: (1) making defects, (2) delays, (3) overprocessing, (4) motion, (5) overproducing, (6) making inventory or WIP, and (7) material handling. Add to these *missed opportunities* (opportunity loss) from using limited resources to support waste, and you have the Seven Deadly Wastes + One (see Figure 2.1).*

FIGURE 2.1. The Seven Deadly Wastes + One (Non-Value-Adding Activity)

---

* Examples of non-value-adding (NVA) shop-floor activity include: double handling products, searching for tools, long equipment changeover times, waiting for parts, waiting for instructions, and unscheduled equipment downtime; value-adding (VA) shop-floor activities include forming, stamping, machining, drilling, heat treating, assembling, and painting.

These wastes are often referred to as rocks, blockages, or debris in the river (the river representing the flow of product through the production system). Only the tops of them are visible above the water line, however; the rest is masked by the enormous inventories a company keeps to buffer against such production exigencies as defects, equipment breakdowns, long equipment changeover, etc. (see Figure 2.2). Getting the product to the end-user on time is not an unobstructed shoot down the pipeline but rather a painfully slow and sluggish meander around the rocks that choke the flow.

The objective of the VAM strategy is to systematically identify and remove those rocks or wastes (the NVA component of the formula), including the inventories themselves. A key element in this attack requires managers to resist "improving" the value-adding (5 percent) component (see Figure 2.3 for details). Their exclusive improvement focus needs to be on the 95 percent that represents waste.

This strategy of waste elimination was raised to both a science and an art by Japan's Toyota Motor Company in the 1970s and, for nearly two decades, has been the focal point of the improvement efforts of many companies all over the world. Today, definitions of the so-called "seven

FIGURE 2.2. Rocks in the River/the Flow of Production—1980s

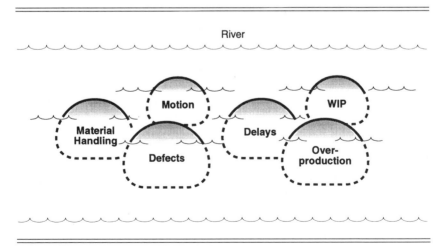

FIGURE 2.3. Value-Adding Versus Non-Value-Adding Activity

A. Many times, when asked to describe what it "does" all day, a company will reply something like this: *"We're busy all the time making products for our customers."* Such a company tends to see its "work" as 100% value-adding (VA).

100% "Busyness ~ VA"

B. The reality is more likely to look like the following: 95% of the activity does not add value (NVA), with only the other 5% adding value (VA). In other words, 95 out of 100 hours, the company is generating waste—and cost—not value.

95% NVA	5% VA

C. When a company wants to improve its profit margin but is not aware of the level of waste it is generating, it will often attempt to improve that portion of its effort that is adding value (average 5%). So, if such a company targets a 100% profit improvement this year, it will probably conceptualize it something like this: "Last year we made and sold 50 widgits. This year we'll make and sell 100 and double our profit for sure." The company then proceeds to improve the VA portion. But, because the relationship between VA and NVA is a ratio, success will automatically cause the VA portion to shrink and NVA simultaneously to increase. In this case, success resulted in the 95% NVA expanding to 97.5% NVA because the 5% VA shrunk to 2.5% VA.

97.5% NVA	2.5% VA

D. A more strategic application directs the company to focus improvement efforts on the non-value-adding component *first* so that NVA steadily decreases. Only when the ratio between VA and NVA reaches parity (50%:50%), should any effort be focused on improving the VA portion.

50% NVA	50% VA

deadly wastes" are practically burned into the brain cells of self-respecting executives, managers, and shop-floor employees everywhere, along with the methods and techniques used to reduce these wastes and shift the VA:NVA ratio into greater balance.

Quick changeovers, kanban, statistical process control (SPC), fail-safe/*poka-yoke* devices, cell design, supplier-customer partnerships, kaizen improvement proposal systems, policy deployment, Quality Function Deployment (QFD), and other powerful continuous improvement techniques have entered the mainstream of the way companies now do business. And they are working! In many companies, processes have been streamlined or completely re-engineered, work-in-process (WIP) has been drastically reduced, lead times have shrunk, inventory turns have improved, single-minute changeover times have become commonplace, and transportation distances have collapsed. The non-value-adding side of the ratio has receded.

On the value-adding side, the demand for new products and market-in design has quickened. Many manufacturing companies face this reality: Successful new products are the lifeblood of the enterprise. Today, zero defects quality, nearly instantaneous delivery, and broad product selection are virtual givens in the marketplace.

But as the markets of these same businesses approach middle age, they face a new category of challenge—product glut.

The Push for New Products

Ours is an age of choice. We live in a time of abundant products. And the customer is hungry. It wasn't always that way—but it is now. The past hundred years has witnessed a revolution in the industrialized world of what, why, and how people buy—the birth and ascendancy of consumerism.

In the late 1800s, constrained by rudimentary production techniques and poor roads, most Americans bought goods that were locally made and locally sold. This was the epoch of *commodity* wares, general products that met the practical needs of the day—boots, clothes, carriages, and "isinglass curtains that'll roll right down in case there's a change in the weather . . ." Availability was the defining competitive characteristic.

As national transportation networks evolved and production technology improved, companies extended their reach, and the buying public gained access to a wider choice of wares and higher-quality goods that were more uniformly made. This was the era of Henry Ford's great contribution: the assembly line and the standardization that made it possible, an extraordinary leap in concept and execution. Think about it. Ford tested his first automobile in 1896, four years before the national census reached 76 million Americans and 21 million horses. By 1903, 11,235 cars had been sold in the United States, a number that jumped to 43,000 by 1907. The year 1908 was to become the watershed between *commodity* and *standardized* products—between the purchase motivator of *availability* and that of *affordable sameness*. That was the year Henry Ford introduced his famous "any color as long as it is black" Model T, the ultimate universal product. In an era when one product was perfect for everyone and price defined the competition, Ford's Model T became a national brand, the ultimate perfect-for-everyone product. That 1908 standard remained unchanging and unchanged for nearly two decades until the Model T was retired in 1927, with over 15 million sold. The age of universal products reached its peak during World War II, with its urgent need for highly standard, mass-produced goods.

As a result of that war, the public had grown more discerning, more sophisticated, and wealthier. People wanted special things, products that reflected their personal life-style and values. Product diversification was born. What started back in the 1920s, when General Motors debunked Ford by introducing the concept of different cars for different people ("a car for every purse and every purpose"), turned into a headlong rush of annual model changes, market segmentation, and products that were differentiated on the basis of ever more finely delineated sets of demographics. Americans, above all other people, had come to cherish their right to choose. The day of the consummate consumer was just around the corner.*

That corner was turned in the 1980s with the advent of mass customization, a customer-driven strategy that combines the best production systems with a never-ending series of product choices. B. Joseph

---

* For more about this fascinating period in American commerce and a first-rate read, see Richard S. Tedlow's *New & Improved: The Story of Mass Marketing in America* (New York: Basic Books, 1990).

Pine II, one of mass customization's leading advocates, makes no bones about it: The way to create products that sell is through optimizing relationships with your customers. He goes on to say:

> Mass customization is first of all a mindset that places the needs of each individual consumer paramount. It holds that no customer should have to sacrifice what he or she needs and wants because of a company's internal inability to provide it. Once you grasp that mindset, you are ready to consider how to go about differentiating and customizing your products—and doing it at low cost. You generate a strategy and then, still holding fast to that fundamental customer mindset, you develop the technology you need to be able to deliver it.*

Once again the auto industry is a perfect reflection of new trends. In their admirable and exhaustive treatment, Kim B. Clark and Takahiro Fujimoto observe: "Where 20 years ago the American car buyer had to look long and hard to find a model with anything but a traditional V-8 engine with rear-wheel drive, today choice in engine-drive train spans 4, 6, 8, and 12 cylinders, multi-valves, front-wheel drive, and 4-wheel drive."** Variations in brake, suspension, and engine control systems, electronics, and interiors widen customer choice even further. Similar to the disposable diapers market discussed in the previous chapter, the range expands again exponentially when automobiles are segmented psychographically—you get passenger cars, hatchbacks, luxury sedans, economy cars, sports cars, sports coupes, station wagons, vans, mini-vans, recreational vehicles, and so on and so forth. More variety than you can—or want to—shake a stick at!

Whether or not customers really want all those choices is another story and one we will address later in this book. Right now, let's look at other forces driving product variety.

* From a private conversation with Joseph Pine. For further discussion, see his excellent book, *Mass Customization: The New Frontier of Business Competition* (Boston: Harvard Business School Press, 1993).

** Kim B. Clark and Takahiro Fujimoto, *Product Development Performance: Strategy, Organization, and Management in World Auto Industry.* (Boston: Harvard Business School Press, 1991), p. 8.

Expanding Choices—Collapsing Cycles

Businesses cannot survive, much less prosper, without continually bringing out new products. Few companies can rely on markets secured ten or twenty years ago—or even one year ago. Whether to respond to a new consumer demand or create one, new products drive markets, and companies dedicate enormous time and effort each year to introducing them. Some new products are simply extensions, flankers, improvements, or "me too" entries. Others are new to the company or even new to the world. Some sell and some fail.

Whatever the case, it is no longer enough for a product to be of the best quality, and delivered the fastest and at the lowest price. In a marketplace where winning and keeping customers is the name of the game, companies must offer all this *in addition* to the widest possible choice of products. Consumers expect and demand greater convenience, higher performance, and an ever-widening variety at equal or greater value—more features that are personalized to them. These requirements drive the market and the pace is accelerating.

Contributing to the speed of product proliferation are two other factors—collapsing time-to-market and product life cycles. Ten years ago, it could take anywhere from three to five years, in most industries, to get a new product introduced; other industries, such as automobiles and other heavy equipment, could require upward of 10 years. Now, more often than not, you or your competitor, aided by CIM (computer-integrated manufacturing), CADCAM (computer-aided design/computer-aided manufacturing), and a concurrent engineering approach, can get the job done in 18 months or less. Once the new product is launched, productive life expectancy, which was formerly three to five years, now ranges between 14 to 24 months—and is shrinking.

The benefit for the consumer is practically unalloyed—an endless stream of exciting new "things" to buy. But for the manufacturer, accelerating times-to-market and collapsing product life cycles act as a double-edged sword. On one edge, they represent a significant competitive advantage (if the company is positioned to take that advantage). On the other, products that come and go quickly give a company less time to recoup its development investment and less time to justify product costs or to make or order components in sufficient quantities to reach important economies of scale. And when products fade and are retired, the cycle continues and these products get swiftly replaced by "new and improved" ones. The net effect of these factors is an ever-widening spiral of variety, a virtual explosion of products.

EXPLODING VARIETY, COMPLICATED ORGANIZATIONS: THE HEART OF THE PROBLEM

There is no question: To prosper, companies must develop successful new products, products that offer distinct and meaningful points of difference in the eyes of the customer. But "successful" does not only mean valued, wanted, and bought by the consumer. "Successful" must also mean greater profits for the manufacturer. To be a true success for the company, new products must represent a *least-cost sum* (achieving maximum customer selection with the least amount of resources or cost).

Too Much of Too Much

What companies often fail to see in their rush for more new products is the increased stress each new product adds to the company. The first sort of stress derives from the strain on resources required to develop new products. New consumer products can cost a million dollars or ten millions to get from concept to final prototype, with associated production technology and marketing eating up millions more. The stress on the organization of this repeating level of investment is significant and observable.

But there are other, less evident categories of stress beyond those generated by the cost of development. The category of stress we want to draw attention to is one that a company usually "sees" but rarely sufficiently appreciates—the stress of adding one new part.

A survey of 18 companies and 30 divisions conducted by Brisch, Birn & Partners, Inc. (BBP), a Fort Lauderdale, Florida, consulting firm specializing in classification and coding systems, found that the introduction of a single new part can cost the organization between $123 to nearly $6,000, or an average of approximately $1,500 per new part.* Engineering costs associated with that part averaged around 20 percent of the total cost. When you multiply the impact of that single part occurrence by the host of parts that enter a system annually, it should be enough to make a company sit up and take notice. Even more so when it finds out that this BBP survey, which spanned nearly 100 manufacturing plants, was conducted between 1967 and 1968. William F. Hyde, BBP president, recently commented that the average cost of introducing a part *today* is "no less than $4,000 per part, conservatively speaking,"** and may require weeks—even months—to effect. And, according to BBP research, designing the part represents only 19.7 percent of the cost.

When a company introduces a new product, you can be sure that at least one new part gets added to the parts universe. Does this surprise anyone? Certainly, not. "What? Only *one* new part!" you may say. "When we come out with a new product, we add anywhere from 20 to 200 new parts to our base! What's the big deal of only one new part?" The big deal is that every single added part puts a new, however small, burden on the organization. Let's look at what happens in the wake of introducing one new part, which we define as follows: A new part is *one not currently in use or available inside company walls.*

In the wake of the addition of a single new part to a company's parts universe come legions of secondary activities. At the low end, a new part triggers the need for at least one new drawing. Then comes the need to contact a supplier (or possibly to find a new one). Contacting a supplier triggers a purchase order, various phone, fax, and computer transactions, and at least one check. The part then needs to be handled in some

---

* Brisch, Birn & Partners, Inc., *What You Don't Know* Can *Hurt You*, Fort Lauderdale, Fla., 1968.
** Discussion with William F. Hyde, president of Brisch, Birn & Partners, Inc., Fort Lauderdale, Fla., August 1994.

manner, which might mean all or some of the following: receiving, counting, inspecting, shelving (whether point-of-use storage or in the stores—that is, if space can be found), and when the part is summoned, it gets handled again. There may be some other "minor" requirements as well. If the company is lucky, for example, the new part will need only one new tool—a special wrench, perhaps—and only one new operation sheet or procedural write-up. But it might also require the purchase of new fixturing or even a new piece of equipment; in either case, in addition to the purchase cost, another cycle of paperwork and computer transactions gets triggered. And then there is the question of the added load on the production control schedule.

In and of itself, each of these activities could be said to be individually indispensable. As a whole, however, they trigger stress in the organization that is observable and problematic, over time creating a tight web of actions that adds cost, complexity, and complication.

The Eight By-Products of New Product Expansion

Just as in the 1970s, specific waste categories were named (above) as burdens to traditional manufacturing operations, so too can we define and label the excesses or wastes associated with new product introduction. In effect, these wastes are the internal *by-products* of new products, and when a certain level of critical mass is reached, they get the upper hand and "run away." We therefore call them: *The Runaway By-Products of New Product Expansion.* They fall into eight broad categories:

Runaway By-Product 1—Exploding Active Parts Count

When new products are developed, new parts get added; the question is: Is each of these new parts required and unavoidable? Even if a new part is required, it may bring an escalation in the number of service parts the company must stock.

Runaway By-Product 2—Pressurized Procurement Activity

As a part number is added, purchasing responds; the continuous need for new purchased or made parts can exert massive pressure on the parts procurement function.

Runaway By-Product 3—Unwarranted Processes, Dies Tooling, Fixtures, Equipment, and Changeover Times

New parts often require new production processes, and new equipment, dies, fixtures or tooling, and accordingly extra changeovers; these can burden already-loaded shop-floor activity.

Runaway By-Product 4—Congested Floor Space, Shelving, and Storage Racks

As with parts in general, new parts need homes, however temporary, and can add clutter to floors, racks, shelving, and stores; over time, multiplying service parts and dead stock (obsolete but not yet retired parts) can further cramp already-congested storage areas.

Runaway By-Product 5—Overburdened Material Handling

If the company accepts material handling as a given, added parts can tax an already-burdened transportation system, as each new part requires its share of handling in the form of receiving, counting, inspecting, storing, retrieving, and otherwise moving it.

Runaway By-Product 6—Ballooning MIS Input and Upkeep

Each part that enters or leaves the system must be individually logged in and maintained; pressure to keep data systems up to date can be staggering.

Runaway By-Product 7—Mushrooming Control Points

Literally hundreds of paper, computer, and other transactions across all departments (known as control points) support each new product and its new parts—drawings, catalogs, cost estimates, supplier searches, purchase orders, faxes, invoices, receipts, tracking checklists, inspection sheets, etc.

Runaway By-Product 8—Loss of Opportunity

The resources needed to support runaway parts proliferation are astounding. They can rob the company of assets it could otherwise use to develop and grow (see Figure 2.4).

Look at the first eight runaways on the list. Taken as a series of single events, it is not hard to justify the need for each of them in the successful running of the business. But look again. In the actuality of profit and loss, they are each non-value-adding in the same sense as the previous set of operational wastes are. That is, while many of the by-products of new product expansion do not create problems for the organization in and of themselves, each one becomes a significant problem when it is recurrent—when it happens in sufficient multiples. Then it becomes a runaway and a genuine source of complication and unwarranted cost.

In multiples, these by-products provoke day-to-day entanglements that, in turn, can cause the company to tilt into overload and go into organizational gridlock. If we are to head this off, or be empowered to make a midcourse correction, we must first recognize these by-products for what they are—*waste!*

Rethinking the 95:5 Ratio—Death by 10,000 Cuts

In the decades preceding the introduction of JIT, inventory was erroneously presumed to be an asset at best or a necessary evil at worst; as a result, the wastes it created remained invisible for a very long time. Similarly, many companies continue to consider the *by-products of new*

FIGURE 2.4. The Eight Runaway By-Products of New Product Expansion

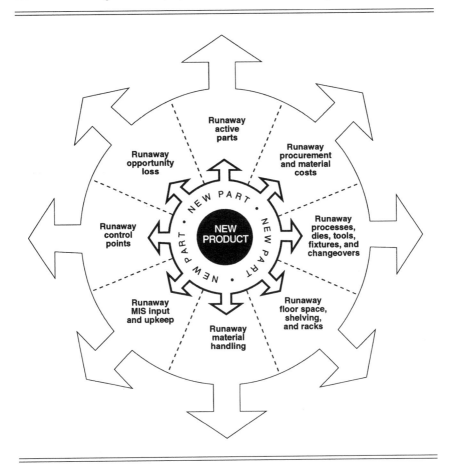

products necessary and required—the price paid for market share. In actuality, they are exactly like the evil of inventory was discovered to be twenty years ago: a monster, hidden deep in the infrastructure of the company, that drains life force from the organization but, without a mechanism such as VEP, never willingly comes out into the open to be seen and confronted. You will remember that VEP (Variety Effectiveness Process) is a systematic approach for helping companies prevent or reduce unwarranted product and parts variation while offering maximal customer selection at a least-cost sum.

Having said that, let's take another look at the 95:5 ratio we previously discussed in light of new product expansion. There is a valuable insight there that should not be overlooked.

We begin by stating the obvious. The sale of a product and subsequent revenues are critical to a manufacturing company—the doorway to its profits. The development of new products initiates that process, and so we place new products on the value-adding (VA) side of the ratio (5 percent). The 95 percent or non-value-adding side is comprised of those wasteful activities that occur in the process of getting new products introduced. These are the equivalents of the seven *deadly wastes of production* (making defects, delays, overproducing, overprocessing, motion, etc.). Until you are aware of them, these can often be as invisible as non-value-adding activities in production were—just "part of the way business gets done around here" (see Figure 2.5).

FIGURE 2.5. Equivalents in Product Development to the Seven Deadly Wastes in Operations

7 Deadly Wastes of Production	Equivalents in New Product Introduction
Making Defects	Making Mistakes in Design
Delays	Waiting for Specs, Waiting for Approvals
Overprocessing	Reworking the Design, Conducting Multiple Proofs
Overproducing	Creating Multiple Prototypes
Motion	Searching for Information, Missing Drawings, etc.
Making Inventory	Adding New Parts
Material Handling	Circulating Designs, Prototypes, Test Data Results
Missed Opportunities	Loaded down with current design work, the company cannot move on to new product opportunities

In reality, these wastes are concealed, embedded in the 5 percent or value-adding side of the ratio. If we explode them out and into their true 95 percent impact, we begin to recognize their enormous non-value-adding drain on the organization (see Figure 2.6).

The challenge of the 1980s was to eliminate the Seven Deadly Wastes from the flow of production. In the 1990s, the challenge is to remove the silt accumulating on the river bottom from the runaway by-products—unneeded drawings, processes, dies, tools, racks, change-overs, etc. These are making the river of production increasingly shallow and congested and threaten to choke off the flow. But they are, like the silt itself, mere symptoms of a deeper blockage, the true cause of the decelerating production flow. The true cause lies under the silt—those myriad small, tangible objects lodged in the riverbed. We call those objects *unwarranted parts*. Their removal is the focus of VEP (see Figure 2.7).

Many manufacturing companies release an avalanche of new parts into their systems every year. Like the famous Chinese proverb describing a slow and initially painless death by ten thousand cuts, each part exerts its tiny stress on the enterprise. Eventually, the company tips over into chronic complexity and organizational gridlock.

Let's look a little closer at this phenomenon.

NEW ENGLAND FARMHOUSE EFFECT—
THE Y-TYPE COMPANY

Profit-making is a constant trade-off between revenue and cost. But many businesses nowadays buy increased sales through new products and make no attempt to control the runaway by-products; as a result, any sales increase gets bought at an inflated cost rate. Too few new products are commercialized as a result of a carefully defined and executed product introduction strategy. In many instances, an organization's new product

FIGURE 2.6. 95:5—Runaway By-Products Hidden in New Product Activity

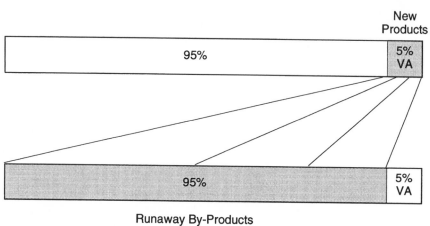

FIGURE 2.7. Blocks in the Production Flow—Revisited

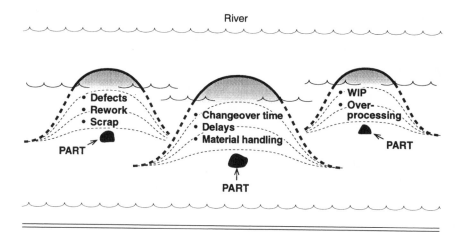

approach resembles how farmhouses in New England often get built—expand as needed in any shape and direction (see Figure 2.8).

When new products are introduced, sales appear to respond and grow. The number of parts, however, is escalating at a rate parallel to or greater than those sales, and a dangerous Y-shaped curve begins to emerge as the rate-of-parts increase overtakes the rate-of-revenue increase (see Figure 2.9).* Profits begin to erode and the company wonders why.

Even when a company achieves genuine market-driven product diversity, there is no guarantee that profit will improve. In fact, the reverse often happens. Product variety increases, but output grows only slightly, stagnates or even declines. Concurrently, costs escalate, sales slow down, and profits erode.

FIGURE 2.8. The New England Farmhouse Approach to New Product Introduction

New product "strategy"—expand as needed in any shape or direction

* The contribution to this discussion of Toshiro Suzue and Akira Kohdate is gratefully acknowledged. For more, see their valuable book, *Variety Reduction Program: A Production Strategy for Product Diversification* (Cambridge, Mass.: Productivity Press, 1988).

FIGURE 2.9. The Y-Type Trajectory: Profile of a Company in Trouble

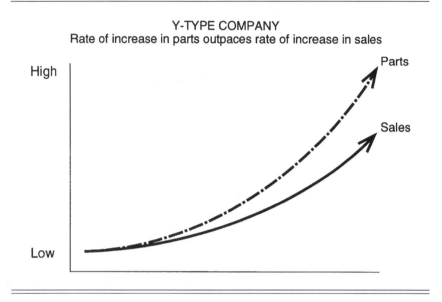

In the face of this, the company may attempt to regroup and bolster flagging sales by developing still more new products in the desperate attempt to rectify the cost curve. Gross sales may go up in response, but profits usually do not recover; meanwhile, sales on existing products can shrink. Marketing looks for new product opportunities. Design and Product Engineering try to speed up new product development. Production introduces more high-performance equipment and acquires more storage space and purchases more forklifts to speed up material handling. Production control labors through the introduction of new computers and next-generation software. Neither production nor sales can keep up with the burden of increased product variety. Generating more costs than revenues, the company sinks deeper into financial quicksand with each new product offering. The entire company engages in a futile attempt to build a box big enough to hold its burgeoning product line.

Companies caught in this Y-type trajectory pay for their products twice: once as part of the official product introduction budget, and again in the cost of managing the complexity added to their systems as a result of introducing new products.

PUI: When Variety Is Negative

In retrospect, Parts Unlimited Inc. became a victim of its own growth. Product variety, and the ancillary activities it triggers, are completely out of control. Although company leaders failed to recognize the implications at the time, every new product that got introduced served to fold in yet another micro-layer of cost and complication. Like many companies, PUI took decades to blunder its way into trouble.

What went wrong at PUI was not its commitment to maximizing customer selection and seizing market share. Product variety is never wrong. What went wrong was the company's lack of an equal and parallel effort to regulate and control the negative side effects of that selection. Negative variety—the sum effect of the runaway by-products of new products—got the upper hand.

The fact is, the central premise of PUI's product approach is both erroneous and dangerous. In order to continue to meet and exceed the need of its customers for new products and retain market share, the company believed that its parts inventory *had* to increase, along with the other "obligatory" add-ons. Negative variety, say the managers, was inevitable.

VEP: THE ALTERNATIVE

Negative variety is not only *not* inevitable—it is avoidable. But in order to avoid it, organizations must systematically head off the negative aftermath of new product introduction—the downside of product expansion—

before it takes root. Managers need an approach that will help control and then reduce their parts inventory and dismantle existing complexity from the inside. And they need to do this even while they initiate new practices and policies that prevent negative variety from recurring.

Attempts to eliminate the problem by stemming the flow of new products will not only *not* solve the problem but are likely to sink the enterprise. The only solution is to understand and eliminate the true causes of the problem and stop the downward spin.

Variety Effectiveness Process (VEP) provides a solution. VEP enables companies to step back and dismantle the layers of complication that cover and choke the organizational infrastructure. Through VEP, unneeded products, parts, production processes, and control points are identified and minimized.

VEP is a systematic team-based methodology directed at maintaining or expanding customer selection while reducing negative variety in parts, processes, and control points and preventing their future recurrence. Its goal is to lower costs dramatically and de-complicate systems while maximizing a company's ability to respond to the demands of the market. Effective implementations of VEP can result in reductions of 25 percent to 40 percent in parts count, 15 percent to 40 percent in production processes, and as much as 60 percent in control points (those transactions aimed at procuring, receiving, inspecting, storing, counting, and retrieving parts and products).

The Rewards

Such reductions create deep and far-reaching benefits for the life and flow of the enterprise. When effectively implemented, VEP does not simply reduce the number of parts, processes, and control points. It frees the system from the inside to achieve new levels of health, flexibility, and vigor. From single-product industries like bricks to multi-product ones specializing in household appliances, furniture, or control equipment, companies that adopt the VEP perspective can experience impressive rewards:

Reward 1—Reductions in Total Active Parts

Through VEP, parts are eliminated or combined, and sub-assembly levels simplified. As a result, Bills of Material (BOMs) are streamlined and flattened, requiring fewer layers because products are developed based on the principles of effective variety. Reduced parts count, by association, triggers all the other rewards that follow.

Reward 2—Fewer Production Processes, Special Equipment, Dies, Tooling, and Machine Changeovers

Eliminating even a single part often triggers parallel reductions in production processes, dies, tooling, and the number of machine changeovers. The cumulative impact of this can be immense.

Reward 3—Reduced Storage Space and Less Material Handling

Reductions in products and parts automatically erase the need for their handling. The need for shelving, racks, and other storage shrinks along with the space formerly required for associated production processes, conveyors, material handling, fixtures, equipment, and the office and support areas that were needed to control and maintain such units. Literally miles of square footage can get freed up.

Reward 4—Accelerated, Complete, and Accurate Parts Information Retrieval

Because intelligent design is closely linked to the capability of the parts database, VEP works to ensure that a company's parts classification system can support strategic design decision making.

Reward 5—Strengthened, Functional Alignment Between Engineering, Operations, and Sales and Marketing

VEP is a team-based approach that utilizes information and insight from all the players involved in product design, procurement, and manufacture. This multifunctional approach breaks down the barriers between functions as people focus cooperatively on the task at hand.

Reward 6—Reduced Product Introduction Lead Time

With an efficient database and design practices in place, it now takes much less time to go through the development process. Marketing becomes fully cognizant of the implications of product and parts variety, as does Engineering; in addition, Design and Product Engineering can access significant, complete, and accurate information for making sound decisions about new parts.

Reward 7—Reduced Levels of Paperwork and Other Control Transactions

Since VEP sees the part as the ultimate cause, the cumulative addition of a single part number can, over time, trigger a vast range of activity that would never exist without it. As parts are eliminated, procurement and other supporting activity are simultaneously and dramatically reduced. In addition, the VEP method provides for specific efforts to streamline and reduce remaining control points, independent of parts-reduction procedures.

Reward 8—Upgraded Policies and Practices That Prevent Future Proliferation

VEP seeks the root causes of product and parts proliferation. In many cases, these causes are concealed in seemingly blameless policy directives and day-to-day practices, such as those related to purchasing, equipment, and design. When a company's corporate policies and practices are revised to align with VEP principles, many causative factors disappear.

Reward 9—Streamlined Procedures for Engineering Change Notices (ECN)

When engineering changes must happen, they are moved through a simplified procedure governed by now-familiar principles and practices that prevent unneeded variety from entering the system (see Figure 2.10).

FIGURE 2.10. VEP Outcomes—A Chain of Rewards

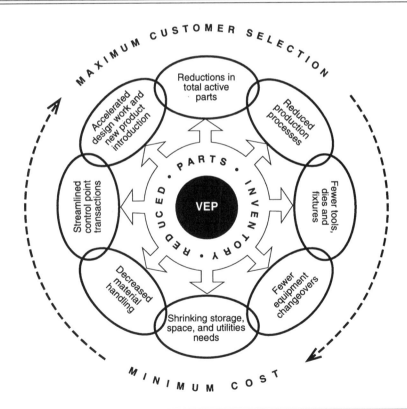

Companies adopt the VEP approach because it is quite simply too expensive for them not to.

VEP is especially relevant in any company in which product diversification is a strategic issue and proliferating costs, a persistent concern. Companies in the audio equipment business, electronics, home furnishings, and appliances can all benefit from VEP. From the machine tool industry to shoes and clocks, companies can gain a significant competitive advantage by applying the VEP methodology. As you will read in subsequent chapters, with VEP's emphasis on cross-functional analysis and aligned change, it cuts through the issues that cloak negative variety and illuminates its causes and solutions. The VEP process represents a new way of designing and developing products that can positively impact not just those products but all the activities and transactions that support them as they move through the workplace on the way to end-users.

What Is Variety Effectiveness?

Variety effectiveness is a new way of looking at product expansion. No one can deny the criticality of a company's introducing new variety into its product lines. But this variety must keep cost and complication to an absolute minimum. When it does, the variety that results is said to be *effective*. By the same token, *negative* variety does not appreciably expand selection but adds cost that the company may or may not be able to pass on to the customer. In short, *variety effectiveness* refers to the extent to which variety in new products contributes to profit.

The job of the VEP methodology is to assist companies in cleaning up the negative variety from the past as well as insuring that *all* new variety is as positive as possible. With its negative elements removed or minimized, the true profit potential of a company's products is achievable. When this happens, the Y-shaped curve previously described makes a midcourse correction, with sales steadily rising even as parts take a downward slide and plummet (see Figure 2.11).

FIGURE 2.11. The X-Type Curve: Profile of a Company Succeeding

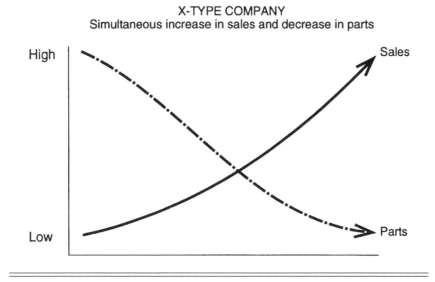

The X-Type Company

In a Y-type company, sales and parts count escalate in parallel. Negative variety reigns. In X-type companies, the reverse happens—sales increase even as parts count and costs shrink. This does not happen by accident. The X-type profile emerges over time as a result of a well-defined, intentional, carefully implemented strategy of variety effectiveness. Products are made for profit from the get-go.

Levels of complexity are manageable. They are designed to balance the quality and speed required for low-cost and high-impact production with the richness and ingenuity that are needed to offer truly viable new products and expand markets. Penalties for creativity are kept to an absolute minimum. People know what levels of variety are warranted for specific levels of output and return. They can spot negative variety at a glance.

In the X-type company, products increase in response to market demands, but the total number of new parts and processes increases at a lesser rate. The company's approach ensures no deterioration in profitability throughout the life of its products, even after the market peaks and begins its decline. The business has already found satisfactory answers to the key questions:

- At what market niche are the characteristics of each product in a product group targeted?
- How many parts are now used to provide the characteristics of each product, and how many are optimal?
- How many production processes are now used to produce each product at the required level, and how many are optimal?
- How many control points are now used to ensure quality, delivery, and customer satisfaction, and how many are optimal?
- What specific corporate policies and business practices are in place to support effective variety and enhance market share and profit? What new ones need to be developed?

In such an enterprise, smart, simple design is a strategic commitment and a living reality.

The goal of VEP is to help mature companies make the shift from a Y-type to an X-type profile, and to guide new organizations toward practices that create X-type results and avoid Y-type triggers.

VEP'S MULTIDIMENSIONAL APPROACH TO EFFECTIVE VARIETY

How does VEP help companies avoid becoming Y-type organizations or make the transition from Y to X? VEP meets this challenge by linking five powerful dimensions: (1) a comprehensive view of cause, (2) an in-depth analysis of complexity, (3) an insight-rich, team-based approach to improvement, (4) the unraveling of complexity through engineering-based tools, and (5) a prevention-based orientation. These are summarized below and discussed in detail in subsequent chapters (see Figure 2.12).

FIGURE 2.12. The Five Power Points of the VEP Approach

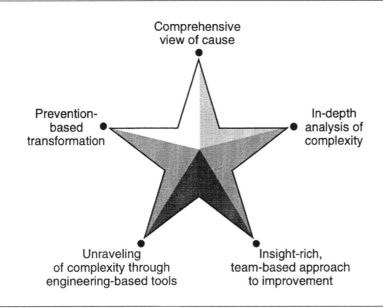

1. A Comprehensive View of Cause

Product, product function, and product structure are primary concerns of many improvement techniques that support product development. For example, value analysis/value engineering (VA/VE), Quality Function Deployment (QFD), and other market-in techniques can successfully reduce part costs and increase product value on a unit-by-unit, customer-by-customer basis, but costs across the board can increase along with organizational complexity. Standardization is another excellent cost-cutting approach; it is focused on normalizing products or commonizing components and subassemblies, but customer selection is often sacrificed. (These techniques are discussed in fuller detail in Chapter 4 "Triggers of the Variety Explosion.")

By contrast, VEP adopts a wider view without losing a precise product focus. Its goal is to de-complicate and dismantle all troublesome obstructions within the company caused, directly or indirectly, by the introduction of new product variety. To succeed in this, a company must identify and address all the causes or triggers of by-product runaway. Broadly speaking, these fall into five areas:

Trigger Area—Marketing and Sales

In a sometimes overzealous search for differentiation between products, certain marketing practices trigger layers of variety that are unwanted by the customer and unmanageable for the company.

Trigger Area—Product Development

There are many ways that unwarranted variations in products and parts can creep into the design process—high designer turnover, lack of a unifying development strategy, designer preferences, changing technology, the absence of sound information to support design decision making, and shifting design criteria, to name a few.

Trigger Area—Data Systems

A company's computer database and classification systems often make it difficult for Marketing and Engineering to make decisions in favor of effective variety because the information housed in these systems is often inaccurate, incomplete, obsolete, and/or difficult to retrieve.

Trigger Area—Accounting

Few accounting approaches recognize unwarranted variations as the framework within which costs and complications escalate. Traditional accounting procedures, for example, can mask these costs, the hidden price of doing business. Still concealed, these costs tighten their grip on the company and continue to drain off its resources.

Trigger Area—Operations

Flawed operational assumptions, such as the belief that large lot production is required, can trigger unneeded variation. This problem is further exacerbated, for example, when the company feels compelled to purchase equipment capable of running high volumes and considers high inventory an asset.

Chapter 4 is devoted to discussing these and other trigger areas in detail.

2. An In-Depth Analysis of Complexity

De-complicating enmeshed internal systems is no easy task, particularly in mature organizations where negative variety has taken root over a number of decades. One must sometimes start at the perimeter and work inward.

VEP does this through its central approach, *3-View Analysis*. This analysis focuses equal attention on: (1) the marketing factors that trigger the expansion process, (2) the structure of the products themselves, and (3) variation found within each part type in the company's parts inventory. The objective of this three-way approach is to identify opportunities to optimize positive variety, reduce negative variety, understand the causes of negative variety, and implement changes in the organization in order to remove those causes and ensure that future negative variety is minimized. Each of the three views described above (market analysis, product structure analysis, and part type analysis) represents an independent framework of inquiry—in essence, a series of questions that, when answered, show us where the greatest opportunities for reduction lie.

In another sector of in-depth analysis, VEP shines its light directly on the unwarranted proliferation of production processes and control points. Further reductions are then made.

3. An Insight-Rich, Team-Based Approach to Improvement

Organizational complexity is not triggered by single causes but rather by a network of highly diverse, interlocking variables. Many hands are needed to unravel it and get the company back on track.

In doing this, a company can choose one of two VEP implementation options. It can adopt a narrow focus (called the *select* approach) that uses a crack task force of internal experts to analyze and improve a specific product line. Or it can adopt a comprehensive application (called the *deep-dive* approach), bringing people from all over the organization to work together on cross-functional teams to reduce negative variety company-wide.

In either scenario, VEP recognizes people as the resource for insight and creativity, and encourages a team-based process that capitalizes on the knowledge and experience of a wide assortment of company employees. VEP provides the logic, tools, and structure for them to succeed.

4. The Unraveling of Complexity Through Engineering-Based Tools

The job of de-complicating the infrastructure of a company can be daunting, particularly when, for decades, product expansion has not been guided by a unified development approach that builds on the principles of variety effectiveness. VEP turns to an engineering tool chest for six techniques to organize and analyze product- and parts-related data into the meaningful format required to solve the problem through implementable improvements. VEP teams adapt these six tools (called the 6-VATs or VEP Analytical Tools) to the focus of their individual inquiry—whether that be marketing, product structure, part types, control points, production processes, or corporate policies and business practices. (See Chapter 7 for a detailed discussion of the 6-VATs.)

5. A Prevention-Based Transformation

The work of a VEP implementation is not considered complete just because parts inventories shrink by 30 percent or because 25 percent of all production processes is eliminated, or because control points are reduced by half. VEP's job is not done until the *roots* of negative variety have been dug out of the organization and replaced with practices and policies that will prevent recurrence. To do this, VEP also knows that an array of stakeholders (all departments and suppliers, *plus* the customer) must be satisfied that their interests are respected. A balance must be struck between many competing organizational forces.

VEP is about transformation that is prevention-based and looks to the long term for its results. What is your parts count one year after victory was declared? Two years after? Ten years after? Has the company stayed the course, maintained its optimal parts count in the face of even greater competitive threats? Has it remained a *least-cost sum* company? VEP sets up a dynamic infrastructure that ensures that the answers to all these questions are positive, and negative variety cannot regain a foothold in the organization.

VEP: NOT MAGIC—WORK!

The Variety Effectiveness Process is far more than the latest entry in world-class improvement methodologies. The issue of the effectiveness of the variety a company offers, whatever the market, has been long *un*recognized as a success factor. For many companies, this is where a true competitive lever lies. De-complicating systems that have evolved over decades is not an easy task; inevitably some painful restructuring must occur. But for those who recognize the potential rewards, such an undertaking will be welcomed and diligently implemented. The stakes are high and the perils of failing great. All-around business excellence is the only goal worth seeking. VEP is a core element of that quest.

Before we examine the details of the VEP method (the *how*), let's find out more about how VEP views cost and how traditional cost approaches may blur not only the problem but its solution.

CHAPTER THREE

TRUE COST: PRODUCT PROLIFERATION AND THE BOTTOM LINE

The cost system you are now using may not take into consideration the true cost of your products or the true cost of diversifying your product lines.

VEP AND WORLD-CLASS EXCELLENCE

Creating a world-class organization requires a total change in the way a company approaches the design, production, and distribution of its products and services. In its goal of achieving *truly effective variety*, VEP can play a key role in that change by helping a company track and reduce the level of its parts inventories and internal complexity. VEP offers two tools to point the way and measure the company's progress toward greater profitability. Those two devices, which will be discussed in detail later in this chapter, are VEP's *Parts Index* and VEP's *Tri-Cost/True-Cost Model*. As a result of applying these tools, a more valid, immediate, and practical tracking approach emerges, one that helps the company valuate and understand the complexity of its internal systems and the true cost of making product.

In this sense, these two VEP mechanisms offer an alternative perspective on cost when compared to the more traditional approach known as GAAP (generally accepted accounting principles). The GAAP approach tends to gauge company progress almost exclusively on outputs and past performance. With its focus on measures such as labor, material, and overhead, its practices can actually interfere with the improvement efforts and often run counter to world-class values and objectives. Created nearly a century ago at a time when accumulating parts inventories were not a key corporate concern, the traditional approach was not designed to track negative variety and the unwarranted proliferation of parts. The reverse was more often the case: Because they could not and did not assess burgeoning parts counts, they often provoked further parts accumulation and masked the direct and the indirect consequences of negative variety.

Let's visit Parts Unlimited Inc. again and find out more about its accounting approach and the problems facing Tom Vargas and his company.

A CASE IN POINT: ACCOUNTING GONE AWRY

Parts Unlimited Inc. (PUI) now generates revenues of about $25 million a year from the sale of mechanical and electronic process controls. Selling to both distributors and end-users, its products can be found in applications ranging from food processing to oil and natural gas exploration.

The Vargas family has owned PUI since its founding during the Depression. Over the years, the workforce has grown steadily from a 15-person garage shop operation to more than 200 people currently employed. Today, that work force is composed of 40 percent direct manufacturing employees and 60 percent support personnel. Ten years ago, the work force was 50 percent direct labor and 50 percent support. Twenty years ago, the work force was 55 percent direct labor and 45 percent support.

PUI operates a single manufacturing plant and relies largely on hand assembly to build most of its 50 different product series. In order to build more than 100,000 standard end-item configurations, supporting processes include: welding, cutting, filling, machining, wave soldering, Computer Numerical Control (CNC) machining, testing and setting, and component burn-in.

As we found out in the last chapter, PUI management has become alarmed at the company's ballooning inventory figures. Despite a relatively low growth in revenue (2.3 percent a year) over the past five years, inventory has risen from $4 million in 1986 to $5.6 million last year. In the same period, PUI's active parts count grew from 9,454 to 13,156, an average increase of 6.8 percent per year.

A variety of reasons has been offered to top management to explain this increase:

- New products require new parts.
- To get more market share, PUI must offer whatever the customer wants (be everything to everybody in the market—whatever it takes).
- Customers want things faster, so PUI has to have more inventory.

In addition, lead times from suppliers are horrendous; parts shortages often threaten to—and often do—close down lines.

As we heard, Tom Vargas is unwilling to accept these conditions, particularly in view of the current economy and the company's declining profitability. With another year of anticipated low growth on the horizon and a prediction by the materials group that the inventory figure will grow to $6 million by the end of the year if something isn't done soon, Vargas is convinced that the time for action is now.

He is also concerned because he knows that inventory costs are just the tip of the iceberg. Recently he has read about and attended seminars on so-called "hidden" inventory costs, such as those arising from the sheer variety of parts and processes associated with the inspecting and warehousing of massive quantities of goods as well as costs related to planning, organizing, and controlling huge volumes of inventory and production processes. At PUI, these consequences seem to multiply by themselves, and quickly have outpaced any increases in sales. Vargas recently heard his firm described as "a typical Y-type company," a direct reference to this parallel rise in sales and parts inventory, and he knew it was not a compliment to his managerial skills.

Impact on Manufacturing

Coupled with slow or moderate growth are rising inventory levels at PUI. But that's not all that's increasing. More products have triggered:

- More setups and changeovers in production processes
- New tooling and dies
- Additional floor space for production, inspection, and warehousing
- New production processes and investment in equipment to support them
- Additional suppliers and purchasing costs
- New packaging and shipping materials
- Increased design time and expenses
- Mounting quality-control costs
- Increased accumulation of outdated stock
- More time for inventory planning and control
- Additional documentation requirements such as new drawings and procedures
- Rising opportunity costs (money committed to inventory and its support that cannot be used for other purposes)

Allocating True Cost

CFO Helen Leary shares Tom Vargas's concern about the burgeoning inventory values. But she also has severe reservations about the company's ability to measure the true costs associated with all these parts, and with related processes and tasks such as purchasing, paperwork, and drawings. The current computer package at PUI incorporates a costing module that measures product cost based on material cost, direct labor, and an additional amount factored in for factory overhead. This overhead factor is calculated for each product based on the amount of labor in the product and does not take into consideration, at all, the amount of inventory, inventory handling, or control tasks related to the product.

For these reasons, Leary feels the current method of costing is not conducive to a proper understanding of the true cost of a product. For example, she knows of one popular Series 11 product that has few parts in it but requires more direct labor than the comparable, slower-moving Series 8 product that has almost twice the parts. Under the existing labor-burdened system, the Series 11 product absorbs more of the factory overhead and has a higher total cost—even though Leary is convinced that, because it has fewer parts, it actually costs the company less, overall, than the Series 8 product (see Figure 3.1). Leary and her staff see the burden of the mushrooming parts on the company, but it is practically impossible to validate what they see via the principles and techniques available to them in their traditional cost-accounting package.

FIGURE 3.1. True Total Cost: Which Product Costs More?
Comparison of Series 11 & Series 8 Products

Cost Contributor	Series 11 Product	Series 8 Product
Direct Labor	21 minutes	10 minutes
Material Content	$20.50	$21.75
Total Parts	29	46
Production Process Steps	6	16
Tools & Dies	1	4
Fixtures	3	7
Control Points • Drawings	33	51

• Transactions,
  Paperwork,
  Inspection Points
	8	12

Helen Leary's concern with what is happening at PUI is an important one. The dilemma she faces was created long before she came to the company. Let's look at the history of its origins.

THE TRADITIONAL COST APPROACH

History and Logic of GAAP

In the early days of the industrial revolution, *cash flow* was the central barometer of fiscal viability for most companies. And, for all intents and purposes, the tin cash box was the only available cost-management tool. It worked like this:

1. If there was enough money in the cash box at the beginning of the day, certain purchases were made. If not, the purchases had to wait.
2. If money was left at month's end, the business turned a profit and the enterprise continued. If the cash box was empty, the enterprise folded.

As the U.S. economy grew, companies grew with it; manufacturing sites multiplied, more and differing products were offered, and distribution systems began to operate on a nationwide basis. Industrial growth became increasingly dynamic and was no longer manageable in simple cash box terms. Cost accounting was born. By the 1930s, basic accounting concepts and practices were formalized into *generally accepted accounting principles* (GAAP). Many of these same cost-accounting practices are in use today. At their foundation is the following definition of product profit, which is also of special interest to the VEP discussion:

$$Profit = Price - Cost$$

Profit, then, is the difference between product cost and product price. Here's how traditional accounting calculates cost, specifically product cost:

Product Cost = Material Costs + Labor Costs + Overhead Costs

A look at the way that each of these cost terms—material, labor, and overhead costs—is defined is the next step in understanding how the traditional approach can confound efforts to de-complicate the organization.

Material Costs   Direct costs, and a function of adding the purchase price of each component part and/or raw material used to produce the item, as listed on the product's Bill of Material (BOM).

Labor Costs   Also a category of direct cost representing a combination of the level of manpower and the level of mechanization and automation required to convert the parts list (BOM) into the desired level of product.

Overhead Costs   Indirect costs, referring to those expenditures not directly assignable to a given product and, therefore, allocatable across all products on a formulaic basis. Overhead costs include depreciation on equipment, heat, light, power, taxes, research and development, maintenance, as well as salaries and wages for operations-support personnel and fringe benefits for both direct labor and operations-support personnel.

Based on these, the GAAP product cost formula assigns a standard cost to each manufactured product. Standard cost represents the sum of the costs of each individual product part and each labor step in the production process, as well as associated overhead assigned to the product, based on some pre-determined formula. In this sense, the standard cost approach serves as the framework against which actual costs are assigned, entered into the cost-accounting system, and then analyzed for variance. Variance data are then linked to the level of each department's productivity and, if deficient, to production problems.

Straightforward as this procedure may appear, it can pose certain challenges in trying to track proliferating complexity in an organization.

FROM TRACKING THE PAST
TO TRACKING COMPLEXITY

Standard cost accounting is a set of assumptions against which company managers can evaluate organizational strengths and weaknesses to determine if the enterprise is on or off the profit track. Linked to these assumptions is a complex system of performance indicators, measures, and techniques for pricing products and assessing operational efficiency. When GAAP techniques were introduced decades ago, an information conduit was formed relative to the operational and financial performance of the enterprise. Companies used this information for decision making relative to a vast array of strategic, tactical, and day-to-day needs.

In the late 1970s, however, the way companies did business began to change, but the accounting system, developed 60 to 100 years prior, that tracked that business did not. A value divergence developed. To understand the depth of this discrepancy, remember that any accounting approach, traditional or otherwise, is a measurement and reward system at its foundation, a system that defines which performance outputs are valuable and which are extraneous. Given this, the choice of accounting system is as significant to the future of an enterprise as the profit and loss system is as significant to the future of an enterprise as the profit and loss it measures. At their best, performance measures align with the company's vision, pointing the way to the strategic and tactical decisions needed to achieve that vision. At their worst, ill-conceived performance measures deflect an organization off its path of growth and achievement and can cause it to flounder, even if these measures signal otherwise. That is the nature of measurement. And this is part of the problem with GAAP related to VEP.

Variety effectiveness is reached when two conditions are met: (1) The company has achieved optimal levels of parts inventory to support its market growth, and (2) Its systems are sufficiently de-complicated to require *least-sum* resources. As we will see later in the chapter, this understanding can trigger practices that lead to decreases in unwarranted parts and in other direct and indirect wastes.

The problem in traditional managerial accounting is that a product's cost is based almost exclusively on three factors—materials, labor, and overhead (defined above). As illustrated in Figure 2.1 and the discussion that follows, the GAAP approach can cause more parts to be purchased or made, which, in turn, can lead to more, not less, internal complexity and higher, not lower, parts inventories. From there, complications adhering to new parts can skyrocket (see Figure 3.2).

We are *not* suggesting that a company drawn to VEP needs to get rid of GAAP. Many aspects of a traditional accounting system can continue to serve the company during a VEP implementation and beyond. In addition, differing approaches can live side by side with GAAP during an implementation, with each approach making a positive contribution.

FIGURE 3.2. GAAP Versus VEP

GAAP Approach

- Tracks the past
- Assigns disproportionate product overhead
- Focuses on least-cost parts/piece price
- Triggers multiple suppliers
- Triggers large lot production and machine over-utilization
- Promotes price mark-up to attain acceptable profit margins

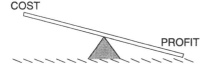

VEP Approach

- Tracks complexity and needless variation
- Tracks total parts count
- Focuses on true cost (F-, V-, and C-Costs)
- Promotes single-source suppliers and global pricing
- Fosters price-targetting and design-to-price practices
- Encourages small lot production

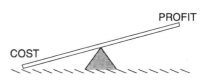

Does your accounting approach focus on the bottom line **or** micro-issues; on total cost **or** the cost of individual products?

Activity Based Costing (ABC), discussed briefly at the close of this chapter, is one such option. Our intention is to bring attention to some of the anomalies in the traditional approach related to VEP goals. What is needed is a new understanding of: (1) how GAAP helped to create the problem of exploding variation, and (2) what GAAP can*not* do to help solve it. In this way, we hope that the discussion in this chapter will help you discern where to take exception to traditional practices because, if a company involved in VEP continues to rely exclusively on traditional cost accounting practices, it may run into a powerful *disconnect*.

The nature of this disconnect is two-fold. The traditional approach is not specifically equipped to: (1) identify or clarify the levels of organizational complexity brought about by negative variety, or (2) illuminate opportunities to reduce or dismantle that complexity. GAAP procedures are simply not designed to track organizational complexity levels or to discover the true cost of product diversification. One reason for this is found in certain flaws in basic GAAP assumptions.

FLAWS IN TRADITIONAL COST-ACCOUNTING ASSUMPTIONS

The overall purpose of cost accounting is two-fold: first, to ascertain how much it costs the enterprise to provide products and services to its customers, and second, to determine how much the company gains in profit from these endeavors. Any flaws in the set of assumptions that govern these two assessments can have serious repercussions for the enterprise. And there are several flaws undergirding GAAP accounting assumptions. The primary ones associated with VEP goals relate to cost and to price, the two elements in the traditional definition of profit.

Flawed Assumptions About Cost

1. Material Costs. A hundred years ago, material costs accounted for about 10 to 15 percent of total manufacturing costs in the ratio among labor, material, and overhead. Due in part to decreases in the two other formula elements (labor and overhead) as well as a shift from labor-intensive work to work done by machines, the level of material cost has grown in recent times to 50 percent or more of total cost. In addition, material costs typically represent the price for which materials are delivered at the facility. But the GAAP formula does not adjust, for example, for procurement or carrying costs.

2. Labor Costs. When accounting techniques were developed in the early days of the industrial revolution, labor costs accounted for 75 to 95 percent of total cost, the largest share by far; material costs came next, followed by overhead costs. But cost patterns have changed significantly in the past 50 years due to new product and new production technologies. The result is a marked reduction in the amount of labor required to manufacture a product. By the late 1980s, the labor content of the average product manufactured in the United States, for example, was 7 percent of the total cost. In isolated cases, where commitment to JIT and other world-class techniques was high, labor costs dropped even lower. At some Hewlett-Packard sites, for instance, labor costs have been reported as low as 2 percent.

In companies where the labor content formula remains unchanged, the accounting departments continue to expend significant time and energy to track and valuate labor elements that have become increasingly less important to the profit equation.

In addition, while standard cost accounting makes it fairly easy to calculate the labor rates (wages paid by category) and time requirements for the operations needed to complete a product, other factors that figure prominently in driving up labor costs are more difficult to reckon. These include: the size of production runs, number of different runs through the same machine or department, equipment changeovers, operator experience plus the detrimental effects of high employee turnovers, fluctuations in production output, and the precise link between a specific product and the processes (production and nonproduction) required to realize it. As a subset of difficult-to-reckon factors associated with product-linked processes, make sure to also include any searching for or moving of parts, tools, fixtures, paperwork, etc.

3. Overhead Costs. According to standard cost-accounting principles, overhead costs are not attributable to specific products; as a result, they are allocated to *all* products. Seventy years ago when this practice was codified, this did not pose a problem because the overhead costs of a product were negligible compared to its labor content. There was little need to track them in great detail.

Now, decades later, the differences between direct/indirect and fixed/variable costs are far less distinct. The boundaries between them are blurred. The overhead portion of product cost can account for as much as 35 to 50 percent of total cost, and, in some cases, can escalate to 75 percent. The net effect is that certain products now get assigned a disproportionately large or small overhead share. Since overhead can now represent a large measure of total product cost, an inequitable formula for analyzing and assigning it can have serious repercussions for the enterprise.

Some companies have adjusted their standard allocations to correct for these outdated cost assumptions. Others have gone over to a system of activity-based costing (ABC), described on pages 86–87. But in many companies, traditional cost-accounting principles remain unchanged. If a company committed to the path of world-class values and results continues to use these, it may get a distorted and misleading picture of its present performance, challenges, and improvement options. This is perhaps the greatest danger.

We now turn to the price component of the profit formula and some erroneous GAAP assumptions associated with it.

Flawed Assumptions About Price

1. **Shift from Margins to Market Share.** Traditional cost analysis is geared to calculate product price based on acceptable margins. Over the past two decades, however, there has been a shift in corporate strategy away from customary pricing practices to one that assigns price based on market share and long-term company viability. The emerging importance of capturing new market share has fueled a rush among manufacturers to introduce a continuous stream of new products at a price the *consumer* finds acceptable.

2. **Cost-Driven Versus Market-Driven Pricing.** In the traditional accounting approach to pricing, a company arrives at a suitable selling price by putting an acceptable profit margin on top of its costs. Product price is a function of cost differential and markup and, over the decades, many a company has improved its bottom line simply by raising the price tag. In this scenario price becomes a matter of what the consumer will bear.

But that day has passed. The economy (both domestic and global) has entered a period of disinflation in which surging demand fuels lower, not higher, prices. Low-ball or target pricing is now king.

These changes in pricing patterns are positive ones and do not diminish the role of cost as a profit factor. If anything, as we discussed in the Introduction, disinflation is forcing organizations to take a harder look at costs and their corollaries in product and organizational complexity. It is because markup is no longer a routine solution to high costs that market-driven pricing can add fuel to all manner of cost-improvement activity. When high costs can no longer be absorbed by jacking up the selling price, companies have no other recourse than to work more diligently on cost-improvement activities.

Unfortunately, flawed GAAP assumptions around price mask the opportunity and the solution. In many companies, GAAP practices that support obsolete markup pricing remain unchanged.

THE ALLOCATION OF TRUE COST

A New Cost Perspective

One of the most significant insights into what makes a successful company in the business ecology of the 1990s is the recognition of the link between product complexity and complexities found in marketing, design, manufacturing, distribution, and support processes. On what basis is this link made? How do we substantiate it? Are there specific costs triggered by this relationship? If so, can they be measured or verified? If so, how? We already know that traditional accounting, with its *cost-masking* properties, will not help us. What we need is a new and more practical perspective on cost.

For over two decades, the Japanese have been giving us lessons in how to build long-term competitive advantage through the systematic identification and reduction of waste—a.k.a. cost. We have learned those lessons well. We have found and rooted out the high costs of manufacturing—making defects, overinspection, too much material handling, building inventory. But, as we are now learning, there are other costs beyond these, buried deep in the organizational infrastructure. In the previous chapter, we labeled these "new" hidden costs (and what is "new" is the awareness of them, not the costs themselves) the *runaway by-products of new product expansion*. They are excesses, rarely seen and almost always ignored, triggered in the push for new markets.

The term that VEP uses to capture this new perspective on the cost of new products is "true cost." "True" here is used in the sense of real and actual. True cost, as we shall see, is not an extension of an abstract formula such as found in GAAP practices but a quantity that makes or breaks the bottom line. It is not so much a redefinition of cost as the decision to look for cost in a different place, in its real abode, at its source—the single source of cost, *the part itself*. VEP defines true cost as "the sum of the chain of costs triggered by the introduction of a new part into the company system." Minimizing true cost is the goal of VEP. In this sense, all organizational activity is reduced to a single source of cost, the part itself. This emphasis on true cost is VEP's way of calling our attention to the need for a new cost perspective, one that factors in the full impact of all our business decisions.

The Origins of Organizational Complexity

In VEP, finding the root cause of variety begins as far upstream as possible, at the initial phases of product conceptualization and design. It is here, as the product moves from concept to prototype and one new part after another is added, that cost begins to accumulate and its various trajectories can be observed ricocheting across the entire organization.

Singular as it may initially appear, it is only when a company discerns waste in this clear and precise manner that the successive layers of complexity triggered by that part can be identified and disassembled. Minimizing these layers is, by its very nature, an iterative process. Like a gem cutter chiseling away at the layers of a rough diamond to expose its brilliant core, you have to systematically remove unwarranted variation and needless differences until variety effectiveness is realized. This effort leads us through the dross and debris of antiquated product practices to the smart, simple designs that our customers will buy. We begin to make products for profit.

Costs Adhere to Parts: The Part as First Cause

Parts Unlimited Inc., our company example, began as a one-product company. Within a decade, its product lines began to rapidly expand, with each new product requiring from one to 25 new parts. Now, 60 years later, the company is awash in products and parts, and complexity threatens to choke off all profits.

Just One New Part

From the VEP perspective, PUI's unhappy plight got kicked off when the first new part was introduced—and nobody "noticed." This is an important point. From the viewpoint of variety effectiveness, the addition of even one new part sets in motion a long causal chain of cost and complication, which is almost impossible, if unaddressed, to trace or restrain.

When PUI decided to differentiate its product line, it *inadvertently* triggered a series of negative effects, and a trail of costs followed in its wake (*inadvertently* because its cost-accounting system was not geared to watchdog for those effects). The first loop of these unintended effects hit the company in four main cost categories—development, materials, production, and facilities. The actual costs spanned a range of activity, from the cost of drawings to copying, from the cost of materials management to product defects, from the cost of purchasing new equipment, tools, and dies to planning and scheduling, and from utilities cost to the rent or mortgage itself, (see Figure 3.3).

But PUI's cost list does not end there. Labor hours for designers, drafts people, and other technicians in the Product Development Department increased due to overtime costs and new hires. As parts plans were fed into the system, drawings and blueprints multiplied. Purchasing began to fight never-ending battles to procure parts and maintain service parts. The shop floor faced a spiraling need for new dies and tooling and a corresponding need for more setups.

Over the years, production processes and methods grew in number and complexity, creating other complications in the flow of production. As product offerings rose even further, dead stock began accumulating in storage.

In its attempts to deal with mushrooming product lines, the infrastructure at Parts Unlimited Inc. became increasingly cost-burdened. Spiraling complexities made it less likely that their root cause could be identified and addressed. Continuing complexity spurred yet further complication, and the company became engaged in a desperate struggle to find a box big enough to hold the consequences triggered by adding "one new part." And all this in the face of ever-shortening product life

FIGURE 3.3. Consequences of Adding Just One New Product with Just One New Part

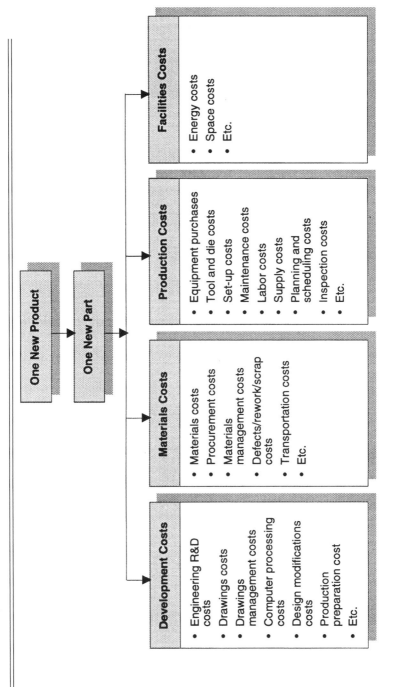

cycles and sales and profits that never seemed to grow in proportion to the increase in product offerings and parts count variety. The cumulative effect was about to drive an otherwise thriving company out of business.

What happened? Like many companies, Parts Unlimited Inc. had not yet realized that complex products create complex organizations; it had not yet understood that *all costs adhere to the part*. Once a company grasps this, it must then operationalize this new understanding into practices that help gauge levels of organizational complexity and valuate true costs. VEP provides two mechanisms for doing this. The first is VEP's *Parts Index** for exposing product and organizational complexity. The second is VEP's *Tri-Cost/True-Cost Model* for differentiating the costs of that complexity. First we'll learn about the index and how it works, and then look at the cost model.

MEASURING PRODUCT AND ORGANIZATIONAL COMPLEXITY

We have already seen how the addition of even one new part can trigger dozens of cost categories. In VEP, this simple but powerful understanding is operationalized through the VEP Parts Index, a universal measure of product and organizational complexity.

To illustrate how the VEP Parts Index works, let's observe what happens as a start-up pen company prepares to manufacture its first product series, the J-190s, a ballpoint pen line. The first model, J-191, is a blue-ink pen, simple as products go: eight part numbers at a cost of about $.23 per pen. The part numbers and description are listed below, along with the cost of each part (standard carrying costs already reflected) (see Figure 3.4).

A success, the blue-ink model led to the introduction of a red-ink model the next year—model J-192. Figure 3.5 shows that the parts list for

---

* See Toshiro Suzue and Akira Kohdate, *Variety Reduction Program.*

FIGURE 3.4. Parts List: Model J-191–Blue Pen

Part #	Part Description	Part Cost
1. 1-R-9	One housing	.010
2. J64T	One cap clip–blue	.035
3. 32-2	One ball bearing	.035
4. 54-BL	Ink–blue	.023
5. J56-3	One pen tip	.025
6. 5K3	One ink retainer	.070
7. 44-44	One pen guide	.025
8. 77-94	One plug–blue	.008
	Total unit cost	**.231**

FIGURE 3.5. Parts List: Model J-192–Red Pen

Part #	Part Description	Part Cost
1. 1-R-9	One housing	.010
2. J65T	One cap clip–red	.035
3. 32-2	One ball bearing	.035
4. 55-RD	Ink–red	.023
5. J56-3	One pen tip	.025
6. 5K3	One ink retainer	.070
7. 44-44	One pen guide	.025
8. 77-95	One plug–red	.008
	Total unit cost	**.231**

this second model is identical to that of the first, except for the ink change and corresponding changes in the color-coordinated cap clip and plug. Simple as this product is, however, the ink change resulted in the addition of three new part numbers, or a 38 percent increase in the company's parts inventory; the five other parts are shared (or commonized) between the two models. The "cost" of the two products is identical, according to traditional cost-accounting procedures in use by the company at this time.

The VEP Parts Index: Universal Measure of Complexity

What was the effect of adding a red model to the pen company's product line? Simple as the product is, the addition of the second model led to complicating factors and unexpected costs—the cost of acquiring and handling the three new part numbers, added paperwork needed to order and track parts, separate storage space for each new part, new shelf and bin labeling, the need for additional machine setups when the ink is changed (and the purchase of dedicated equipment if either product gains popularity and demand grows), etc., etc.

Let's look at the two models via a VEP perspective, as a function of complexity rather than parts cost. To do this, we will lay out the parts lists (a.k.a. bill of material/BOM) for each model in a matrix known as the VEP Parts Index. This matrix allows us to see the number of different part types as well as the number of times each part number within each part type is used across the blue- and the red-ink models. In other words, we can see which, and how many, parts are shared or commonized and which are dedicated or unique. Once displayed, we compute a simple calculation and arrive at an indexed figure. This figure is a relative measure of complexity (see Figure 3.6).

The VEP Parts Index is the sum of all the part numbers in the associated BOMs *multiplied by* the sum of the times each part number occurs *across* those models—16 part numbers, occurring as a part type, 11 times. The multiplied result (product) is an indexed figure, in this case 176. This figure is a relative measure of variety within the product group. In this way, the index is a reconfiguration of the BOM, but unlike a BOM for one product, it shows the intersection of part types and number of occurrences within each of these across the models under scrutiny. *In other words, variety is reflected in the total quantity of parts handled.*

FIGURE 3.6. VEP Parts Index for Model J-191/Blue and J-192/Red

Part Type	Part Number	Model J-191	Model J-192	Part Type Occurrences
Housing	1-R-9	1	1	1
Cap Clip	J64T-BL	1		2
	J65T-RD		1	
Ball Bearing	32-2	1	1	1
Ink	54-BL	1		2
	55-RD		1	
Pen Tip	J56-3	1	1	1
Ink Retainer	5K3	1	1	1
Pen Guide	44-44	1	1	1
Plug	77-94-BL	1		2
	77-95-RD		1	
Parts Count		**8**	**8**	11 / 16
VEP Parts Index (Models J-191 & J-192) = 176 (16 × 11)				

Within a month, the red-ink model began to outsell the blue, and the company decided to add a black model (J-193) and a green one (J-194). We ask the question again: What was the effect, the real impact—the true cost—on the company of adding two more models? To answer that question we begin by looking through the window of a new VEP Parts Index (see Figure 3.7) and comparing it to the previous one.

Looking through the window of the new index, we see that the cumulative number of BOM parts has doubled, going from 16 to 32. That makes perfect sense, you say, since the number of products doubled, going from two to four. And the part type occurrences climbed six notches, from 11 to 17. No worry there. But the index itself is behaving strangely. It was at 176 for two products but jumped to 544 for two more, more than three times the original number and 68 percent higher than the previous index (and not the expected 50 percent). The scene at the pen company is getting "unexpectedly" complex. In the back offices, the

FIGURE 3.7. VEP Parts Index for Models J-191, 192, 193, 194

Part Type	Part Number	Model J-191 (blue)	Model J-192 (red)	Model J-193 (black)	Model J-194 (green)	Part Type Occurrences
Housing	1-R-9	1	1	1	1	1
Cap Clip	J64T	1				
	J65T		1			
	J66T			1		4
	J67T				1	
Ball Bearing	32-2	1	1	1	1	1
Ink	54-BL	1				
	55-RD		1			
	56-BK			1		4
	57-GN				1	
Pen Tip	J56-3	1	1	1	1	1
Ink Retainer	5K3	1	1	1	1	1
Pen Guide	44-44	1	1	1	1	1
Plug	77-94	1				
	77-95		1			
	77-96			1		4
	77-97				1	
Parts Count		8	8	8	8	17 / 32

VEP Parts Index (four J-190 Models) = 544 (32 × 17)

search for suppliers of black and red ink has begun, calls for bids are out, new storage area is being located, and new fields are being entered into the computer. Equipment set-up operators are trying not to think about the messy ink changeovers that'll be required. Things are getting just a little bit more congested. But, excited by the increased sales revenue, Sales and Marketing are talking about adding a new model in sparkling pastel

colors aimed at teenage girls, and another with a mock Mount Blanc®
barrel and cap for the "yuppie wannabe" market.

The VEP Parts Index is not designed to put a judgment or valance on
the parts variation it exposes. It simply displays it. The question of whether
the engendered variety is positive or negative remains to be answered by
the VEP teams, not by the index. The index is first and foremost a measure
and a predictor. As such, the VEP Parts Index is a simple and shrewd
yardstick for measuring product complexity and for predicting corresponding complications that *could* follow in the aftermath. (In later chapters, we'll show how the index is used to support the VEP methodology and
how it can be adapted to index other areas of variation triggered by product
variety—production processes and control points.)

Up to this point, our examples have illustrated an application of the
index on a highly standardized product of few parts (of which many are
shared)—a ballpoint pen. Observing the expansion of variations across
the several models of this simple product helps us appreciate the progres-
sive and accumulating impact of adding new parts. But the index is also
used to expose possible complications associated with complex products.
In VEP, a product is considered *complex* when it has some shared parts
and many dedicated parts (parts unique to it). If the parts are highly
standardized, the likelihood of their being shared across products increases and, inversely, possible levels of organizational complexity drop
substantially. But we're getting ahead of ourselves.

Let's look at the more complex product known as the T-144, a
pressure control made by Parts Unlimited, designed for hazardous, explosive applications in oil refineries, chemical plants, and gas pipelines. The
VEP Parts Index shown in Figure 3.8 is a partial index, calculated on
partial BOMs; it displays 12 part types out of the 25 found across three of
the 51 different models in the T-144 series. (Other more complex PUI
series have models whose BOMs contain from 50 to 200 different parts.)
The index figure of 1,672 for these partial BOMs begins to suggest the
level of complication the company is encumbered by in manufacturing
these three models. From a pool of only 12 part types, 76 different parts
are used, variously occurring 22 times.

One might wonder what it was like in the beginning, as PUI was
ramping up to launch these exciting new additions. Translated in our

FIGURE 3.8. VEP Parts Index: Partial BOM for 3 of 51 PUI Models

Part Type	Part Number	Model T-144-06	Model T-144-08	Model T-144-12	Part Type Occur-rences
Screw	0113-06019	2	2	2	
	0113-08038	1	1	1	
	0125-10025	3	3		6
	0147-08038			4	
	0147-08056	3	3	3	
	0143-40075			10	
Nylon Ball	6219-746	1	1	1	1
Spring Pin	6219-813			2	1
Lockwasher Split No. 1/4	2519-25	1	1		1
Explosion-proof Enclosure	60120-13	1	1	1	1
Insulator	6205-267	1	1	1	2
	6205-387	1	1	1	
Spring	6238-446	1			2
	6238-448		1	1	
Plunger	6240-966	1			2
	6201-298		1	1	
O-Ring	6212-144	1	1	1	3
	6212-281	1	1	1	
	6212-284			1	
Housing	6216-208	1	1	1	1
Mounting Bracket	6222-167	1	1	1	1
I & M Label	6233-543	1	1	1	1
Total Parts Count		**21**	**21**	**34**	**22** / **76**

VEP Parts Index = 1,672 (76 × 22)

imagination, the index is like a TV screen on which we picture product developers scurrying to Drafting with a fistful of drawings, harried process engineers swarming the shop floor in the midst of last-minute ECNs (engineering change notices), procurement specialists upstairs scouring the county for a source for explosion-proof enclosures—located close enough to meet the company's JIT requirements, teams in Cells #930 and #931 scratching their collective head, trying to figure out where to fit 76 new part numbers in their POUS (point-of-use storage). In other words, it's business as usual.

Not an Exact Measure—But an Exacting One

VEP's Parts Index is not an exact measure. It serves, instead, as an approximation of product cost, with cost as a function of the number of part types and their occurrences by product. It can also be adapted for multiple other uses:

- Tracking part types as they are added over time
- Estimating the impact of ECNs on the total parts inventory
- Assessing offerings across diverse markets
- Displaying the intersection of production processes across product models, types, and lines
- Displaying the intersection of control points across control functions and products

Because it is a relative measure of variety, it is possible to use the index to surmise or extrapolate the impact of complex products on the organization.

Companies wanting to make the move from a traditional measurement approach that runs counter to their operational and profit objectives need ways to verify the existence of complexity as an organizational problem and to gain insight into its whereabouts and causes. Depending on how wide its scope, the VEP Parts Index can let us see the impact of part variation (or its potential) from several perspectives:

1. Narrow Perspective—compute an index on all subassemblies within a model group.

2. Broader Perspective—compute an index on all part numbers within a model group.
3. Widest Perspective—compute a single cumulative index on the company's entire product universe.

In each case, VEP's Parts Index exposes internal part jam-ups and helps track down associated causes.

The Index as an Improvement Driver

One of the challenges of a cross-functional improvement process like VEP is to find a simple measure that the organization can use to gauge its overall progress. Similarly, individual departments need a simple and understandable way to assess their respective success levels. Up until now, no device has been available for estimating, even approximately, the impact of product proliferation on the organization. To attempt to do so with a traditional accounting approach would be so cumbersome and intricate, any benefit such knowledge might bring would be nullified. The VEP Parts Index, however, provides such a yardstick. And it becomes more powerful when linked to an improvement-driven approach such as ABC accounting (more about this later in this chapter).

Given that VEP's goal is to reduce parts numbers to a level optimal for the market, and given its central premise that *the part equals cost*, the VEP Parts Index is a useful way to estimate the company's success in minimizing cost as a corollary of parts count. The index is not an exact measure; as we will learn in the next section of this chapter, however, solid awareness of a significant issue is often more potent than meticulous evidence of an insignificant one—or, as someone once said, "a stitch in time would have confused Einstein."

Now that we've explored the VEP Parts Index and how it can alert us to the possibility of hidden costs, we turn to the second cost-related mechanism in VEP to help us understand what form those costs might take—VEP's Tri-Cost/True-Cost Model.

VEP'S TRI-COST MODEL: THE THREE DIMENSIONS OF TRUE COST

We have seen that variety in products and parts can trigger costs and internal complexity. What, then, are the divisions of those costs? What does the complexity look like? Can this information be codified or summarized into a reference model that facilitates inquiry and application? What form does the impact of adding one or a dozen new products to the company offerings take? Is there a way for the company to assess what it will spend—or has spent to date—on meeting customer demands? What is the true cost of a single drawing? To find the answers, we look to VEP's Tri-Cost/True-Cost Model.

In a nutshell, the Parts Index makes complexity evident and the Tri-Cost Model delineates a product's *true cost*. Unlike the traditional labor-burdened GAAP approach discussed earlier in this chapter, this model links up directly to the complicating side effects of manufacturing more than one product, and then reconfigures the expenditure of time and assets along three cost dimensions—function, variety, and control:

- The dimension of function—or what happens as the company fulfills the performance requirements of a single product
- The dimension of variety—or what happens as the company develops and manufactures diverse products
- The dimension of control—or what happens as the company orders, tracks, inspects, or otherwise supports the manufacture of diverse products*

These dimensions are more clearly delineated in Figure 3.9. True cost is the sum of the costs of these three dimensions, expressed as the following formula:

* For more, see Toshiro Suzue and Akira Kohdate, *Variety Reduction Program*.

> **Total Cost = Variety Costs + Control Costs**

The pen company discussed above, for example, will use this cost equation not to assess on the cost of a single product but to delineate the meaning of the index figure (544 in Figure 3.7) and its impact on the organization. In conjunction with the Index, VEP's cost approach looks at the costs, or consequences, of introducing that single new model into an organizational context that is already product-populated. It does not— nor does it attempt to—provide an exact cost reckoning for each product or the dollar amount of those consequences.

We will now examine each of the three VEP cost dimensions in further detail.

Dimension 1: Function Costs

A product is a collection of parts. Function Costs (F-Costs) are generated as the company furnishes a product with its required functions through parts specifications, values, dimensions, and unit structures. F-Costs are triggered in the design of a single product and also include the materials, processing, methods, and personnel involved in developing, fabricating, assembling, and packing and shipping that product.

Design decisions about product and part values are inextricably linked to the functions those values are contrived to fulfill. Ideally, a product's structural and parts specifications are based, first and foremost, on client and market needs. Frequently, however, this is not the case. Too often, a company fulfills product function through a parts structure that is unduly varied and complex.

Many companies facing high Function Costs have attempted to redress this condition through value engineering/value analysis (VE/VA). The intent of VE/VA is to minimize the cost of realizing product function. This can be very effective in minimizing Function Costs on a case-by-case basis, but may cause a simultaneous rise in Variety Costs (more about this in Chapter 4).

FIGURE 3.9. Three Dimensions of True Cost Defined

Cost Dimension	Definition	Details
1. Function Costs	. . . are generated as the company furnishes a product with its required functions through part specifications, values, and unit structures.	*F-Costs* are equivalent to the sum of the labor, material, and processing costs as found in a standard cost-accounting system.
2. Variety Costs	. . . are triggered when a company adds to its stock of design specifications, dimensions, and values in the form of even a single new part, regardless of whether the addition is customer-driven or internally triggered.	*V-Costs* include *added* production processes, machines, tooling, fixtures, shelving, space, etc.—all that is required to fulfill the demands of multiple products, product types, and models—and encompasses the cumulative consequence of diversity on the entire system.
3. Control Costs	. . . refer to tasks and information transactions geared to control, track, manage, or otherwise support a product and its parts as they move through the system to the end-user.	*C-Costs* refer to the myriad of transactions the company undertakes to design, acquire, order, receive, inspect, track, store, retrieve, count, handle, maintain, or otherwise support and manage the manufacture and sale of its offerings.

As a category, F-Costs may be taken as the sum of the labor, material, and processing costs as found in a standard cost-accounting system. Seventy years ago, these costs accounted for more than 90 percent of the cost of a product. Today, in many businesses, they range as low as 40 percent.

Dimension 2: Variety Costs

Variety Costs (V-Costs) exist in companies that have a diversified product line. These costs are triggered when a product line expands, even if only one attribute of a single part is altered, however slightly. Whether such changes are customer-initiated or internally triggered, the result is a variety cost.

Variety costs, then, are the costs that arise from product diversification. These costs include the additional production processes, machines, tooling, fixtures, etc., required for the enterprise to fulfill the needs of additional products and multiple product types and models. This variety factor applies across product lines and encompasses the cumulative consequence of diversity on the entire system. The engine of complexity is variety costs. Overall, they are estimated to constitute 25 percent of the total cost of the product.

An organization may adopt several strategies for dealing with the demands of a proliferating product line. For example, the company may pursue standardization as a remedy. In this event, engineers seek to avoid product designs that call for dedicated or specialized parts and strive, instead, to design parts that can be shared across as wide a range of products as possible—a critically important tactic as far as VEP is concerned. In another case, the company may elect to meet the need of processing the differing parts by investing in additional equipment and/or in flexible manufacturing equipment (e.g., Computer Numerical Control [CNC] machines). Sooner or later, though, the limits of this equipment are reached; the company may then decide to purchase machines and tooling that promise even greater range and flexibility. In such a case, it is not unusual for the company to pass on its dilemma to the customer in the form of higher prices.

Along the same lines a company seeking to meet the needs of ever-burgeoning product lines through equipment purchase can find itself in a double bind. If it continues to allocate resources for new tooling, it may be forced to forgo other investment opportunities. Alternatively, in light of a mushrooming parts count, it may foresee the futility of automation as a long-term solution and decide not to invest in it; as a result, it forgoes its money-saving benefits. In both cases, exploding variety renders these options expensive, and neither of them provides a durable solution to the problem.

Dimension 3: Control Costs

Control Costs (C-Costs) refer to the indirect tasks and information transactions that support the other two cost categories—Variety Costs and Function Costs. C-Costs include costs for design, drafting, ordering, buying, inspecting, transporting, storing, and maintenance. In scope and variety, they are therefore roughly equivalent to overhead.

Each informational exchange is a control point. The wages of all nonoperational personnel involved in these activities are also Control Costs. What, for example, are the cost corollaries of a single drawing? Let's track the cascade of control points triggered by that.

Once the design is generated by the designer, it winds its way through the company to drafting, then prototype, pilot, and revision. There are many other aftereffects of a single drawing, viewed from the opposite end of the plant:

Group 1: Raw material/parts are sourced, ordered, and paid for.

Group 2: Raw material/parts are received on the dock, inspected, handled, and stored.

Group 3: Raw material/parts are retrieved and checked for quality after processing and/or assembly.

Group 4: Finished goods are packed and shipped to the customer.

There are many other kinds of activity, of course, that are not specified here—inventory control (which attempts to answer the question: How much should be kept on hand?), production scheduling, and data processing.

Control Costs, then, delineate the overhead expense incurred to support products, parts, and processes. These are the costs incurred by people—the people in Design, Operations, Material Handling, and other support functions. Control Costs also refer directly to the myriad of transactions that people in the company undertake to acquire, receive, inspect, track, store, retrieve, market, sell, and support products.

Literally dozens—sometimes hundreds—of control points can adhere to a single product, or even a single part. Control points are single-product or part-specific actions and transactions that touch every department and, taken in their sum, create a workplace that is hyperactive with detail and swimming in minutiae. The population size of control points found in an organization goes a long way in making and keeping it clogged with complexity. However committed a company may be to world-class excellence—JIT, lean manufacturing, customer-driven service, etc.—its progress will eventually get stymied if control points are not themselves brought under control and minimized.

Divvying Up the VEP Cost Pie

Seventy years ago, Function Costs accounted for 90 percent of total manufacturing cost, with Variety and Control Costs sharing the remaining 10 percent.

But that was then and now is—different. World War II brought huge changes to the meaning of success in business, with product diversification increasingly viewed as a competitive strategy. With those changes, Variety and Control Costs began to take ever-widening shares of the total cost pie. By cost category, the percentage share of total cost generally assignable to each is as follows (see Figure 3.10):

F-Costs: estimated at 40 percent of the total cost of the product
V-Costs: estimated at 25 percent of the total cost of the product
C-Costs: estimated at 35 percent of the total cost of the product

The shares of the costs shown above are typical approximations at best. These can fluctuate widely according to the type of industry and markets, as well as the ongoing level of improvement activity in specific companies. In specialized industries like brick manufacturing, for example, Function Costs generally hover around 15 percent because the product is highly standardized; Variety Costs, on the other hand, may be

FIGURE 3.10. Divvying Shares: F-Costs, V-Costs, and C-Costs

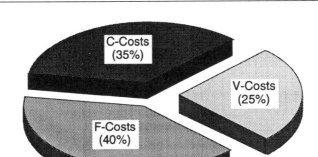

elevated, possibly as high as 55 percent, due to the costly chemicals required to meet the range of brick values needed in that market.

In automotive, mass-production electronics, and other volume industries, Function Costs can reach as high as 50 to 70 percent. Variety Costs in highly standardized sectors can account for as little as 20 percent of total cost, with Control Costs as low as 10 percent. By contrast, special-order industries like furniture, heavy earth-moving equipment, and customized electronics can trigger Control Costs that climb to 45 percent.

A further word on the control cost share. These generally stay steady in the 30 percent to 40 percent range due to the high degree of similarity across industries in standard bureaucratic and administrative procedures. Exceptions include businesses dealing with highly regulated government contracts, which require significantly more documentation and inspection activity than does private-sector work. In these instances, if *all* control points were carefully tracked in terms of VEP's definitions, C-Costs might soar into the 50 percent level or higher.

The Link Between Control Points and Accounting Practices

It is the variety in products, parts, and processes that results in excessive control points. We must also point out that many control points are also triggered by the outdated accounting practices described earlier in this chapter. This labor-burdened approach often overlooks or ignores wasteful variety; it may even encourage or create it because:

1. It spends vast quantities of time and energy measuring the wrong things in the wrong way.
2. It neglects to measure the right things efficiently and effectively.
3. It directs the work force, as a consequence of the above, to pursue irrelevant, and often detrimental, objectives.

Activity-Based Cost Accounting

Part of the beauty of VEP's Parts Index and Tri-Cost Model is that they do not encourage companies to get caught up in ascertaining costs in terms of exact dollar amounts, one of the problems with traditional cost-accounting practices. So much time and effort are spent in getting to the penny-exact figures that the goal is sometimes forgotten. The goal is to improve, to find and exorcise the causes of negative variety, and to expend what resources one must more effectively until they are optimized into least-sum means—until *effective variety* is achieved.

A more helpful alternative to consider is activity-based costing (ABC). While it is not our purpose to promote or explain the ABC approach, we will mention several factors that align it with VEP objectives:

- ABC does not make the strict differentiations among material, labor, and overhead costs defined in traditional accounting principles.
- ABC groups them all as indirect costs and then seeks to link each of them with a specific source activity (known as a cost driver).

Companies select the cost drivers most relevant to their process and their improvement objectives and begin to track them—for example, number of purchase orders, customer orders, engineering change notices (ECNs), material moves, machine setups, tools issued to the shop floor, product insertions, manual soldering tasks, products shipped, etc. A company using an ABC system learns to reassign, in correct proportions, costs that were previously allocated as indirect to specific products. In ABC costing, for example, indirect costs are separated into procurement, production, and support activity.*

AWARENESS IS EVERYTHING

The goal of VEP is to maximize customer selection by reducing the negative effects of product variety and strengthening the positive effects. That means optimizing external variety (varying products so that customers buy them) and minimizing internal variety (how the organization provides those varying products).

In this chapter, we introduced two of the tools central to this effort— first, the Parts Index, to help you determine whether your company might be a shelter for negative variety, and second, the Tri-Cost Model, to help you ascertain how negative variety expresses itself in your organization. Between the two, you can validate the need for action. While you may never succeed in eradicating all traces of negative variety, you can expect to find a balance point between it and positive variety. That balance point is called effective variety. Achieving this balance does not necessarily mean that the enterprise makes more revenue—or even saves more money. It means that the company makes more *profit*.

As much as a company may need reliable accounting procedures, it is equally urgent to cultivate a dynamic awareness in the organization that negative variety creates cost. The VEP Index and Tri-Cost Model are designed to promote that awareness and trigger further insights so that

---

* For more about ABC costing, as well as a brilliant and useful discussion on improvement measures that really matter, see Brian H. Maskell, *Performance Measurement for World Class Manufacturing: A Model for American Companies* (Cambridge, Mass.: Productivity Press, 1991). See also Robin Cooper and Robert S. Kaplan, "Measure Costs Right: Make the Right Decisions," *Harvard Business Review*, September–October 1988, pp. 97–103.

you and your associates recognize the existence of negative variety in your midst. And once you recognize it, you will move to action, to improvement action. You will do something about it.

Next we will look at the *causes* of cost and complexity triggered by new product expansion.

CHAPTER FOUR

TRIGGERS OF THE VARIETY EXPLOSION

Nissan . . . [used to offer customers] more than 300 varieties of ashtrays.

—*WALL STREET JOURNAL,* MARCH 3, 1993

THE VARIETY EXPLOSION

In the 1990s, a new giant was found hiding in corporate closets: riotous growth in products accompanied by a simultaneous explosion in parts inventories. The net effect was a level of internal complexity and congestion unparalleled in the history of business and industry. To a great extent, this condition was both the beneficiary and victim of accelerating capabilities in computer technology. The computer, and the canny software that supported it, allowed companies to generate huge annual crops of new products with levels of speed, ease, and ingenuity previously unthinkable, limited only by the human imagination. The same computers provided organizations with a capability to store and manipulate immense amounts of information related to the design, marketing, and production of these products, and, in the act of doing so, vast new quantities of data were added to an already-swollen base.

But the computer was not designed to manage itself or its output. Few companies were prepared to manage the pool of data or the glut of diversified products that resulted. Few companies had factored in the secret costs of introducing all those exciting new products. Nor were they prepared to absorb their costs, costs that continued to drain even those companies with sterling, super-lean production systems. The cruelest blow, perhaps, was the dawning realization of these businesses that the customer did not always want the high level of choice they had worked so hard and spent so much to provide.

A *Wall Street Journal* article reports that in 1993 Japan was facing "the worst slump in car sales in 20 years." Nissan (one of Japan's top automakers), after "nearly a decade-long quest to build cars in ever more sizes, colors and functions to satisfy the presumed whims of the world's drivers," saw its car model variations balloon to more than 2,200. To support these, the company offered 437 different kinds of dashboard meters, some 1,200 types of floor carpets, and the 300 different kinds of ashtrays mentioned above. In one model alone (the Laurel, now discontinued), Nissan offered 87 types of steering wheels. Under the hood, customers might find (if they cared to look) one of 110 types of radiators. And it was all held together with over 6,000 different fasteners. The number of possible combinations that made for unique products bordered on astronomical. Nissan went on to discover "that 70 of the 87 types of steering wheels for the Laurel accounted for just 5% of the total installed. Indeed, 50% of Nissan's model variations contributed only about 5% of total sales."*

Swelling costs tied to product variety were not confined to Nissan. All 11 of Japan's automakers were expecting "a skid" in 1993. Matsushita Electrical Industrial Co., another Japanese giant, came out of the 1980s saddled with 6,000 models of stereos and portable tape players. And the variety explosion at the OEMs (original equipment manufacturers) rippled through a chain of suppliers that staggered to respond with a supporting medley of components. Calsonic Corp., for example, one of Nissan's biggest suppliers, was forced "to make no less than 2,000 kinds of mufflers alone, the majority of which are used at a rate of only a few units a year ... [and] to maintain the presses, dies, and

---

* Clay Chandler and Michael Williams, "Strategic Shift: A Slump in Car Sales Forces Nissan to Start Cutting Swollen Costs," *Wall Street Journal*, March 3, 1993.

inventory on all those different kinds of mufflers for the lifetime of the cars . . . nine or 10 years. In the fat years, Nissan could afford such excess. But now it considers that array of choices too expensive and ultimately fruitless."* Many companies are reaching the same conclusion.

This chapter focuses on the causes of negative variety. To frame the discussion we start by looking at the goal—*achieving effective variety*—in order to better understand it as a balance point, not a static outcome. We then define three areas of change or forces that are found outside the individual company in the broader ecology of commerce itself. These forces challenge the effort to achieve a balanced approach to product expansion. Inside the company a second set of forces are in motion in the form of company and departmental policies and practices (formal and informal); these challenge the balance point further and can trigger significant complications and costs of their own. The remainder of this chapter (and the bulk of it) is devoted to describing 16 such practices, some or many of which may exist in your own company.

EFFECTIVE VARIETY—THE BALANCE POINT

Unrestrained variety in designs and models is not a requirement for increasing market share. Much of what passes for increased customer selection may be, in reality, needless variation. Nissan's 87 steering wheels is a good example; rare is the customer who buys a car *because* of the steering wheel. When a choice is pointless, it is negative. *Negative* variety adds cost, not value. It burdens the corporation with complexity and expense. Ultimately, the customer pays. *Positive* variety, on other hand, adds value, increases sales, and can cut costs. Understanding the

* *Wall Street Journal*, March 3, 1993.

s between positive and negative variety—and their respective causes—is critical.

The difference is this: Positive variety is *customer-driven*; it is directly linked to verifiable customer interest or demand. Negative variety is everything else; it is the result of the *way the business operates*, its policies, practices, and systems. In other words, negative variety is *internally triggered*. *Effective* variety is the balance point between the two.

What effective variety is not is the static endpoint of a journey. Instead, it is the act of finding the ever-shifting point of balance that is suitable for your organization between what your company wants and the internal requirements of running a successful business (see Figure 4.1).

Though this point of balance is forever being redefined, the goal remains the same: Root out the causes of negative variety and find the least-sum means. And, as we will show before the end of this chapter, those causes are unavoidably linked to specific company practices. Virtually every part of the organization—Marketing, Sales, Design Engineering, Process Engineering, Operations, Purchasing, Systems, and others—can make either a positive or negative impact on effective variety through the formal and informal policies it follows. It is these policies that help or hinder efforts to achieve effective variety.*

THE ROOTS OF PRODUCT PROLIFERATION

Global Forces

The introduction of new products is at the top of the competitive agenda of practically every manufacturer in the 1990s. This agenda emerged over the past two decades, driven by three forces. First, markets have been

---

* This is overviewed here and discussed more fully later in the chapter.

FIGURE 4.1. Effective Variety—An Ever-Shifting Balance Point

Before VEP
- Out of balance
- Negative far outweighs positive variety

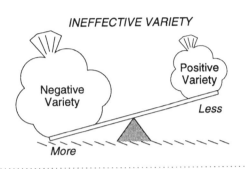

VEP in Process
- In balance
- The balance can now begin to shift

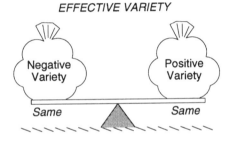

VEP Success
- Positive far outweighs negative variety
- Effective variety achieved

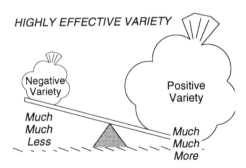

internationalized. Competition has become global. Companies can no longer count on growth and security from success on a regional or domestic scale alone. Even if companies thrive in those domestic markets, the threat of an invasion of foreign competitors is never far from view; protective steps must be taken. *Fortune* magazine reports that in the

1980s Cummins Engine, a top-ranking diesel engine manufacturer, spent "$1 billion, three times the market value of its stock at the time," to expand its engine products simultaneously on three fronts. "Within four years, Cummins had to slash prices on its new products as much as 30% to fend off Japanese imports." Says Henry Schacht, Cummins's CEO since 1977, "You let these guys in, you never get them out."*

A second powerful stimulus for new products are the breakthroughs in science and technology that continually push the edges of the innovation envelope. Advances in technology now make it possible for a company to give consumers the specific differentiations they increasingly demand. This is nowhere more vividly seen than in the computer industry, where advances in technology have resulted in the introduction of a flood of new-to-the-world products over the past two decades. In addition to your basic computers, monitors, and printers, the market offers an ever-widening range of laptops, portables, notebooks, scanners, plotters, modems, plus legion peripherals and accessories.

By the same token, scientific and engineering breakthroughs can spread like wildfire through the R&D departments of the world, making yesterday's product triumph tomorrow's has-been. AT&T used to measure its "product cycles in decades," reports *Business Week*, "not the months that one of today's personal computers lasts before it becomes outmoded."** Every victory is accented by the lurking awareness that your competitors just may be able to purchase or license the same technology—or discover it (or its next generation!) themselves through their own R&D. In short, the same technology that gives you market dominance today may turn around and bite you tomorrow.

The third force driving the new product agenda is the consumer. Consumers, no longer passive bystanders to the process, have become more knowledgeable and more demanding. Markets are highly segmented *and* the buying public exacts more and more for its purchasing

---

* *Fortune*, "Cummins Engine: A Long Term Bet Pays Off at Last," August 23, 1993, p. 79.

** Commentary by John W. Verity, "How AT&T Thrives—As Other Giants Falter," *Business Week*, August 30, 1993, p. 32.

dollar. Customers want choices on much deeper levels than ever before. Where price and basic performance used to be sufficient reason to buy, consumers now look for products with the "right" life-style values. Gillette, where earnings keep rising at a steady 16 percent annually, uses a holistic approach with its wildly successful, high-end disposable razor, the Sensor Excel. According to *Fortune* magazine, "Gillette never gouge[s] its consumers on price. It makes a demonstrably superior product. It innovates constantly, too rapidly for a competitor to copy." CEO Alfred Zeien sums it up this way: "We don't sell products. We capture customers."*

The very act of consuming has sensitized customers to the possibility of more product differences.

The issue of the nineties is not *whether* to diversify but *how* to make that diversification *effective*. First and foremost, that means variety that sells, creates markets, generates new customers, and results in increased profits. If your variety does not do that, it can do only one thing—it costs. It is ineffective.

The right product sells. You know it—and so do your competitors, and they are on the playing field with you. There are more of them than ever before and they are going after the same customer dollar as you are with their own *right* product. The fact is that in 1990, the U.S. market offered consumers some 228,000 branded products for purchase. The marketplace is filled to overflowing with products and brands, all competing for the same consumer. The rivalry continues to heat up.

But launching new products is expensive. They can cost anywhere from $5 million to $50 million or more—a huge investment with no guarantee of a return, let alone success. In *Getting It Right the* Second *Time*, Michael Gershman observes:

> [N]ew products are enormously chancy. In the 1950s, the rule of thumb was that six out of seven new products fail. . . . [Of the] 6,695 new products introduced between 1970 and 1979 . . . only ninety-three, not much better than one out of a

* *Fortune*, "Brands: It's Thrive or Die," August 23, 1993, p. 53.

hundred, eventually achieved sales of $15 million or more per year and had an average cost of $7.4 million each to launch.*

Then, as noted in the case of AT&T and laptops, there is the matter of collapsing product life cycles.

In the face of all this, the only safe move for a company that plans to continue to develop and diversify products is obvious: Ensure *effective* product variety.

Which Way to Diversify?

In the best of organizations, companies like Hewlett-Packard, Panasonic, and Honda, product variation is the result of a carefully considered policy of product diversification, anchored to a well-defined and unified development strategy. Key to such a strategy is clarity on two foundational conditions. First, the company is clear on its long-term goals—where it wants to go, its vision of the future. Second, the company has decided on a growth strategy—how it plans to get where it wants to go, including the role new products will or won't play in getting there. Some firms do not figure new products into their growth plans at all, relying instead on acquisitions, licensing, and/or geographic expansion. But, if new products are named as players, the company then identifies the exact types of new products, ties specific financial goals to each, and designates screening criteria that each product needs to satisfy. From there, it can formulate a process of introducing new products.

If your company is product-driven, your product strategy—whether by choice or deed—is likely to reflect one, or a combination, of the following:

1. Product Innovation
2. Product Improvement, Extension, and Revision
3. Reactive Development

---

* Michael Gershman, *Getting It Right the* Second *Time* (Reading, Mass.: Addison Wellesley Publishing Company, Inc., 1990), page xv. (Partial quote of Edward M. Tauber, formerly chairman of the marketing department at the University of Southern California.)

1. **The Product Innovation Approach.** Companies that adopt *product innovation* as a growth approach are looking for high returns and are willing to take risks. In such companies, new products can typically contribute 20 percent to annual revenues, though sometimes as much as 60 percent.

In this kind of organization new products are the lifeblood—and everyone knows it. Significant dollar and manpower resources are made available specifically to the effort. While the new product mix may include extensions and improvements (see below), the development process is squarely focused on the introduction of fresh, original, innovative products that propel the company into new markets or even entirely new businesses. Hewlett-Packard, 3 M, Sony, and Panasonic are good examples of this type of organization.

Companies that follow this product expansion approach anticipate substantial increases in parts, part types, and corresponding costs that innovation typically triggers. Without the guiding principles and practices of variety effectiveness, parts, part types, and costs can needlessly swell. And, while the enterprise may be successful—even wildly so, as in the case of the companies cited above—profits may fall far short of their potential.

2. **Product Improvement, Extension, and Revision Approach.** In contrast with innovation-centered companies, organizations that adopt an improvement approach to new products want to play it safe. They want strong growth but are also interested in minimizing risks. Advanced products may be a part of their growth strategy, but these companies concentrate on improving, extending, or revising existing successful product lines. Commonly referred to as the upgrade or full-line approach, product improvement is the central stratagem of most carmakers and can also be widely seen in retail cosmetics, clothes, and the nonprescription pharmaceutical industry. The names of these products are often good indicators of their genesis—New Improved Tide, Miller Lite *Ice* Beer, Kraft *Free* Dressing.

Flankers—new products that strengthen an existing market niche by differentiating it further—are another form of expanding a product line through improvements. Pet foods with their extensive age and size group segmentation are a good example; disposable diapers (described in Chapter 1) and jeans are two others. Each flanker caters to a slightly differentiated customer but all plug into the same need as the original product and do not compete directly with each other.

These kinds of new product tactics generally contribute 10 percent or less to yearly revenues but can reach as high as 20 percent.

For companies that do not have a comprehensive practice of variety effectiveness in place, this product strategy is perhaps the most susceptible to exploding costs. With the multiplicity of products this strategy can trigger, there is greater risk that superfluous offerings, unnecessarily complex products, and myriad unwarranted new parts will get introduced.

3. Reactive Development Approach. *Reactive development* is a low-growth approach which responds to product competition rather than creates it. The focus tends to be on *me-too* products that display some slight variation or improvement over rival offerings. Resultant products usually account for annual revenue percentages as low as 5 percent or even less. This is often the approach adopted by companies that have a high degree of security in the marketplace and perceive little threat from competitors. When and if a new product possibility appears, the organization evaluates it on an opportunistic basis. Many banks fall into this category, changing rates, for example, only in response to changes by the Federal Reserve, and offering new services only after the competition has proven them successful.

Since this reactive approach tends to keep new products to a minimum, complexity and parts count triggered by new products can be kept to a minimum as well. By the same token, because such organizations do not grow their offerings pro-actively, they are likely to have few mechanisms in place to protect them against the pitfalls (viz., the eight runaway by-products, Chapter 2) of even their circumscribed expansion. Such companies can end up paying more dearly for their limited efforts than other, more savvy firms.

You Always Ship Your Organization

As far as VEP is concerned, each of these product development approaches can be as good as the other in terms of satisfying customers and building profitable organizations—*if* the principles and practices of variety effectiveness are factored in and implemented *as a part of* that approach. Without that, each strategy can be equally damaging.

There's no getting around it: When you ship your product, you always ship your organization. A *Harvard Business Review* article comments, "If you have seams in your organization, you are going to have seams in your product. . . ."* If your product strategy does not consider the impact on the entire organization of new products relative to variety effectiveness, it'll show in your product—in its quality, performance, cost to you, and/or price to your customer. Whether that product represents an innovation, revision, extension, flanker, or reaction, some one will pay extra for it.

Customer-Driven Versus Internally Triggered Variety

Introducing customer-driven products (positive variety) is just half of the formula for achieving *effective variety*. The other half is minimizing those aspects of product variety that are not linked to a known, valid, or anticipated customer need, expectation, or want. The absence of these links is caused, without exception, by the way the organization operates, however inadvertent that may be. We call these factors as a group, *internally triggered variety*. All variety, customer-driven or internally triggered, generates cost and complexity. But internally triggered variety exacts an often unacceptable trade-off between cost and return.

If a product variation is customer-driven, it is positive. If it results

* B. Joseph Pine II, Bart Victor, Andrew C. Boynton, "Making Mass Customization Work," *Harvard Business Review*, September-October 1993, p. 115.

from some practice internal to the organization, it is negative. Not all sources of internally triggered variety can be completely eliminated. *Effective* variety is a balance point that is struck by achieving customer-driven variety with the minimum amount of internally triggered costs possible for your organization *at that time.*

Customer-driven variety increases market share because it gives customers what they want—really want. Because positive variety is driven or pulled by the customer, it fuels growth in sales revenues. It makes, sustains, and grows markets. In this light, continued product proliferation becomes a corporate imperative. We want to make this perfectly clear: The era of the universal "any-color-the-customer-wants-as-long-as-it's-black" product ended with the Model-T Ford. In this day and age, businesses cannot survive, much less enjoy consistent profits, without continually bringing out new products.

But do car buyers really need (or want) 437 different dashboard meters from which to choose? Does such an extended range of choice ever actually clinch the sale of a car? Will the fact that 6,000 different fasteners are used across a product line ever help a consumer make the choice to purchase a car from one company over another? It is hard to imagine even one instance where this could be true. Even when variations are identified as customer-driven, they must genuinely be so. Authentic customer-driven variation occurs as the result of careful market research, using proven market techniques. In its absence, variation can sneak in as someone's notion of a "good idea." The annals of sales and marketing are littered with such costly notions. As reported by *Fortune*, Borden Foods brought new meaning to the term *niche market* with its 3,200 different varieties of snack foods.* What organization, we ask, could possibly manage this truckload of differences? In a blinding flash of the obvious, Borden is now in the process of simplifying its offerings.

Joe Pine makes a related point in the *Wall Street Journal*, when he says, "Customers don't want choice. They just want exactly want they want. Profitable product-line expansion requires that you not overload

* *Fortune*, August 23, 1993, p. 53.

your customers with too much information and too many choices, forcing them to spend too much time figuring out if you have what they need."*

Pine's solution to getting the customers "exactly what they want" is mass customization, already cited in Chapter 1. As he puts it in his book, *Mass Customization*, it "is a synthesis of the two long-competing systems of management: the mass production of individually customized goods and services."** Accordingly, mass customization is predicated on operational systems that are capable, flexible, responsive, and low-cost. But the first tenet of mass customization is: A product gets created *only* in response to a direct customer request. Positive variety only, please! Everything else—strategy, design, operations, and all other levels of technology and systems—flow from that. The way to create products that sell, then, is through optimizing relationships with your customers. The way to ensure maximum profit from these sales is to build the principles of variety effectiveness into all layers of your organization.

POLICY: THE SOURCE OF NEGATIVE VARIETY

Negative variety is defined as: *Any variation that is not in response to a validated customer need or request.* Unintended as it may be, negative variety is always internally triggered by the way a company does business—on the inside and the outside. Internally triggered variety originates in, as well as further burdens, the inner workings of a company, making them more complicated, extending lead time, lowering margins, inflating costs, and, very often, swelling prices. Everybody loses.

---

* Joseph Pine II, "Customers Don't Want Choice," *Wall Street Journal*, Manager's Journal, April 18, 1994.

** Joseph Pine II, *Mass Customization: The New Frontier in Business Competition* (Boston: Harvard Business School Press, 1993), p. 48.

By definition, internally triggered variety (negative variety) does not add value for the customer; it always adds cost. *But it is also not always avoidable.*

Achieving effective variety is a two-fold task: Minimizing negative variety and enhancing positive variety—the kind that is genuinely customer-driven. The challenge is to find *and* maintain a balance point between maximal value and least cost. In the process, the organization is de-complicated. Here we include not just proliferating parts but the after-effects we have repeatedly mentioned—exploding production and nonproduction processes, dies, fixtures, control points, and so on and so forth.

This need to de-complicate the organization extends to all departments and all functions and refers not only to simplifying products, parts, and processes, but also to refining and improving specific behaviors and practices which encourage or provoke needless variety and, hence, cost. We group all such behaviors and practices under a single term— *company policy*. Whether officially sanctioned or not, policy refers to any activity that has become standard or usual within the organization. Formal or informal, policy reflects what is expected and, to a large extent, what is done.

The policy roots of negative variety can be found in five areas of the organization:

1. Accounting
2. Marketing and Sales
3. Product Development
4. Data Systems
5. Operations

Some sixteen negative triggers can be found in policies and practices across these five areas. In the remainder of this chapter, we examine these areas one by one, analyzing *policies* in each that hinder positive variety (see Figure 4.2). At the end of each analysis, we suggest alternative practices, call "improved policies," that are geared to promote the VEP goal of effective variety.

FIGURE 4.2. 16 Policy Triggers of Negative Variety

Accounting	Marketing and Sales	Product Development	Data Systems	Operations
1. Overhead Cost Allocation 2. Make Versus Buy Decisions 3. Supplier Base Selection	4. Response to Customer Requests 5. Margins, Product Pricing, and Discounting 6. New Product Market Requirements 7. Cost Targeting/Cost Reductions	8. Products as Separate Entities 9. Long Lapses Between Products 10. Different Designers/ Different Design Concepts 11. Cost Targeting in New Product Development 12. Technical Solutions 13. Product Life-Cycle Decisions	14. Product Documentation, Classification Systems, and Computer Support	15. Lot Sizing 16. Capital Equipment and Process Improvement Justification

Negative Triggers in Accounting

Accounting practices can be dangerous variety proliferators. Here are three:

1. Overhead Cost Allocation
2. Make Versus Buy Decisions
3. Supplier Base Selection

1. Overhead Cost Allocation. As discussed in Chapter 2, the traditional approach to allocating overhead costs still used in many companies assumes that a product with heavy direct labor should absorb a lot of overhead. But that product might also have few parts, making its *true* total cost lower than that of another product which requires little labor but contains many parts, some of which may sit in stock and rarely turn over. This was the point in comparing Product 8, which had 46 parts, with Product 11, which had only 29 parts but to which a heavier overhead portion was applied because of its higher labor content (Product 8: 10 minutes versus Product 11: 21 minutes; see Figure 3.1, page 57).

Many companies do not readily realize the relationship between part count, stock-on-hand, and operating expense (cf., Control Costs) and the fact that operating expense is, in some measure, a reflection of the sum total of parts warehoused and shipped on products per year (as opposed to total labor per year). These companies' widespread use of traditional allocation systems proves it. Operating expense in an assembly factory, for example, is very much a function of part variety (as are the number of processes). Therefore, an allocation system that burdens parts count rather than direct labor would provide a more reasonable gauge of costs.

The same issue with the allocation of direct labor pertains to turn-overs in parts inventory, which typically take place once a year. Again,

TRIGGER 1: Overhead Cost Allocation Policies and Practices

RECOMMENDATION

- Replace the flawed accounting policies that allocate product and inventory costs based on an obsolete Labor + Material + Overhead (L+M+O) formula with the following improved policies:

Improved Policy 1

- Develop a costing system that allocates overhead based on: (a) number of parts in a product and (b) inventory turns per part.

Improved Policy 2

- Do not use a direct labor-based overhead cost structure for determining inventory costing, except in valuating it for taxes.

this policy fails to recognize that overhead associated with inventory is actually time-based—the longer we perform activities associated with parts, the higher the control costs associated with that material. Companies that do recognize this would do well to consider a secondary inventory modifier: the quantity of stock-on-hand as it deviates from the previous fiscal quarter.

2. **Make Versus Buy Decisions (Cost Per Piece).** Most often, decisions regarding the *manufacture of parts versus purchase of parts* (make versus buy) are based on the cost per part, as determined by internal costing methods applying overhead based on direct labor costs. As a result of this practice of applying overhead expense to each part, subcontracting and outside purchasing often become a company's first choice for handling as many production operations as possible. In other instances, the make/buy choice comes down to whether a process already exists in the plant. If it doesn't, common practice usually dictates: Let someone else make it. On paper the company may appear to be saving money, but people and machines often stand idle and could be used to make those same parts.

TRIGGER 2: Make Versus Buy Decisions Policies and Practices

RECOMMENDATION

- Replace flawed procurement policies that result in automatic parts out-sourcing due to (a) cost-per-piece accounting, (b) restricted internal capacity, (c) limited process capability, or (d) "just not feeling like making it in-house" with the following improved policies:

Improved Policy 1

- Design parts to favor existing or planned in-house part production process capability.

Improved Policy 2

- Design parts to standardize on the most robust material where a choice of raw materials exists to provide a specific function across many products.

Improved Policy 3

- Let raw material cost, capacity, and process capability be the only constraints in determining *make versus buy* decisions. Do not consider overhead costs.

The same cost issue (cost per piece) can cause a company to purchase parts in a variety of materials instead of standardizing and using a single, superior material that can meet the needs of multiple applications. For example, a plunger or screw may be stocked in several materials—brass, brass/nickel, aluminum, and stainless steel. In the interest of value engineering, each part is matched to the nominal environmental specifications for its function. This often creates dis-economies of scale (three years of stock-on-hand) for each material variety. By choosing a more robust material (the one with the broadest range of applicability),* the quality of all products will be improved while true costs (including such control costs as drawings, purchase orders, expedites, and billing) are reduced.

3. Supplier Base Selection. The driving philosophy at many companies is to have multiple suppliers for each purchase part. The idea is to create a competitive atmosphere among suppliers in order to keep the piece price down. Unfortunately, antagonistic behaviors and poor working relationships are often the chief by-products of this practice, especially when competing suppliers catch wind of some of the deals "pet" suppliers are striking with their favorite buyers.

In any given year, a company may have hundreds of active suppliers, with half again that many designated as secondary suppliers in case of emergency. We can see the burdening effects of this policy, for example, in Accounts Payable, where supplier payments are fulfilled by a burgeoning number of employees.

Traditional purchasing practice also seeks to spread the sourcing of parts over several suppliers in order to create a competitive atmosphere and to protect against line shutdown in case of supplier calamity (e.g., a fire at one supplier's factory). Over time this practice creates an adversarial relationship between a company and its suppliers. And so-called "calamities" rarely, if ever, occur. Be that as it may, it is hard to imagine a disaster serious enough to justify the sometimes dozens of different suppliers a company will retain for a single commodity. Excess suppliers equals excess cost.

* This is part of a larger set of considerations forming the VEP methodology, and is discussed in more detail in Chapters 7 and 8.

An improved policy would promote supplier-customer partnerships, requiring that "we put all our eggs in one basket and then watch that basket." Adherence to this guideline reduces sourcing activities, ranging from telephone calls and faxes, to delivery and quality standards, drawings, and checks in payment. A word of caution. If a company should choose to adopt this policy, the supplier reduction target must be aggressive enough to force a fundamental revision in how the company deals with suppliers. A 20 percent reduction, for example, could be achieved without a substantive change in sourcing strategies.

Since maintaining a dynamic equilibrium between parts and processes is a long-term goal of VEP, another improved policy would require that a new supplier be added only if an existing supplier providing the same item is first removed.

TRIGGER 3: Supplier Base Selection Policies and Practices

RECOMMENDATION

- Replace flawed supplier policies that make selections based on (a) cost-per-piece only, (b) purchasing "pets," and (c) calamity protection with the following improved policies:

Improved Policy 1

- Establish partnerships with best suppliers and provide 90 percent of the business for a particular commodity to the primary supplier that can best serve the company's requirements for service, quality, price, and delivery.

Improved Policy 2

- Set a target for supplier reduction that is aggressive enough to require a genuine change in policy (e.g., reduce supplier base by 40 percent in the next year).

Improved Policy 3

- Do not add a new supplier to the supplier base without direct offsetting of another supplier providing the same commodity.

Negative Triggers in Marketing and Sales

Triggers of negative variety found in marketing and sales functions are:

4. Response to Customer Requests
5. Margins, Product Pricing, and Discounting
6. New Product Market Requirements
7. Cost Targets/Cost Reductions*

4. Response to Customer Requests. Some organizations have a reputation, both inside and outside the company, for "doing anything for the customer—no matter what." As one manufacturer related, "We build quantities of 10,000 once. And we build quantities of one once. You name it and we do it and somehow get the order out the door. But we usually get stuck with lots of new parts, equipment, and paperwork. Last week, we built a product we hadn't seen in two years. It took us three days to unearth the special fixtures used to calibrate it. We never did locate the right drawing, so it took a manufacturing engineer two days to mark up a standard product drawing for us to meet the special specs. This happens all the time. It seems as if every engineer wants to build the product just a little different, and every new project that hits the floor needs just one or two different jigs or fixtures."

Companies that provide open-ended support for customer-specific products often experience serious disruptions in service to their other customers. Typically, support for such products is not predicated on contracts stating preagreed customer usage levels. Such contracts also rarely contain language that states the company's policy on product obsolescence. In reality, many companies do not have one.

In addition, salespeople may inadvertently add to a company's inventory woes because they have not been educated about the link between giving the customer everything and increased parts inventory levels. Indeed, traditional accounting principles provide no motivation

---

* The numbering of these items is in sequence across the five organizational trigger areas.

TRIGGER 4: Response to Customer Requests Policies and Practices

---

RECOMMENDATION

- Replace flawed customer-response policies that (a) give customers whatever they ask for, (b) provide indefinite product support, (c) obsolete a product only when internal complaints get loud enough, or (d) obsolete a product in response to periods of product nonactivity of seemingly arbitrary duration with the following improved policies:

Improved Policy 1

- Base product obsolescence on the tracking of product life cycle.

Improved Policy 2

- Determine and publish an obsolescence timetable (for example, three-year notice before obsolescence; five years for maintenance and repair).

Improved Policy 3

- Provide quotes for customer-specific products that state minimum annual usage amounts required for continued company product support.

Improved Policy 4

- Provide ongoing education on effective versus ineffective variety to all sales and marketing personnel.

Improved Policy 5

- Establish the implementation of these improved policies as a marketing function.

---

for salespeople (or engineers) to keep parts count and excess variety to a minimum in all products.

5. **Margins, Product Pricing, and Discounting.** Products that cost the company more in the long run often have a much lower selling price than products that are a breeze to plan and manufacture. One marketing vice president, defending her company's current pricing policies, put it like this: "In management meetings, I am constantly called on the carpet to get profit margins up. The only data my people have to go on are the cost figures in the computer. So we price, based on these figures. How are we supposed to know which parts are turning over and which aren't?"

Product discounts are often made in a similar information vacuum. A company may decide, for example, that a price reduction (discount) on its more mature products will spur on new sales and gain profit; but, in reality, additional revenues may not offset the costs of continuing to support those products. In keeping with VEP, it may be wiser to retire them if they cannot be made more variety effective.

Another common (and often unstated) policy is to price products according to market value—what the consumer will bear; but if the company sets prices above market value, market share may be lost. Other troublesome results may ensue if factors related to LMO (labor, material, and overhead) are used to drive the company's pricing and discounting decisions. Because traditional costing can generate wide swings of over- and under-valuing per piece cost, for example, pricing policies based on them may be equally unreliable.

In addition, minimum order releases for customers, a vestige of a policy of economic order quantity (EOQ), dictates that a minimum number of items must be ordered so that the company can justify the costs of filling an order (e.g., cost of machine changeovers). This practice forces customers to buy and stock unneeded material and the company to produce it while needed material waits in line.

TRIGGER 5: Margins, Product Pricing, and Discounting Policies and Practices

---

RECOMMENDATION
- Replace flawed pricing policies for setting price based on (a) profit margin as calculated by the traditional L+M+O formula, (b) economic order quantities, and (c) what the market will bear with the following improved policies:

Improved Policy 1
- Provide product discounts based on total order quantity, without regard for minimum releases.

Improved Policy 2
- Figure product price based on market forces, not L+M+O.

Improved Policy 3
- Hold prices of mature products constant in mature markets.

Improved Policy 4
- Base profitability on the comparison of net selling price to total cost, in which material and overhead are allocated on a part/product basis.

6. New Product Market Requirements. Many companies do not have a well-defined strategy in place for evaluating new product requests. Instead, Marketing or Sales initiates a new product request and supports it with some data on market size, projected sales, competition, and a laundry list of product specifications and cost constraints. Little consideration is given in the early stage of product review to separating the functions needed by the market from the actual and possible product structures, production processing, and support methods that might need to be established to accomplish perceived product requirements.

In companies where evaluation of consumer needs is inadequate, products tend to be offered piecemeal as a passive response to individual demands. The timing of product introduction is usually random.

Without a unifying approach, new products often cannibalize the sale of existing ones. As a consequence, economies of scale are reduced and sales volumes split between old and new products. In almost all instances of this cannibalization, parts and processes proliferate as a direct result, and costs increase for the older lines. Negative variety explodes.

TRIGGER 6: New Product Market Requirements Policies and Practices

---

RECOMMENDATION

- Replace flawed new products policies that result in the introduction of (a) products into new markets without sufficient research, and (b) so-called "new" products that are simply revisions of existing products with the following improved policies:

Improved Policy 1

- Develop a well-defined new product development strategy that includes screening criteria for evaluating new product requests.

Improved Policy 2

- Develop new products that fill voids within previously targeted markets instead of ones that are redundant.

Improved Policy 3

- Sell existing products to any market, but do not undertake new product development for markets not specifically targeted.

The cannibalization issue, however, hides a deeper problem: A company may tend not to develop products that fill voids within defined target markets. Instead, new product requests can reflect a desire for one or more of the following:

- Another "me-too" product for markets already well served by existing products
- A product with a higher profit margin in an existing but competitive target market
- An existing product, re-engineered for cost reduction to make it more price competitive (see below)

7. Cost Targeting/Cost Reductions. Many companies develop new products for existing markets which do not constitute a new technology or a "first to market" strategy. In these cases, product cost is the driving force in an effort to achieve an attractive market price and undercut the competition.

This policy often causes designers to favor lower-priced *new* parts over existing parts that may be slightly more expensive. Other costs associated with the requirements of new parts, more processes, more support tasks, numbers of parts, and expected inventory turns are rarely considered.

TRIGGER 7: Cost Targeting/Cost Reductions Policies and Practices

---

RECOMMENDATION

- Replace flawed cost-targeting policies that trigger new products, which are differentiated from the competition only by a least-cost parts criterion, with the following improved policies:

Improved Policy 1

- Validate any target market by specifying key operating characteristics required by that market that differentiates it from all other markets.

Improved Policy 2

- Avoid entering markets on the basis of a least-cost product.

Negative Triggers in Product Development

The triggers of negative variety in product development are many and, for the most part, related to one central problem: the lack of a unifying product development strategy. These can be grouped under several specific categories:

8. Products as Separate Entities
9. Long Lapses Between Products
10. Different Designers/Different Design Concepts
11. Cost Targeting in New Product Development
12. Technical Solutions
13. Product Life-Cycle Decisions

(Recommendations on improved practices for these six triggers are presented as a group at the end of this section.)

8. **Products as Separate Entities.** One of the first issues related to the absence of a unifying new product development strategy is that products are handled as separate entities. When they are developed, it is on an individualized basis with no seeming relationship to other products. No attempt is made to group these disparate products into coherent family categories or follow a line of logic that would link them to one another, either conceptually or structurally. The internal result is many more products and parts than would otherwise be required, plus ballooning complexity of processes and control points. Externally the company exhibits a seemingly haphazard, confusing array of products that often vie with one another for customers.

9. **Long Lapses Between Products.** Long lapses can occur between the introduction of new products. There are legitimate, market-driven reasons for this as well as reasons connected to the internal availability of resources. But when new products are not anchored in a well-defined development strategy, product fragmentation occurs. The net effect is that new products often appear to be unrelated. This is

especially true nowadays when technology and the needs of consumers are evolving so rapidly.

10. Different Designers/Different Design Concepts. Companies pay designers handsome salaries for their imagination and creativity. But some designers tend to work in isolation and, either by default or intention, promote their own individual ideas about products. Many prefer to work as individual contributors. Others do not take care to integrate their work into a larger concept of product line or to work cooperatively with other designers or other organizational functions that have a stake in effective design. Isolation between designers is intensified by the differing developmental concepts held by their managers or groups, making coordination between individual designers or groups that much more difficult.

As a result, company products as a whole do not reflect a group consistency or design coherence. Variety in products and parts can appear arbitrary and random. This haphazard effect is often further aggravated if design managers come and go.

11. Cost Targeting in New Product Development. Engineers work hard to meet cost constraints handed over to them by Sales and Marketing. Unfortunately, this sometimes results in new products that do not reflect consideration of existing capabilities or inventory.

Many employees do not have a good understanding of the true costs of inventory and process proliferation, especially when a company's profound focus on labor, material, and the overhead burden factor has played a part in encouraging design engineers to dismiss the use of existing parts and processes if it means hitting product-by-product cost targets.

In addition, a company's parts and process classification systems, even when computerized, often do a poor job of meeting the needs of design engineers. Specification information on existing parts and processes can be extremely limited, and designers often complain about the running around they have to do to find the data they need (see below).

12. Technical Solutions. Companies put certain techniques at the disposal of their engineers in the belief that these can result in improved products. In reality, they often do. But, if improperly applied or if applied outside the context of a larger and unified product approach, they can trigger negative variety. Value engineering, computer-aided design/computer-aided manufacturing (CADCAM), and Quality Function Deployment (QFD) are three techniques that fall into this category.

Value engineering is a technique aimed at satisfying the functional requirements of specific, individual products at the lowest possible cost and the highest value (hence the term "value" engineering). The result is a product for which functional costs have been minimized but variety costs, across the company's product universe, can increase severely.

CADCAM is a powerful computerized system for integrating the product design and development cycle with the manufacturing process. Because of the ease with which CADCAM allows engineers to develop new products, less attention may be paid to possible product carry-overs (the process of utilizing existing parts or components in new product design). Without specific policies to the contrary, product engineers usually find it "more convenient" to design from scratch. The result is that many more parts can get introduced into the system than necessary.

QFD is a very effective tool for aligning product features and characteristics with a specific customer base and identifying cost trade-offs. While QFD can help a company develop verifiably customer-driven products, it does not specifically track, across the company's product spectrum, the impact of the variety it generates.

13. Product Life-Cycle Decisions. As products move through their life cycles, they reach a point at which sales volumes drop off, economies of scale are reduced, and margins erode.

Engineering departments often express concern over mounting requests to *value engineer* products on the down side of their product life cycles. Under their own set of pressures, Sales and Marketing employees often find themselves badgering the Engineering group to "get the cost out" of the same products so margins remain high despite eroding sales. When this practice is predominantly margin-driven, the company usually pays the hidden costs. Additionally, the organization may be all too ready to meet any request from an OEM customer interested in Value Engineering an existing order in the name of cost-cutting.

TRIGGERS 8–13 (COLLECTIVELY): Product Development Policies and Practices

---

RECOMMENDATION

- Replace flawed product development policies that (a) treat products as separate entities, (b) isolate designers and don't provide them with a unifying development approach, (c) promote product costs based on what the market will bear, (d) expect engineers to meet cost targets without first understanding true cost and/or without access to accurate and complete data on existing parts and processes, (e) use technical and/or computerized systems that let negative variety enter unchecked, and (f) use value engineering to get the cost out of mature products with these improved policies:

Improved Policy 1
- Educate marketers and engineers in VEP principles, including the difference between effective and ineffective variety and true cost.

Improved Policy 2
- Utilize existing parts and processes in developing new products (shared versus unique).

Improved Policy 3
- Assume that existing parts and processes are the least-cost solution; record these at the lowest comparable "standard" cost.

Improved Policy 4
- Base cost targeting on (a) number of parts in the product and (b) inventory turns of parts in the product.

Improved Policy 5
- Arrange all product lines in categories along a projected life-cycle curve.

Improved Policy 6
- Develop procedures for regulating or controlling the introduction of new parts resulting from the use of technical and/or computerized techniques that lack or cannot provide a product-wide perspective on product development.

Improved Policy 7
- Develop criteria for qualifying a product for value engineering based on its life-cycle curve placement (e.g., those in the latter third of the curve); do this for all products except where an outright defect is present or a part or process may be totally removed from the product.

Improved Policy 8
- State that customer-specific products that have no economies of scale will not be candidates for "cost reduction" except where a part or process may be totally removed.

Improved Policy 9
- Develop a costing system that allocates overhead as described under Trigger 1 (above).

The question is: Are the processing and control costs associated with the value engineering practice compensated for by the remaining sales? In these cases, the true costs of the products probably go up—not down. Cost reduction of small subclasses of products is a wasteful use of resources and a major cause of unwarranted variety. Control costs and costs of stock-on-hand required to support this artificial improvement far exceed the "cost per piece" reduction effected through this.

Again symptomatic of the absence of a coherent product development approach, many companies do not have any formal procedure for planning the improvement or discontinuation of products or product lines. An operations manager in this kind of company once quipped: "If there is any hint of life left in the product, Sales will demand that we still support it 100 percent." So no one is surprised when, a week before a product line is declared dead, one thousand sets of parts are brought in for it. Two months prior to that, the same amount of money spent on those thousand sets may have been spent on repairing dies and upgrading assembly drawings for the same product line.

Negative Triggers in Data Systems

Negative variety related to data systems is triggered in: 14. Product Documentation, Classification Systems, and Computer Support.

14. Product Documentation, Classification Systems, and Computer Support. Document maintenance can be a bear in any business where drawing maintenance is performed manually. "Simple" changes can often result in the revision of literally hundreds of drawings and routings. Drafting managers and staff get frustrated by a never-ending backlog of maintenance requests, sometimes dating back months or longer. The plea to management is often to invest in computer-aided design (CAD) technology so the area can begin to have the flexibility and organization to support systematic part and process revisions.

But these departments are also responsible for setting up new parts descriptions and Bills of Material (BOMs) in the company's computer system. Often, however, no real model or standard is in place for assigning descriptions or structuring BOMs. A company's computer system may also do a poor job of meeting the needs of design engineers. Typically, the designer or draft person uses descriptions and part-number sequences used in similar—or seemingly similar—products. Specification information on existing parts and processes, however, is often inaccurate or incomplete, and designers often complain about the need to chase down data on parts and processes (see Chapters 5 and 6 for further discussion).

In addition, and again due to a drafting department's workload, it can happen that little emphasis is placed on standardizing descriptions and making sure part numbers carry the right computer codes and reflect the proper code-number sequencing. The descriptions that are entered are not always entirely useful for the engineers since these descriptions

TRIGGER 14: Product Documentation, Classification Systems, and Computer Support Policies and Practices

---

RECOMMENDATION

- Replace flawed MIS policies that (a) do not provide engineers with the data they need to make effective design decisions and (b) do not provide for systematic additions and changes to the database with these improved policies:

Improved Policy 1

- Do all drawings using CAD or photo capture technology.

Improved Policy 2

- Establish criteria for exempting certain changes to old drawings.

Improved Policy 3

- Develop attribute templates and a database system, maintained by the engineering function, that support designers in making variety-effective decisions on parts and processes; make this database available to all employees.

Improved Policy 4

- Have the Systems Department take a lead role in revising the computer model to more accurately reflect organizational and policy changes supporting VEP.

often do not adequately describe the characteristics of the parts or the attributes needed by engineers to decide, for example, if an existing part might be sufficient for a new design.

Negative Triggers in Operations

In operations, the two main trigger areas of negative variety are:

15. Lot Sizing
16. Capital Equipment and Process Improvement Justification

15. Lot Sizing. Unwritten practices around lot sizing have their impact on inventory. Economic order quantity (EOQ) assumes that setup time and defects are unavoidable. Despite progress in quick equipment changeovers and fail-safe devices (*poka-yoke*), many organizations continue to accept batch production as a given. As a result, work-in-process (WIP) continues to pile up, prompting the need for more storage. This in turn creates ever-widening geographical distance between operations, with further variety in processes an inevitable consequence. This same practice serves to camouflage what is in reality high levels of parts variety as simply high levels of WIP.

For internal orders, manufacturing and planning in many companies still rely on large lot sizes in making components and end-items. Setup time and loss due to defects are often cited as the reasons for building excess stock and maintaining buffer quantities. Even when a company adopts process improvements in order to increase quality and reduce setup times, management will often have a tough time selling supervisors, production planners, and manufacturing employees on the idea that inventory is not a saving grace but a costly waste.

In a similar way, purchase-order release quantities often reflect a "more-is-better" attitude. Companies adopt an informal least-cost policy in purchasing parts; suppliers offer significant price breaks on large-order quantities. In addition, while Material Resource Planning (MRP) systems may be in place and monitored faithfully, planners often increase

TRIGGER 15: Lot Sizing Policies and Practices

RECOMMENDATION

- Replace flawed policies relative to lot sizing that (a) promote large lot production and decision making based on EOQ or other formulas, (b) valuate inventory as an asset, and (c) seek price breaks from suppliers for ordering parts in large quantity with these improved policies:

Improved Policy 1

- Institute lot size of one as the ideal for all manufactured parts and end-items.

Improved Policy 2

- Purchase parts in quantities of no more than one-quarter stock-on-hand, regardless of the cost per part.

---

the suggested MRP quantities before handing off requisitions to Purchasing. Purchasing, in turn, often factors in "a little extra" for problems in the supplier's process or a supplier's inability to deliver small lots. Unfortunately, the end result is often a lot of extra quantity on hand, and complexity gets a stranglehold on internal systems.

Coupled with this, inventory turns of less than one per year are not untypical for many purchased components. Accepting low inventory turns not only ensures that activities surrounding parts inventories will continue for extended periods of time, without any compensation to the company or its employees, it also does nothing to force an examination of those parts that might be combined, eliminated, or replaced.

16. **Capital Equipment and Process Improvement Justification.** Many companies have long used efficiency and utilization calculations to justify investing in equipment capable of massive overproduction. As a measure used in isolation, efficiency can suboptimize a process without regard to actual market need. Utilization as a measure discourages changeover, which, once again, serves to generate overproduction and storage problems. In turn, these impede the reduction of parts and processes.

Cost-per-part and large lot production continue to be the two key

TRIGGER 16: Capital Equipment and Process Improvement Justification Policies and Practices

---

RECOMMENDATION

- Replace flawed policies that allow for the justification of equipment purchases and process improvement expenditures to be based on (a) cost-per-part consideration, (b) large lot production, (c) machine efficiency (overproduction), and (d) equipment pets with these improved policies:

Improved Policy 1

- Do not use efficiency and utilization calculations or cost-per-part and machine efficiency considerations for justifying process improvements or investing in equipment.

Improved Policy 2

- Establish a documented procedure for qualifying an investment to improve a process and/or purchase equipment.

---

considerations in evaluating the soundness of equipment and process improvement expenditures. In addition, Operations often selects certain kinds of equipment based on personal preferences (equipment pets) rather than on a sound and well-researched rationale.

NO ONE IS EXEMPT

The causes of negative variety in an organization are myriad but not countless. Sooner or later, they all get linked to formal and informal company policies. The power of these policies cannot be underestimated. When these are formalized, watchdogs can be put in place to make sure they are followed. But informal policies are dangerous because they are held in place by habitual behaviors, and a silent, mutual, and often damaging agreement to sustain the status quo.

Every segment of the organization makes its silent contribution to the continuation of "things as they are." By the same token, every department is in a position to be self-reflective and make a positive (or negative) contribution to the goal of variety effectiveness. No one is exempt.

An active and searching inquiry into formal and informal policies can surface many triggers of unwarranted variation. Such an inquiry is a fact-finding mission. The information and templates given in this chapter are presented to provoke discussion, with a single driving question: What is the impact of this policy on our effort to reduce or prevent unwarranted variety? Either the policy makes a positive contribution to reduce or prevent unwarranted variety or, by default, it is promoting it.

The goal is to trace the causes of unneeded variety to their roots— and then eliminate these causes, inadvertent as they may be. Certain policy behaviors distort and obstruct the effort of so many in the organization to grow, expand, and flourish in today's competitive markets. In changing these behaviors to support effective variety, we begin to stem the tide of unrestrained variation and redirect it toward higher profitability.

CHAPTER FIVE

HOT PRODUCTS
The Power of Design

A hit product goes beyond just selling well. A true hit product establishes an entirely new franchise in the marketplace. You can design these products, and they not only win awards but sell like crazy.*

—BOB BRUNNER, MANAGER
OF INDUSTRIAL DESIGN,
APPLE COMPUTER INC.

Leveraging the power of design is the game today. Industrial design is a core competency that smart companies are using to drive their entire product development process. The prize: hit products—billion-dollar sellers.

The *Business Week* feature on award-winning designs of 1993 spotlighted nothing but billion-dollar products—Gillette's Sensor Razor, Reebok's Pump sneaker, Motorola's MicroTac cellular phone, Chrysler's LH cars, Apple's PowerBook, and IBM's ThinkPad notebook computer. "These design-driven products are transcending the traditional norms of market success. [They are defining] whole new [product] categories."**

Let's begin by defining terms. *Industrial designers* are responsible for conceptualizing and pre-inventing all aspects of a new product—its function, geometry, style, and visual impact. Industrial designers (sometimes called "stylists") understand the needs of the customer and

---

* Bruce Nussbaum, "Hot Products: Smart Design is the Common Thread," *Business Week*, June 7, 1993, p. 54.
** Ibid.

create the total product with that in mind. Their job is to shape a vision of the product that works aesthetically and functionally, often creating results that expand market boundaries.

Product engineers are inventors and validators. They find ways to realize the form, fit, and function of the product concept the designers generate. Product engineers make things work; they solve problems. They take what designers conceptualize and determine the precise geometry (geometric functionality) required to make the product perform in real time and real space, and all within the cost constraints of their product developmental budget. Part of their challenge is to preserve in the final product as many of the original design elements as possible—the appeal that the company spent big design bucks to create.

It is inaccurate—though all too easy—to say that designers focus on the outside of a product and engineers focus on the inside. Even when housed in different departments, the two groups work in tandem. When co-located in teams (and that's the growing trend), engineers help design and designers help engineer. To invent and create: That's why they both went to school in the first place—to get a license to devise hot new products. Working together, industrial design and product engineering get new technology out of the lab and into the hands of the buying public.

CAD—SO EASY TO BE DIFFERENT

Geez, I must be more efficient—I'm on CAD.

—Anonymous

A two-page *Industry Week* ad (February 15, 1993) for Autodesk, maker of computer-aided design (CAD) software, said: "What you can do with affordable technology these days is amazing. . . . Companies are turning out a constantly changing array of products with uncanny efficiency. You can create new designs by just plugging in new parameters. Now we design our new products ten times faster than if we used conventional design methods."

It *is* amazing. When CAD came on the scene two decades ago, it revolutionized the product development process. Lead time was axed, product features reached new levels of imagination, and the differentiation between products became increasingly subtle. Companies that invested in CAD enjoyed tremendous success and short payback periods, providing their designers and engineers with a tool that gave them a wondrous new window on innovation as a competitive advantage. Plus CAD* linked with CIM (computer-integrated manufacturing) took so much of the pain out of making and delivering new products.

OVER-DESIGNING—OVERUSING YOUR STRENGTHS

Yes, CAD offers companies a vast new creative capability, allowing engineers to develop innovative, highly differentiated products at a fast clip. But while it is a breakthrough technology of enormous significance, its strengths can be and have been overused. It is a double-edged sword.

Driven by a nearly universal call for market-in design, every new and existing product in the 1980s seemed subject to upgrade and enhancement. Distinctive products—and distinctions between products—became obsessions. In the search for new products, many companies sent designers out in droves to "be with the consuming public" and have their innovative capacities probed and prodded. Armed with CAD, lean production, QFD, and other world-class methods, manufacturers were

---

* CAD was recently joined by CAID (computer-aided industrial design), a new creative tool used for early surface and product volume definition. Linked closely with CAD, it's starting down the same path and may, like its predecessor, hold some surprises.

confident that they could provide customers with everything they wanted. A market that had been highly segmented went ballistic, fragmenting into thousands of slightly differentiated bits. The age of mass customization had arrived.

Recall Nissan's 437 different dashboard meters and 1,200 types of floor carpets. Flush with revenue and determined to grab market share from Toyota, said the *Wall Street Journal*, "Nissan hatched a brood of winning vehicles, including the rakish 300XZ sports car and a succession of whimsical limited edition vehicles such as the S-Cargo, a petite delivery van shaped like a snail. [The company] pumped out all the subtle variations its designers could dream up. . . . Toyota [was] also diversifying its product line at a mind-boggling clip—nearly car for car [with Nissan]."* Not to be left in the dust, Honda, too, got diversification fever—according to *Business Week*, "even [its] subcompacts got bigger and sprouted Lexus-like gadgets such as vibrating side mirrors to shake off the rain."**

In the United States, automakers got on the variety band wagon. General Motors Corp., for instance, boasted 62 separate vehicle lines, with at least three to four models in each. This is not to mention the variable packages GM made available as options were combined. In the booming 1980s, there was something for everyone—whether it was *really* wanted it or not.

The computer, and the canny software that supports it, allowed businesses to generate huge annual crops of new products with levels of speed, ease, and ingenuity previously unthinkable. The same computers provided organizations with the capability of storing and manipulating the immense amounts of information needed to support the design, development, marketing, production, and sale of these products. But these accelerating computer capabilities were never designed to manage or regulate themselves or to put a lid on their prodigious output.

---

* *Wall Street Journal*, March 3, 1993.
** Karen Lowry Miller, "Japan's New Credo: Average Can Be Good Enough," *Business Week*, May 3, 1993, p. 124.

REVISING THE MIND-SET—DESIGN FOR OVERALL COST

Throughout the 1980s, designers and product engineers had a free hand in coming up with new products, but the playing field has once again shifted. Product life cycles are collapsing. Time-to-market is a fraction of what it used to be. Today's competitive edge evaporates as access to new technology widens. In the United States, new safety and emissions requirements are taking a big bite out of margins. Companies won't risk safety, reliability, or performance, but they have to find new opportunities to cut costs just to stay even.

It is time to revise the product design and engineering mindset. In Chapter 4, we recommended that companies review and, where needed, revise their policies and practices to better support the principles of effective variety. And we mentioned five specific policy improvements related to product development.

In the remainder of this chapter, we want to discuss two dimensions of revising the design and engineering mind-set. The first identifies some new thinking around designing for overall cost. In it, we propose four practices aimed at helping designers and product engineers minimize negative variety. Then we look at the second dimension—some of the barriers to adopting these practices.

Our four proposals for designing for overall cost are:

1. Design from the outside in
2. Know when average is good enough
3. Use fewer parts—use shared parts
4. Get sales involved from the get-go

1. Design from the Outside In—Put Value Near the User. The old two-step of product development used to run something like this: One, company stumbles upon a great new technology; two, company finds some place (or some way) to sell it and designs a product around that. The product got designed from the inside out.

More and more, that's just not working anymore. Today, hot products begin from the *outside in.* "Make the customer's use of the product, not the technology, central to all product development," advises *Business Week* in its "Hot Products" article.*

That's what Apple did in 1990 when it began work on its billion-dollar seller, the PowerBook. It designed from the outside in—from the point of view of the user. Apple engineers "discovered that people didn't really want small computers *per se*, they wanted mobile computers. Size was just one dimension to that."** That led Apple to a whole new set of features and to an award-winning product—one that sells wildly.

This was the core—and the magic—of Chrysler's approach to designing the Neon, its latest compact. The challenge wasn't just designing a great new compact; that would have been daunting enough. The challenge was to do it at a cost that let its sticker price—$8,995—be a major competitive feature and beat the Japanese at their own game. But that wasn't all. Chrysler also wanted the Neon to be first-rate in performance, inexpensive to buy, and low-cost to make. And, while you're at it, said the boss, bring this baby in at, or under, a $1.3 billion budget, and inside an accelerated time-to-market window of 31 months. Those last two items were big ones, considering that Ford needed $2 billion and 5 years to develop its latest Escort, and GM required $5 billion and 7 years to launch the Saturn.

Where to begin? Early on, the team (a cross-functional group Chrysler calls a "platform team") set its priority: Design the car from the outside in. Put the money where it really counts. Don't scrimp on features, performance, or safety, but cut costs where the customer won't notice or won't care. They sang the variety effectiveness song.

Small-car owners told Chrysler researchers, for example, that "power windows weren't important so the team chose the crank variety ... [and that they] saw nothing special in the four-speed automatic

---

* *Business Week*, June 7, 1993, p. 57.
** Ibid, p. 55.

transmission most competitors offer. So engineers adapted an existing Chrysler three-speed, saving more than $300 million dollars."*

The idea is to spend money where it really counts. "Small-car owners worry a lot about safety. So team members swallowed hard and made Neon the first subcompact with standard dual air bags. . . . [adding] a whopping 10% of the car's total parts bill. But supplier TRW Inc. lowered that substantially by designing a single, cheaper impact sensor to replace the usual three. . . . In addition, Neon will have reinforced doors that will meet the tough 1997 federal side-impact standards three years early."** That's variety effectiveness.

We would be mistaken to think that the maneuvers Chrysler used in designing the Neon should be restricted to the low end of products. Here is a story about the other end of the product spectrum, told to us by a VP of Design at a successful automotive supplier:

"Back in 1990, a few of us went to Lotus cars to see its short-run production system. I grew up a car nut and Lotus was always one of my favorites. So we get there and I'm looking inside these cars and I see— plywood and fiberglass! You would have thought they were building boats, not $75,000 cars! And yet, as they added the layers in, you saw that they put all their money where the end-user was. The leather, knobs, sound system, carpets, glass, and all the other things the customer saw was just the best! Two inches away was this stuff called 'plywood.' I walked away thinking, 'Whew. What a cheap car underneath!' And then I said, 'Boy, is that smart!' "

2. Know When Average Is Good Enough. Companies are always challenged to surprise the user. Often this is taken to mean: Build customer loyalty by delivering more than the customer buys. A great concept *if* you can afford it. In Japan where manufacturers are facing a sharply stronger yen, companies are scrambling to cut costs. The result is a major shift in thinking for Japan and a realignment of priorities.

According to *Business Week*, Honda, for example, succeeded

---

* *Business Week*, "Chrysler's Neon: Is This the Small Car Detroit Can't Build?," May 3, 1993, pp. 199–222.

** Ibid.

in cutting costs on its latest Today (a mini-car sold in Japan only) "without losing features that appeal to the car's mostly female owners."* First Honda substituted a regular trunk for the more expensive hatchback in an earlier version and racked up considerable cost savings due to the less expensive superstructure required by a trunk. These and other efficiencies (see below) let Honda cut the price of the 1990 model by $400, add an air bag, and still post unit sales in the first selling quarter that were 21 percent above target.

The facts are plain: Japanese designers, who were given full creative rein in the eighties, are shifting away from "insisting on perfection, [and] looking for areas where average will sell." The carmaker is also questioning whether to continue spending big bucks to ensure particularly tight seams between body panels for the U.S. market, where buyers don't seem to notice. "If the market accepts lower standards, is it really a good idea to keep standards at our level?"**

To do this, product designers and engineers need to have their priorities straight. As mentioned, they need to design the product from the consumer's viewpoint, adding a delightful surprise or two but also making sure the product is not overdesigned. That means the insides of the product need to function properly—but they do not need to make a fashion statement.

3. Use Fewer Parts—Use Shared Parts. In today's disinflationary marketplace, consumers will buy a product strictly on the basis of low price—as long as its quality, performance, and value are comparable to its rivals'! Low-cost product development requires companies to practice *design-to-price*, or target-pricing: setting the price based on an acceptable profit margin and backing out cost targets from there.

The third prong of the revised mind-set is: Use *fewer* parts and make sure as many as possible of those are *shared*. We have already advocated rating products on the basis of their ratio of unique versus shared parts. The absolute goal is: as many shared parts as possible. Put the value where the customer can see it. Cut costs where it is invisible to the user.

---

* *Business Week*, May 3, 1993, p. 124.
** Ibid.

Compaq computers has put this practice to good use, after years of battering by its low-cost competitors. In 1992, Compaq came out with computers that cost up to 60 percent less than its competitors. How? Using target-pricing as a guide, engineers designed products with fewer parts and reused parts from existing designs to achieve cost targets. It was as simple as that—and as smart. And the results were amazing. "The first products manufactured under the new pricing system, the Polinea personal computer and the Contura notebook, came out in less than eight months. [By] the third quarter of last year [1992], Compaq's sales volume ha[d] skyrocketed 64%, and profits [had] nearly doubled."*

Milacron Inc., a machine tool manufacturer based in Cincinnati, is another company with the same strategy. In an article that describes how companies are coping when they can't raise prices in the face of disinflationary pressures, *Business Week* reports that Milacron

> now builds machine tools with 30% to 40% fewer parts. On the new Maxim 500, a machining center it introduced ... to replace its T-10, design streamlining reduced the number of fasteners from 2,542 to 709 and cut assembly time from 1,800 to 700 hours. Altogether, the approach cut production costs by 36%—and the selling price for the Maxim is the same as it was for the machine it replaced. Plus, the Maxim takes up 60% less floor space, can be installed in two days instead of two weeks, and makes much more rapid changeovers, which sharply increases productivity.
>
> Similar tactics paid off in lower production costs for Milacron's plastic injection-molding machines, which now typically sell at 7% to 9% below list price. "Five years ago, we couldn't be profitable with that [discount]," says Milacron CEO Daniel J. Meyer. "Now, we can not only be profitable, we're gaining market share."**

In the redesign of the Today car (mentioned above), Honda engineers succeeded in reusing 40 percent of the parts from an earlier

---

* *Business Week*, November 15, 1993, p. 150.
** Ibid.

version. The automaker is learning to share parts across product lines as well. The new Domani, a Civic that's sold in Japan only, holds 60 percent of its parts in common with other Hondas. And there's more. By using fewer and simpler parts, Honda has also managed to shave some $700 in costs from its all-new Civic.

Nissan faced—and met—the same challenge. Recently, said the *Wall Street Journal*, "the company's top designers [were] ordered to renounce a nearly decade-long quest to build cars in ever more sizes, colors, and functions to satisfy the presumed whims of the world's drivers. That effort [had] spun out of control. . . . Nissan ordered its designers to slash the number of unique parts in its vehicles by 40%"*

4. Get Sales Involved—From the Get-Go. Sales is the first interface with the customer, the first point of contact where the need and the opportunity for new products get identified. The place to champion the practices we mention above is at the earliest possible phase of the product development process—when customers register their needs.

Here's a scenario: You're the top salesperson for a company that designs cab interiors for trailer rigs. After years of hard work, your company is designated the global source supplier for MacTrucks, your biggest client, with plants all over the world. You are planning to meet with the client to discuss a possible new console product. Three hours later, you return with a stack of requirements which you take directly to your design team to spec out. Within an hour they contact you, saying there's absolutely no margin in the product. They don't really want the job, but you and they both know that you're going to have to bite the bullet and take it so your company can hold on to its global-source status. You can't afford to not do it.

Now let's imagine you as top salesperson in a slightly different scenario. Same client, same meeting. You go in to pick up the requirements for the new console, and are meeting with your design team. The team scans the requirements and whistles—"Whoa! No margin!" A

---

* *Wall Street Journal*, March 3, 1993.

SWAT team is immediately dispatched to search the company's product universe for common elements that might be pulled out and applied to the console. In the end, a number of existing components and structures are identified that could keep engineering work to a minimum. When the team rethinks the project, it's clear that the cost savings could be substantial and the margin definitely worth it. You call the client with the good news, mentioning that, if it all works out, you can even sweeten the deal by passing a percentage of the cost savings on to them. The customer gets what he or she wants *and* your company gives him or her a product it can afford to make. Everybody wins.

Considering the speed of change, and the turbulence of the market, your sales force can be a principal partner in the quest for variety effectiveness. To be so, salespeople need to be trained and involved in fostering this awareness. Hooking sales and design early on as a team, during initial consultations with clients, increases the likelihood that the client will be steered toward design solutions that are variety effective and products that are not going to bury the company. This kind of approach can go a long way to ensure that your honey-of-a-deal doesn't beat you up in the end.

BARRIERS TO MOVING FORWARD

When properly supported, the four practices described above can be instrumental in taking out big chunks of parts inventories and designing products with greater levels of effective variety. But there are barriers to implementing them. Here is a story where the right thing *almost* happened *several* times—but barriers got in the way:

Sid is a young designer at Parts Unlimited Inc. About a month ago, he joined a new product launch team. At last week's meeting, the team realized that if it was to stay on track, it would have to collapse the design

cally—from eight to four weeks. Team members got ready to
ɔrner necessary. The burning question was where and how.

The use of shared or carry-over parts came up almost immediately,
and Sid was asked to check out a particular latch (44R) as a possible
candidate. It would be his job to dig up the specs from the database, grab
the actual part(s), and discuss all of this with the team's engineering
partners.

When Sid called up 44R on the CAD system, seven latches turned
up, but only one had full specifications (specs)—and that one did show
some potential. That was two days ago. Since then Sid has searched for
specs on the other six, but they were either not on the database or the data
was incomplete. Not wanting to give up, Sid launched a search for the
drawings themselves, all the while wondering why they weren't available
on CAD. After about three hours of drawer pulling and paper sifting, he
had ascertained the following: Two of the 44R latches had been obsoleted
over a year ago (but part numbers had not been pulled), two more were
entirely too large, and three of them had possibilities, if the product
geometry could be slightly adjusted one way or the other.

Today's meeting was just starting as Sid slid into his chair and put
various drawings and his completed report on the table. The discussion
quickly moved to carry-over parts, and he was asked to show what he had
come up with. Sliding two parts across the table for the team to inspect, he
began to talk about shifting the geometry. By the middle of Sid's third
sentence, the two parts had already completed the table circuit, and the
team leader interrupted, saying, "Thanks, Sid. Great job! But neither one
of these will work." It was over in a flash.

For the designers and product engineers concerned with carry-over parts
and assemblies, scenarios like the above can make a strong case *against*
looking for existing parts and *in favor of* developing 2-D and 3-D geometries from scratch. That would certainly be quicker than wading through
cabinets or CAD files in search of specifications, and then still needing to
scrutinize the product geometry for a fit. Even when engineers have a
complete set of drawings at their disposal on CAD, they don't always
look. In the world of MIS technology, as one manager said, "there

are a gazillion ways to create geometry." When you try to use what someone else has created, you first have to figure out how it is meant to work; only then can you determine whether you can use it. "Well, let's see," says the well-meaning engineer, "how does this work? Ah, heck. I'm not going to fool with it." It is a bother that many times will not pay off—despite the effort, the engineer ends up having to create a new part after all. Easier to create it for starters, this logic goes.

Still, lots of designers and engineers use carry-over parts—from time to time. Gerrie is at her desk working on a design element for a new product—a cover. Remembering a previous cover design, she pulls up the specs and reflects: "Hey, I'll bet this will work. If I carry over this existing cover, we're not going to have to prove it out or do a feas [feasibility study]. We can just use it. It's a given—and I can spend more time in surface development, in how great I'm gonna make my product look."

In the two illustrations above, organized efforts to promote positive variety happen by default rather than as the result of established practices. In the absence of such practices, product development decisions in support of effective variety are left to chance. In many companies, the infrastructure has so many areas of deficiency that it becomes a coin toss whether negative or positive variety ends up in the lead.

Many deficit areas were discussed in previous chapters. We will touch on six here—some new, some already mentioned: (1) no formal policy, (2) limited database capabilities, (3) cost as an accounting worry, (4) no supporting measures and rewards, (5) inadequate training, and (6) no unified strategy.

1. No Formal Policy. Few companies have formal policies that establish the primacy of practices that support effective product variety. When such policies are in place, they ensure that all employees involved make a concerted effort to avoid overdesign, share parts and assemblies, design from the outside in, and steer clients in the direction of effective variety. When such practices are not made explicit as developmental *policy*, design economies are never fully achieved or happen on an *ad hoc*, case-by-case basis only. Without *a priori* design criteria to guide the process, reductions in product costs, complexity, parts count, and development time are haphazard at best. The development process is driven by the will and discretion of individuals or teams, instead of by corporate strategy.

2. Limited Database Capabilities. The company's computer database can be instrumental in the overall reduction of part inventories and the design of new products with fewer and simpler parts. Or it can be the unsuspecting cause of soaring inventories. A computer database can have that effect when the data on the attributes of existing parts, levels of product complexity, and trends in ratios and designs are not accurate, uniform, complete, or easy to access.

The company computerized database is more than an information storehouse. It can and should be a dynamic tool in design decision making, a linchpin in launching products that represent effective variety.

3. Cost as an Accounting Worry. Designers and engineers sometimes mistakenly consider cost primarily as an accounting concern. In their minds, they may segregate cost into a remote silo of function, separate and apart from new product activities. It is not unusual to hear managers say something to this effect: "Designers know what the product should look like, how it should work and perform—but not what it should cost. That's what accounting is for. Let designers stick to their knitting." In fact, until recently, the norm seemed to be: The higher the caliber of design team, the less likely they would factor cost into their work. The same could be said for product engineers further down the line: "Cost is an accounting worry."

This kind of mind-set may be more the exception than the rule in these days of cross-functional product launch teams, but it is an exception that can be very costly. The name of the game today is *total* cost and the critical need to recognize *all* cost drivers.

4. No Supporting Measures and Rewards. Product development is the creative center of many companies, yet these same companies will often hesitate to put measures around it. They tend to consider product innovation and creative design as off-limits, not core competencies. It is rare to see indicators in use in product design and engineering that track product complexity, overdesign, overall cost, unique versus shared-parts ratio, internal versus external value, and the like. Similarly, reward structures may not use the considerable clout they can have to recognize and therefore promote practices that build effective variety.

5. **Inadequate Training.** Closely linked to the absence of formal policy and measures is the lack of adequate training or orientation in the importance and practices of effective variety. The vast majority of employees do their very best to make positive contributions to their employer, but newcomers are often at a disadvantage, finding themselves on their own in discovering what that means in their new departments. Opportunities to increase positive variety and/or minimize the negative kind happen by chance—from time to time. This accidental approach can never be enough to forge an authentic strategic advantage for the enterprise.

6. **No Unified Strategy.** All of the above adds up to the greatest barrier to effective variety in the product development arena: the lack of a unified product development and diversification strategy. Many companies have operated for decades with no such strategy. Others think they actually have one in the single sheet of paper that lists their new product plans for the year. A unified strategy defines and pulls together a multitude of critical factors related to the why and how of introducing successful new products. In addition to defining the overall growth direction of products and specific objectives for each entry, such a strategy also details management's resource commitment to new products as well as the criteria, process, and people framework by which products will be developed and commercialized.

Even with a bona-fide, well-considered strategy, 100 percent success is never assured. But developing new products without one is like asking designers and product engineers to hit a bull's-eye with blindfolds on. Or as a manager once quipped, "Going into the design department of our company in pursuit of profitable products is like looking for cattle in a butcher shop. They are there but in a rather peculiar form."

A NEW ROLE TO PLAY

New products are the lifeblood of modern manufacturing. Designers and product engineers are constantly juggling a host of competing priorities to make great products happen—product geometry, ease of use, life-cycle costs, cost constraints, innovative design, packaging, and launch deadlines, to name a few. Under the VEP umbrella, they are asked to play a new role—as champions of the riches of the imagination *and* the economics of effective variety.

They know that effective variety means a balance point between positive (customer-driven) and negative (internally triggered) variety. Balancing the two kinds of variety on the effectiveness continuum fuses the strengths and weaknesses of a company's current development process and helps an organization arrive at the very best it is capable of *today* but not as good as it will be capable of tomorrow. This is a subtle procedure, one that requires a series of trade-offs. Because of this, designers and engineers have a powerful leadership role to play.

In a recent meeting on just this topic, two engineers were bantering back and forth, one highly skeptical about the possibility of assuming a new role, the other much less doubtful. The first one remarked, "Expecting designers and engineers to come up with a system for reducing parts variety is like asking an alcoholic to come up with a program for quitting drinking." The other quickly replied: "Hey, look who started Alcoholics Anonymous!"

Engineers and designers are in an ideal position to keep their eye on the big picture, instituting policies that can take a substantial chunk out of cost and complication. They are also the only ones who can put such policies into day-to-day practice, exercising high- and lower-level diplomacies to short-circuit the non-value-adding chain that is triggered by unwarranted parts variation. Strategic cost-cutting used to mean finding cheaper ways to manufacture. Now it means finding cheaper and better ways to design and engineer products.

*   *   *

With this chapter, we have completed the first section of this book, and its survey of the problem and explanation of the rationale behind the VEP process. In the four chapters of Part II, we present the VEP methodology, including details on how to prepare for a successful VEP implementation and how to conduct the analysis process that is at the center of the approach.

PART TWO

VEP: The Way to De-Complicate

CHAPTER SIX

DE-COMPLICATING THE ORGANIZATION

Where and How to Begin

Resistance to change is a biological fact of corporate life. After decades of product expansion and building the skills to manage the ensuing complexity, managers rarely welcome the notion of disentangling the web they have carefully woven to handle that complexity and the huge parts inventories hidden beneath it. For most companies, an authentic commitment to parts inventory reduction through variety effectiveness means— a heck of a lot of work! Is it worth it? As reported in the *Wall Street Journal* in 1993, "If Japan's car makers cut parts cost just 3%, they would triple industry operating profits from the fiscal 1991 level."*

Dismantling organizational complexity so that customer selection can be maximized and negative variation minimized is a challenge of the first order. To undertake it, you need to be equipped with a powerful methodology that systematically roots out the full range of negative causes, builds new positive practices, and keeps the vision clear. VEP: Variety Effectiveness Process is that method.

The purpose of this chapter is to introduce the VEP methodology. First we'll provide a brief overview of the four stages of the method so you get the big picture. Then the focus will shift to the details of Stage 1, the process for preparing for an effective VEP implementation.

* *Wall Street Journal*, March 3, 1993.

OVERVIEW OF THE VEP METHOD

The Variety Effectiveness Process (VEP) is a systematic team-based methodology directed at maintaining or expanding customer selection while reducing negative variety in products, parts, processes, and control points and preventing their recurrence. Its goal is to lower costs dramatically and de-complicate systems while maximizing a company's ability to respond successfully to the demands of the market.

As a systematic approach, VEP spells out what needs to change, how, and in what order. To do this, the method is divided into the following four levels or stages (see Figure 6.1):

Stage 1—Prepare for an Effective Implementation.

Get the people, information, and organization ready to interact in meaningful, cooperative ways on variety effectiveness objectives.

Stage 2—Identify Valid Reduction Opportunities, Applying the Six Tools.*

Find and analyze for all instances of negative variety, using specific techniques, and develop valid proposals to reduce their number.

Stage 3—Coordinate and Prioritize Reduction Opportunities.

Compile, align, and schedule all valid reduction recommendations into an integrated plan of change.

Stage 4—Implement and Sustain the Improvement.

Activate and sustain the implementation process until all valid recommendations are in place; stabilize prevention procedures.

* Explained in detail in Chapter 7.

FIGURE 6.1. Overview of the VEP Methodology

STAGE 1
Prepare for an Effective Implementation

STAGE 2
Identify Valid Reduction Opportunities, Applying the Six Tools

STAGE 3
Coordinate and Prioritize Reduction Opportunities

STAGE 4
Implement and Sustain the Improvement

This four-stage approach is designed to help your company:

1. Assess its true capacity for change and mobilize the needed resources.
2. Walk through a change pattern that turns over the assorted rocks under which negative variety hides.
3. Separate valid reduction proposals into ones with low resistance to change that can be implemented quickly and in the near term, and those that require a deeper stratum of support and planning to effect.
4. Move through the change process successfully, so that the payoffs are commensurate with required efforts.

From the first, we look for ways to make and keep company systems simplified and parts inventories on the decline—even as we expand our product offerings to customers. Threaded through this process is an ongoing prevention objective that results in the codification of new policies and practices that strengthen positive variety and deter the recurrence of negative variety. VEP's four-stage paradigm provides the company with a road map for change, showing the organization where it needs to go and how to get there, reliably and safely. The organization can follow the idealized route until it gets where it wants to go, or it can modify or adapt the model route, factoring in the special strengths and idiosyncracies of the enterprise, and fashion some shortcuts.

Before we look at Stage 1 in detail, we will talk about these options related to the scope of the implementation.

What's the Scope?

Embarking on a comprehensive implementation of VEP can be a substantial commitment of company resources. Before making that commitment, it is important to decide on the right size of the project for *your* organization—the scope. You can go one of two ways.

The first way is called the *select approach*. More of a tactic than a strategy, it focuses on winning some battles against negative variety, but not the war. In it, a task force of experts (mostly engineers and perhaps some marketing representatives) selects a single product line, or a subset, for analysis and reduction. The team focuses on it, applying those segments of methodology directly aimed at parts reduction (as Chapter 7 explains, the 3-View Analysis is the primary tool). Depending on a number of factors, a single implementation cycle of this nature could take two to six months to complete. Afterward, the team may elect to cycle back to another single-product focus and go after another set of reductions—then another and another, methodically lowering inventory levels, product by product.

The select approach is a perfectly valid improvement mode, especially in the face of limited company resources. A focused and sustained effort can, over time, result in considerable reductions in parts count on a product-by-product basis; generally, it can measurably lower the number of production processes or control points, and seek impact through policy upgrades and revisions. Its low-profile, contained style is also a good choice when a company wants to take a wait-and-see attitude before making an all-out VEP commitment.

The second option is an all-out attack on negative variety. We call it the *deep-dive approach*. Embracing variety effectiveness as a corporate vision and VEP as the company-wide strategy to reach it, this implementation modality aims at shifting awareness of the entire organization and achieving dramatic reductions in parts inventory, production processes, and control points as well as installing a new set of practices that support positive variety by revising policy. *Awareness training* is a key element in its agenda. The deep-dive approach is a long-term effort that results in the eventual scrutiny of the company's full line of products. Because of this, a full complement of VEP teams is activated (see below), with representatives from most, if not all, departments. Immediate and measurable results happen quickly, within the first 30 to 90 days, and more widespread changes continue to unfold over a period of 8 to 12 months.

Whichever approach you choose, remember, VEP's goal remains the same: to lower costs and complexity dramatically, directing all product-linked expenditures toward *a single source of costs*—the part.

Now let's look at the specifics of Stage 1, the steps the company takes to ensure its investment in VEP pays off handsomely. We will use Parts Unlimited Inc. (PUI), our prototype company, as our focal point. As luck would have it, PUI opted for a deep dive into VEP.

STAGE 1: PREPARING FOR AN EFFECTIVE VEP IMPLEMENTATION

This first of the four stages begins after senior management has committed company resources to a strategy of variety effectiveness. PUI's CEO Tom Vargas sent out a memo to all associates to launch the initiative after that decision had been made (see Figure 6.2). Now that the company has committed, it needs to get ready. In essence, this is a three-part effort:

- Prepare the People—Set Up and Train VEP Teams/Provide Awareness Education
- Prepare the Information—Assess/Upgrade the Parts Classification System
- Prepare the Focus—Select the Priority Product Line for Analysis

FIGURE 6.2. Memo from CEO Vargas to All Company Employees

TO: All Associates
FROM: T. M. Vargas
RE: Kick-Off for Variety Effectiveness Process

As we discussed last month at the company meeting, our parts inventory costs are exploding and must be brought under control.

Last month, the entire management team attended a one-day briefing on a powerful, systematic methodology aimed at reducing high levels of parts inventory and de-complicating the organization. The method is called VEP—Variety Effectiveness Process®.

As a result of subsequent research and discussions, in which most of you have been involved, we are ready to commit. *On February 22, we kick off VEP at PUI.*

Our goal is a challenging one:

> By December 31 we will reduce our parts inventory by 40%, production processes by 30%, and control points by 25%

Here is the calendar for the next four weeks:

> February 2: VEP Steering Team and other VEP teams are formed
> February 15: All VEP teams attend 3-day Training Course
> February 22: VEP KICK-OFF—teams begin
> February 24: First VEP Awareness Session—all associates

Our company is committing substantial time and money to get our parts inventory under control and our organization de-complicated. I need you to get involved and help make it happen. PUI needs your knowledge, skill, and enthusiasm. It won't be easy—but it will be worth it.

Working together, our product designs will improve, our internal systems will become streamlined, our customers will be happier—and our profits will improve.

Thank you for your support in this very important project.

PREPARE THE PEOPLE—PART ONE

In today's fast-paced, decentralized workplace, preparing people for improvement means three things: getting them into teams, getting them trained, and getting everyone else on board through awareness education.

Getting People into Teams

A comprehensive VEP implementation is carried out through the work of eight cross-functional teams (see Figures 6.3 and 6.4 for overviews).

FIGURE 6.3. The Eight VEP Teams Are Closely Linked Together

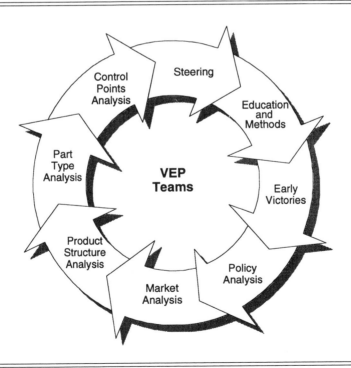

FIGURE 6.4. Teams Organized for an Effective VEP Implementation

VEP Teams	Objectives
1. Steering Team	• Set up other VEP teams. • Provide leadership, direction, and support to overall project. • Review, coordinate, and finalize reduction recommendations from other teams. • Serve as liaison to senior management.
2. Policy Team	• Identify/review/revise company policies and practices (formal and informal) so that they support positive variety and avoid negative variety in the future.
3. Market Analysis Team*	• Identify reduction opportunities in company's existing product offerings that do not endanger the company's market position or limit customer selection.
4. Product Structure Analysis Team*	• Identify reduction opportunities on model-specific parts and structures across all product lines, based on the analysis of product architecture.
5. Part Type Analysis Team*	• Assess existing parts classification system; validate or upgrade as needed. Then develop and implement attribute templates and input new data accordingly. • Identify opportunities for reduction in parts commodities across the company's entire parts universe.
6. Control Points Team	• Identify and reduce all transactions (paper, electronic, or otherwise) that support the design, procurement, sorting, retrieval, scheduling, inspection of parts, etc.
7. Early Victories Team	• In the first ninety days, identify parts and processes with low or no resistance to change and reduce these aggressively by a targeted amount.
8. Education and Methods Team	• Arrange for VEP Team Training.** • Conduct VEP Awareness Sessions. • Assist teams in using and adapting the VEP method. • Promote employee involvement and publicize successes.

* One of the three teams involved in VEP's 3-View Analysis.

** *Note:* A separate team for reducing production processes is not included in this framework. A company may elect to set up a separate team for this purpose or, as suggested here, allow that reduction to take place as a consequence of the efforts of the three 3-View Analysis teams.

These teams provide the process with (a) leadership and integration, (b) detailed analysis, and (c) promotion and support. These three areas can be likened to parts of an automobile. Leadership and coordination are roughly equivalent to the steering wheel, detailed analysis (reduction ideas) is the engine, and promotion and support are the wheels. The first team we'll look at is the first team that gets formed—the Steering Team.

THE STEERING WHEEL—LEADERSHIP AND INTEGRATION

VEP Steering Team

Multiteam implementations such as deep-dive VEP need clear direction and ongoing integration. The first team that gets formed after management commits is the VEP Steering Team. Its purpose is to provide leadership, direction, and backing to the overall project. It also serves as a clearinghouse for the improvement recommendations from the other teams (see below), regularly reviewing, coordinating, and, when the time comes, prioritizing the reduction proposals developed by the several analysis teams. The Steering Team also serves as gatekeeper and regulator of the rate at which change/improvement is introduced into company systems. This is one of its most important functions.

The team, which is comprised of the leaders of each of the other VEP teams (with the exception of the Policy Team leader, who is an executive), is usually led by an engineer, who reports directly to senior management and serves as a liaison or bridge to keep management and other key thought-leaders informed and on board.

The Policy Team

The battle lines are drawn once a company understands that parts trigger cost. While the three teams known as the 3-View Analysis (see below) are charged with scrutinizing the specific substance of the company parts explosion, the VEP Policy Team presses even further. Its mission is to discover the policy roots of the problem, which means identifying and naming those official and unofficial policies and practices that, however inadvertently, promote negative variety. Discussed at length in the previous chapter, this investigation requires digging into the fabric of how the company conducts its business. Because of the power of policy to direct, no department can be spared. Once the roots of the problem are found, the Policy Team then recommends revisions and upgrades. Finally, team members, under the auspices of the senior manager who leads them, undertake the process of gingerly shepherding improved policies through the system in such a way that stakeholders are kept on board. In this sense, and through the documented vision of the company (called "policy"), the team plays a key role in forging the company's future direction toward effective variety. By design or not, policy is the driver.

Change on the policy level is challenging. For one thing, policy changes can shake the status quo at its foundation. For another, though bad policy may be inadvertent, it casts a long shadow, often making it difficult to illuminate all the dark corners it masks. A well-working Policy Team, therefore, fuses a discerning examination with substantial political sensitivity. For this reason, it's advisable that the team leader is a senior executive—preferably, the VEP champion—someone in a position to lubricate the inquiry and facilitate the needed changes. Steering Team members make up the rest of this team; in their role as liaisons to all other teams, they are in a perfect position to advance policy improvement.

The work of policy analysis begins early in Stage 1, as soon as possible after teams are trained in the principles and goals of variety effectiveness. The policy analysis team needs little else to start up. The mechanics are straightforward; for that reason, we describe them here, rather than later in the chapter. First, team members collect and then scrutinize the company's formal and informal policies and practices.

Their job is to tag ones that appear to provoke negative variety. They can use the template of sixteen trigger areas found in Chapter 4 (Figure 4.2, page 103) as an initial guide, adding and deleting in keeping with the needs of their organization. They can also pinpoint policies and practices that support positive variety, using these as models for what "goodness" looks like.

The team next has a choice on how to proceed. It can come up with recommended revisions, with each member bringing these to the attention of his/her respective departments for review and input. Alternatively, members can bring the troublesome policies and practices directly to their respective peers, initiate an open-ended dialogue on what might be changed, and carry any recommendations back to the Policy Team. Depending on your organizational culture, the first approach may be expeditious and satisfying—or it may be entirely too pushy; if you sense this, jump to "Plan B"—the open-ended dialogue option. After that, the process becomes iterative until all the policy bases are covered. Along the way, it is always helpful to have management officially sanction "new" policies. When the new foundation has been laid, designate a small group in each department to watchdog for incursions.

THE ENGINE—ANALYSIS*

The heart of the VEP method is the analysis process that results in specific improvement proposals for optimizing products and minimizing parts inventory levels. This process is the shared effort of three separate but linked teams, each named for the particular analysis window it adopts for scrutinizing the company's offerings—the Market Analysis Team, the Product Structure Analysis Team, and the Parts Type Analysis Team. Collectively referred to as the *3-View Analysis*, these three teams are the

---

* In actuality, there are one to two other analysis teams: the Control Points Analysis Team and the Production Process Analysis Team, both introduced below and explained in detail in Chapter 9.

engine that drives the VEP approach. Between them, products and parts are analyzed, and specifics opportunities for reduction are developed.

View 1—Market Analysis Team

The purpose of the Market Analysis Team is to analyze company products from a marketing perspective and propose reductions that eliminate unneeded variety without limiting customer selection or endangering the company's market position.

In essence, this requires cataloging and comparing company offerings in order to identify instances of overlap, redundancy, indistinctness, and other anomalies. This analysis can extend across the full scope of product features and functionality, so the core of the team must have sufficient experience to handle a wide range of questions and possibilities. Minimally, the core composition of the team should include representation from Marketing (also a good choice for team leader), Design Engineering, Manufacturing Engineering, and Finance.

View 2—Product Structure Analysis Team

Another of the 3-View Analysis teams, the Product Structure Analysis Team, studies the architecture of company product offerings for reduction possibilities—that is, how the product is put together and its functions realized. This team, for example, could conclude that complex housing and bracket assemblies can be simplified and five part numbers eliminated by combining two of the five part-elements in those assemblies.

Due to this team's heavy engineering demands, its core composition is likely to include design engineers as well as representatives from Manufacturing Engineering, Drafting, Purchasing, and Marketing.

View 3—Part Type Analysis Team

The Part Type Analysis Team is the third team involved in the 3-View Analysis. As its name suggests, this team concentrates on negative variety found in part commodities, also known as part types, as exemplified in housings, fasteners, windshield wipers, knobs, labels, lids, brackets, side mirrors, handles, washers, steering wheels, gaskets, side panels, hinges, facings, and so on and so forth.

As with the other two 3-View teams, this team works hard to develop reduction proposals that do not compromise customer selection. Team members may notice, for example, that the outer-diameter specifications on the company's 22 varieties of gaskets are very close and, in some cases, overlap; they see an opportunity to cover the same requirement range with eight fewer gaskets. In a comprehensive VEP implementation, this team eventually surveys all the part types in the company's parts universe. In addition, this team is in charge of the Stage 1 task of assessing and upgrading the organization's parts classification system and developing the attribute templates discussed later in this chapter.

As with the Product Structure Analysis Team, this team's strong engineering focus is the reason it includes representatives from Design and Manufacturing Engineering; typically, people from Systems, Purchasing, and Marketing also serve.

OTHER ANALYTICAL TEAMS

While the 3-View Analysis teams are at the core of VEP's analytical approach, additional VEP teams may be formed for two other areas of analysis—production processes and control points.

Process Analysis Team

The job of the Process Analysis Team is to simplify the shop floor by reducing the number of required production processes. As presented in the PUI case study example, this team is optional, not required. There are two reason for this. First, while process reduction is critical to de-complicating the organization, it can be done as part of the work of the Product Structure and Parts Type Analysis teams (described above). That is, as products are simplified and parts reduced, associated production processes will be tagged for elimination as a matter of course. No special extra effort is needed. The second reason a separate process reduction team may not be necessary is if the company has already done substantial work in process reduction—as PUI did in cell design and die and fixture standardization prior to its implementation of VEP. Companies interested in VEP—but new to process improvement techniques—might well benefit from a separate effort targeting those reductions.

Control Points Analysis Team

A control point is any transaction—paper or electronic—that supports a product, a part, or a production process; this includes drawings, purchase orders, bills of material transactions needed for receiving, retrieving, and inspecting parts, billing, customer service, faxes, and memos of all orders. The mandate of this team is to identify the company's control points and reduce their number.

Because of the extensive number of control points in most companies, the Control Points Analysis Team often includes representatives from most departments—Purchasing, Systems, Drafting, Design Engineering, Materials, Manufacturing Engineering, Finance, Quality, Marketing, Customer Service, etc.

Any representative with good knowledge of the company and strong leadership skills is suitable to lead this team.

THE WHEELS—PROMOTION AND SUPPORT

The changes brought about by VEP can be exceedingly positive and long-lasting, but don't expect everyone to be enthusiastic from the outset. As in any profound organizational change, there will be no shortage of naysayers, skeptics, and resisters. While some negativity is to be expected, it can nonetheless be destructive during the start-up. Certain steps must be taken to harness or diffuse the pessimism. This is the purpose shared by the Education and Methods and Early Victories teams.

Education and Methods Team

In VEP, the majority of the work force does not serve on a team, but their cooperation and quiet support are still vitally important. That support depends on their knowing what is expected of them. One of the main functions of the Education and Methods Team is to make sure everyone knows what VEP is, why it's important, what the broad-stroke timeline is, and how they can contribute. Part of this is done by providing, during the opening months of the implementation, a concise overview of the process (a three- or four-hour VEP Awareness Session) for small groups until the entire work force is informed.

This team is also responsible for promoting the VEP victories—early (see below) and otherwise—and highlighting the positive benefits. VEP bulletin boards spotlight the work of individual teams as well as collective results. A column in the company newsletter can also be of great help in keeping everyone on board and alert.

A third function of this very important team is to help the Steering Team customize the VEP method to fit the needs of the company more exactly, working with all other VEP teams to clarify targets and objectives and keep on track. The Education and Methods Team may, for example, work with the Control Points Team in adapting the VEP Parts Index so that it can capture the number and frequency of the forms used in

Purchasing and Finance. Or it may help the Steering Team think through its timing issues.

The team consists of representatives of the training function (trainers, facilitators, internal consultants) and Human Resources.

Early Victories Team

The Early Victories Team, which moves into action directly after the team training (see below), has a predetermined life span of 3 months—90 days. Its target is very specific: Identify parts and processes with low or no resistance to change and reduce their number by a preset amount within the first 90 days of the implementation. The target, for example, might be stated as follows: *Reduce part numbers with low or no resistance to change by 1,000 and production processes by 100 in the next 90 days—by September 15th.* The idea here is for this team to score the easy successes, early in the VEP implementation, and then, with the assistance of the Education and Methods Team, get them publicized. These so-called *early victories* keep the skeptics at bay while the harder work of preparing for and beginning in-depth analysis gets under way. This is an end-run around those who may want to torpedo the project in its infancy.

For 90 days, then, this team works on getting rid of the easy stuff. Cleaning up the parts database of obsolete part numbers is an obvious and necessary part of this, and as these part numbers are eliminated, certain corresponding production processes are eliminated as well.

The team purpose, therefore, is two-fold: (1) soft-core reduction and (2) hard-core promotion. This promotional component is further enhanced by including full company representation on the team—Purchasing, Marketing, Sales, Drafting, Design and Manufacturing Engineering, Systems, Finance, Customer Service, Materials, Quality, Human Resources, Shipping and Receiving, etc. One immediate benefit of a widely representative team is the likelihood that team members will tell their colleagues what VEP can do and why it is important. This simple mouth-to-mouth promotion can go a long way in keeping dubious tongues from wagging and the atmosphere around the fledgling implementation open and upbeat.

In one company, which eliminated more than a thousand part numbers in three months, the Early Victories Team promoted its efforts through an imaginative device called "The Chuck Wagon," so named because team members would "chuck" each eliminated part onto the wagon on display in the company lobby (see Figure 6.5 for illustration. Notice the plastic arm at the top of the wagon to "catch" unnecessary parts.)

FIGURE 6.5. The Chuck Wagon of the Early Victories Team

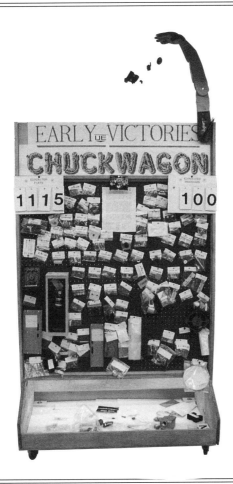

PREPARE THE PEOPLE—PART TWO

VEP Training

In addition to providing the VEP Awareness Sessions described in the previous section, companies pursuing the comprehensive, deep-dive VEP approach schedule formal team training for all VEP teams. This usually requires a multi-day workshop so team members can learn about basic VEP principles and concepts, the big picture, and the various missions of the individual teams, as well as learn and *practice* the technical procedures and supporting team behaviors. As a result, teams gain a strong sense of the purpose and direction of the implementation and build confidence in their respective team tasks and the VEP process in general.

Once a company gets its VEP teams organized and trained, it is ready for the next part of the Stage 1 process—preparing the information. In a nutshell, this means assessing data requirements and, if necessary, upgrading the existing parts classification system.

PREPARE THE INFORMATION—CREATING A VEP-CAPABLE CLASSIFICATION SYSTEM

In Chapter 2, we cited a recent conversation with William F. Hyde, president of the Fort Lauderdale classification systems consulting firm Brisch, Birn & Partners, Inc. (BBP), in which he stated that, based on BBP research data, today's average cost of putting a single new proprietary-designed part into production is $4,000 (representing costs that range from as low as $400 per part to $40,000 per part). In another

study, BBP surveyed more than 500 companies and found t
new part is designed for a product, "the odds are 1 in 11 that an existing
[part] design already tooled and produced is similar enough to be used—
and 1 in 29 that the 'new' part is an exact duplicate."* The key to whether
that existing part gets used or a new one is created rests squarely on the
company's ability to access existing design data efficiently and validate or
refute the need for that part.

The moral of the story is a familiar one: A decision is only as good as
the data on which it is based. Good analysis and good improvement
decisions depend on good information and a good data system—
accurate, relevant, complete, and accessible. We call such a system
"VEP-capable."

VEP teams (no less than the company that houses them) require
sound data systems to do their work. This is especially true for the 3-View
Analysis teams. Each team faces a multitude of data-dependent decisions
related to part types, part specifications, Bills of Materials (BOMs),
product structure, quantity-on-hand (QOH), sourcing, as well as marketing facts and figures. The quality and scope of the company parts classification system is of crucial importance here. If not addressed early in a
VEP implementation (Stage 1), a problem system can stall the initiative
indefinitely and bring the implementation to a complete halt. It is important, therefore, to assess the existing system expeditiously so that needed
upgrades can get under way immediately. By way of reminder, VEP's
Parts Type Analysis Team is in charge of making the classification system
VEP-capable.

Classification systems in too many companies are brimming over
with inaccuracies, redundancies, and useless or incomplete data. Let's
look at the problem and the VEP recovery procedure through the lens of
trouble itself—the parts classification approach at Parts Unlimited
Inc. (PUI).

---

* Brisch, Birn & Partners, Inc., *Helping Manage Better Through Classification and Coding the Data Base*, Fort Lauderdale, Fla.

A CASE IN POINT: A BULGING, BUNGLING, BLUNDERING DATA SYSTEM

PUI's product and parts classification system dates back to the company's founding in 1932. Although logical, the system is inconsistent in some respects and not always adhered to when new products are added to the line. The introduction of a computerized system in 1970 tightened the classification framework to some extent.

Since then, however, the computerized classification system has grown each and every time someone has needed—or thought he or she needed—a new classification, be it for a product, part, or production process. And it's worth noting that the last time PUI updated its computer system, software, and parts classification approach was in 1983. Here is a laundry list of the system's key trouble areas.

1. Part Number Prefixes. At the parts level, similar parts usually share the same prefix designation. For example, all springs should have <6318> as the first four digits in their designation. Later digits in a part number are simply assigned sequentially as new springs are added to the parts universe.

Unfortunately, this means that Engineering usually does not have a clue as to whether *Spring 6318-01* has any attribute in common with *Spring 6318-903*, without sifting through drawing files.

2. PUI Computer Codes. When PUI updated its computer in 1983, it purchased state-of-the-art hardware and the latest MRP-based software. The MRP software required PUI to further refine its parts and product classification system since the system relied on a number of computer codes in order to support sales, production, procurement, and inventory control processes. The logic and consistency used to establish and maintain these codes, however, leaves something to be desired. As a result, the computerized codes do not necessarily provide a classification system that is VEP-capable.

Some examples of code fields that were judged inadequate as people began to consider VEP applications are described below.

3. **PUI Class Codes.** Parts and products also carry computerized class codes. The purpose of these codes is to allow for the grouping of like items, such as sensing assemblies or enclosures. Unfortunately, several class code categories overlap, and there are no concrete rules for deciding how to assign a new part or product to a class code category.

As of last year, the number of active class codes at PUI was 104. The codes (as they existed *before* VEP) and their descriptions are shown in Figure 6.6. Codes 1 to 10 are reserved for completed product configurations. The bulk of the remaining codes are used for grouping parts, with a handful of codes for tools or fixtures. Drafting is responsible for assigning class codes to products and parts.

Recently, Manufacturing Engineering Manager John Sedgwick asked Data Processing for a list of screws used in the company. After two weeks of programming and another week of examining the reports, Sedgwick and Denise Andrews, Data Processing Manager, determined that most screws were in Class Code 91, but that other screws could be found in:

Class Code 38 (switches, parts for)
Class Code 33 (miscellaneous commercial parts)
Class Code 63 (commercial fasteners)

Figure 6.7 shows a portion of their final report on all active screws at PUI.

Both Sedgwick and Andrews suspected that they would have similar problems if they used existing class codes to search for other groups of parts. They noted, when reviewing their report, that they could not use the four-digit prefix <6277>—the one, theoretically, that *all* screws are supposed to carry—for locating all screws because that method, too, had plenty of exceptions.

They wondered whether this mess could be sorted out—and, if it could, whether there was a way to keep it from recurring.

FIGURE 6.6. Active Class Codes *Before* VEP (104 Total PUI Class Codes)

	Code Description			Code Description
1	Mechanical Stock		40	Commercial Wire
2	Non-Mechanical Stock		41	Packaging Materials
3	Electronic Stock		42	Capacitors
4	Electronic Non-Stock		43	Series 4 Head Assemblies
5	Replacement Sensor Stock		44	Printed Circuit Boards
6	Replacement Sensor Non-Stock		45	Relays
7	Electronic Parts & Accessories		46	Meters
8	Mechanical Parts & Accessories		47	Transformers
9	Process Stock		48	Electronic Software
10	Process Non-Stock		49	Planning Bills
11	Miscellaneous Parts		50	Tools
12	Common Parts—Heads		51	Electronic Accessories
13	Common Parts—Sensors		52	Probes
14	Pressure Assembly		53	Series 1 Software
15	Vacuum Assembly		54	Common Parts Sensors
16	Adjustment Assembly		55	Gear Box Assemblies
17	Switching Assembly		56	Enclosure Assemblies
18	Electronic Switching Assembly		57	Printed Circuit Board
19	Bracket Assembly			Assemblies
20	Switch Back Assembly		58	Lead Wires—Electronic
21	Differential Rod Assemblies		59	Welding Electrodes
22	Housing & Bracket Assemblies		60	Nameplates—Mechanical
23	Knob Assemblies—Mechanical		61	Nameplates—Electronic
24	Knob Assemblies—Electronic		62	Flanges
25	Relay Assemblies—Solid State		63	Commercial Fasteners
26	Relay Assemblies—Mechanical		64	Plastic Parts
27	Lead Wire Subassemblies		65	Springs
28	Miscellaneous Assemblies		66	Plastic Stampings
29	Essential Parts-Head Assemblies		67	Springs
30	Miscellaneous Purchaser-		68	Rolled Tubing
	Supplied Parts		69	Mineral Insulated Cable
31	Dialplates		70	Thermistors
32	Diaphragms, Gaskets & Seals		71	Transistors
33	Miscellaneous Commercial Parts		72	Wiring Diagrams
34	Insulators		73	Special Probes
35	Screw Machine Parts		74	Overtravel Assemblies
36	Wells & Connectors		75	Adjusting Screw Assemblies
37	Metal Stampings		76	Miscellaneous Actuating
38	Switches, Parts for			Assemblies
39	Miscellaneous Metal Tubing		77	Cover Assemblies

FIGURE 6.6 (continued)

	Code Description		Code Description
78	Cam Assemblies	91	Screws
79	Printed Circuit Boards—Auto	92	Valves & Fittings
	Insertion	93	Contacts, Switch
80	Armored Cable Assemblies	94	Plastic Mouldings & Knobs
81	Armored Cable	95	Plastic Tubing
82	Common Parts—Final Assembly	96	Fixtures, Miscellaneous
83	Contacts	97	Fixtures—Electronic
84	Spirol Pins	98	Fixtures—Mechanical
85	Washers, All Types	99	Castings
86	Diodes	101	Castings, Painted
87	Potentiometers	101	Insulating Parts
88	Miscellaneous Resistors	102	Wire
89	Prototypes—Mechanical	103	Brackets
90	Prototypes—Electronic	104	Fittings

4. PUI Description Field. Currently, each product or part record on the PUI system carries a 30-character alphanumeric description field, but it is widely known that information loaded into this field is often inconsistent and seldom maintained once it's added to the system. In addition, the descriptions do not provide sufficient information for PUI to make sound decisions relative to new product design. (See Figure 6.8 for examples of 30-character code descriptions that appear on the PUI computer.)

5. Other Codes. To make matters more complex, the computer also carries a number of other codes for each part or product which help determine how they will be planned, manufactured, or bought. While these codes are typical of a traditional MRP-based system, they too are not always consistently applied and are generally not considered an effective means for assessing variety or supporting an inventory reduction program.

Andrews is a great supporter of PUI's efforts to reduce the number of active parts and processes. For her group, every new part or process swells an already-bulging database. Perhaps more than anywhere at PUI,

FIGURE 6.7. Report of All Active Screw Part Numbers *Before* VEP (as taken directly off the computer)

Part Number	Class Code	Description
6261-258	91	Brass Screw
6261-299	91	Fastener, Screw
6276-091	38	Screw, ¼-20 Master Switch
6277-001	91	Set Screw
6277-008	33	S/S Screw, Flat Head
6277-035	33	Stock S/S Screw
6277-109	63	S/S Screw
6277-110	91	1″ Hex Screw
6277-125	91	Brass Screw
6277-221	38	Screw, Binding ¼″
6277-231	91	Screw for 2 Series Bracket
6277-485	91	Screw, Same as -125 but S/S
6277-497	91	Commercial Stock Screw
6277-104	91	S/S Hex Head

this area recognizes how difficult it is to sort out PUI's voluminous data in any meaningful way. Yet department employees are constantly asked for reports on parts, part characteristics, part usage across the product population, and so on. Although they eventually produce some order of report, they are quite sure they are *not* doing it effectively or efficiently.

For the most part, Andrews feels the computer system is adequate—but not when it comes to supporting decisions about new parts and products. She also feels the Data Processing Department should and *must* take an active role in making revisions to support variety effectiveness.

FIGURE 6.8. Examples of Thirty-Character Codes *Before* VEP

M	/	S		6	-	3	2		X	1	/	4		B	/	H		S	/	S									
O	V	E	R	H	A	U	L		H	S	G																		
P	R	E	S	S	U	R	E	,		N	O	N	-	I	N	D	I	C	A	T	I	N	G						
C	O	N	T	R	O	L		C	O	M	P	O	N	E	N	T													
S	C	R	E	W	,		1	/	4	-	2	0		M	A	S	T	E	R		S	W	I	T	C	H			
C	O	M	M	E	R	C	I	A	L		S	T	O	C	K		S	C	R	E	W								
S	/	S		H	E	X		H	E	A	D																		

167

MAKING THE DATA SYSTEM VEP-CAPABLE

From the VEP viewpoint, PUI's classification system exhibits many areas of deficiency. Here are some of them:

1. The terminology used at PUI to describe parts and products is inconsistent and confusing.
2. The classification database is filled with data that are conflicting, duplicate, obsolete, inaccurate, and/or incomplete.
3. Procedures for adding a new classification for a product, part, or production process are informal and often result in inconsistencies.
4. Part numbers do not provide adequate attribute information for decision making.
5. Product life cycle, sales, and other marketing-related data are not easily available to analysis teams.
6. Class codes overlap; no rules are in place for assigning class codes to a new part or product.
7. What rules are in place are weakened by myriad exceptions.
8. Information encoded in the 30-character alphanumeric description format is often inconsistent and is insufficient for making VEP decisions.
9. PUI's data system has rarely, if ever, been maintained; no stated policy to do so exists.

The short of it is: The computer system does not contain the data needed for engineers to make sound decisions relative to the design of parts and products, nor does it allow data to be sorted meaningfully. As it stands, this classification system is a barrier to effective variety. Further, not only is it not able to assist in solving the problem but is actually one of its prime causes. An overhaul is needed.

What to Do? What to Do First?

With so many deficiencies and problems in the parts classification system, where—you may ask—does one begin the clean-up?

Begin. Begin by standardizing the parts terminology. That means define a single set of terms or names for part types and stick to it. Over time, this nomenclature becomes a common language people use on a regular basis. A screw is no longer referred to also as a fastener. Lids are not also covers. Angle stays are not also brackets and/or braces. Without standard terms for parts, a company cannot shore up its class codes. And without that, it is not equipped to move to the next steps.

The benefits of establishing a common nomenclature are immediate. Figure 6.9 shows you the revised set of codes after the Parts Type Team at PUI made the terminology uniform. Note that the number of terms was reduced from 104 to 76, a 27 percent decrease.

Next. Next, decide what kind of information your classification system needs to contain to help you find negative variety in parts specifications so you can propose workable reductions. To do this, VEP recommends developing a set of parameters that define which part attributes are meaningful. These parameters are then converted into an attribute template that becomes standard and is used each time a new part enters the database. That is, parts can be described in a number of ways, using any one of several attributes. Which ones are key, not just for design purposes but for the goals of variety effectiveness? Determine this.

Previous to VEP, PUI described screws in a nonstandard way (see Figure 6.6), but now that a standardized VEP attribute template on screws has been developed, the specifications are presented in an organized, consistent manner (see Figure 6.10). These templates took the confusion out. They made it possible for product engineers to access the vital information they need in the product development process to answer the question, for example: "Can I use this part for this new product, instead of introducing yet another new one?"

Our illustration on screws is a simple one and impressive enough when economies are achieved. Imagine the multiple impact on parts inventories and system complexity when applied, for example, to *all*

FIGURE 6.9. Active Class Codes at PUI *After* VEP (Down From 104 to 76 Class Codes)

	Code Description		Code Description
1	Mechanical Stock	39	Brackets
2	Mechanical Non-Stock	40	Knobs
3	Electronic Stock	41	Packaging Materials
4	Electronic Non-Stock	42	Capacitors
5	Replacement Sensor Stock	43	Relays
6	Replacement Sensor Non-Stock	44	Printed Circuit Boards
		45	Resistors
7	Electronic Accessories	46	Meters
8	Mechanical Accessories	47	Transformers
9	Nuts	48	Electronic Software
10	Rivets	49	Planning Bills
14	Pressure Assembly	50	Tools
15	Vacuum Assembly	51	Covers
16	Adjustment Assembly	52	Probes
17	Mechanical Switching Assembly	55	Gear Box Assemblies
18	Electronic Switching Assembly	56	Enclosure Assemblies
19	Bracket Assembly	58	Lead Wires Assemblies
21	Differential Rod Assemblies	59	Welding Electrodes
22	Housing Assemblies	60	Nameplates
23	Knob Assemblies	62	Flanges
25	Relay Assemblies	65	Springs
30	Miscellaneous Purchaser-Supplied Parts	66	Plastic Stampings
		67	Commercial Electronic Connectors
32	Dialplates	68	Tubing
32	Diaphragms, Gaskets & Seals	69	Mineral Insulated Cable
33	Gaskets	70	Thermistors
34	Insulators	71	Transistors
35	Seals	72	Wiring Diagrams
36	Wells & Connectors	74	Overtravel Assemblies
37	Metal Stampings	75	Adjusting Screw Assemblies
38	Micro-Switches, Purchased	76	Actuating Assemblies

commodity parts. This, of course, is the concept behind the work of the Parts Type Analysis Team in the clean-up aspects of VEP. As we will see in later chapters, the questions asked by its members are slightly different from those asked by the new product engineer; what the Parts Type Analysis Team asks is "Do we really need this part? Do we really need

FIGURE 6.10. Report on Active Screws *After* VEP (Using a VEP Attribute Template)

Part	Material	Length	Threading	Head
6277-001	Brass	⅛	6-32	Flat
6277-002	Stainless	¼	6-40	Flat
6277-003	Stainless	2	6-40	Hex
6277-004	Brass	2¼	8-40	Socket
6277-005	Brass	1	6-32	Binding
6277-006	Stainless	1	6-32	Binding

this particular variation? Can we eliminate, combine, or substitute this part in some way?"

Then. Hand-in-hand with developing standard attribute templates, the company initiates (and later maintains) sound data-input procedures. Assigning class codes can no longer be a matter of expedience or personal preference. The PUI Parts Type Team, which is responsible for upgrading all procedures related to the classification system, worked hard to develop good guidelines for determining class codes for parts. Part of the process of doing this—and of ensuring widespread buy-in—was getting ideas and feedback from all concerned parties. You can bet that the Drafting Department, as one of the main recipients of uncontrolled parts variations, had plenty of suggestions.

As shown in Figure 6.11, PUI came up with a set of simple guidelines. But these are also powerful because they serve as the base for further systems upgrades.

That summarizes the three-part process for improving the parts classification system so it is capable of supporting VEP decision making. Doing this harnesses the power of the information in your data banks so it can join in the battle against high parts inventories. For some companies, this may mean either a slight modification or none at all in the existing approach. For others, completing these three steps may seem roughly equivalent to hopping up Mt. McKinley on one foot.

FIGURE 6.11. Class Code Guidelines for Parts

1. All parts within a class code will carry the same prefix numbers in the part number designation followed by a dash (e.g., "All screws should begin with *6277*").

   Numbers following the dash (-) in a prefix designator will be assigned sequentially as new part numbers are required.

2. Any new part must be assigned to only one approved, existing class code, based on the most current class code list.

3. Each new part number shall be assigned to the existing class code category that carries all similar parts. If one does not exist or if there is any question whether a part fits within a certain class code, the VEP Parts Type Team Leader together with the Drafting Manager will determine how to classify the part.

4. Predefined attributes for each class code shall be the deciding factor in determining if a particular part fits within a particular class code.

5. The Parts Type Team Leader or the Drafting Manager must review and approve the coding of all new parts before they are entered into either the computer system or the attribute database.

6. The Parts Type Team Leader or Drafting Manager must approve any requests for class code changes in an existing part.

7. A class code shall not have overlapping or redundant parts within it *unless* special agreement has been reached with the Part Type Team Leader or the Drafting Manager.

Attribute Templates—More on the How-to

In the VEP scheme of things, the often-arduous task of creating attribute templates is assigned to the Parts Type Analysis Team; it is their first objective. Though not easy, it becomes easier when undertaken in increments and when effected through the team members themselves.

After deciding on the parameters (see above), the team designs a template for each part type and attribute data to plug into the fields. In many companies, this may mean taking values off the drawing directly and inputting the data manually. If you are thinking that this is a task that can be easily delegated to others, you'd best think again. Because of the huge likelihood of error, engineers and technicians are best suited to this job; it may not be as easily or reliably done, for example, by clerical staff.

Assuming this, then (that engineers and technicians will do the work themselves), here is a step-by-step procedure for accomplishing it:

1. The team's starting point is the part types (shared parts) of the targeted or priority product series (the meaning of "targeted series" is explained in the next section).
2. The part type population in that series is divvied up among the team's members.
3. Each team member defines an attribute template (a.k.a. computer screen or field) for his or her assigned part type.
4. Templates are submitted to the team for review.
5. According to the feedback, each template is improved and, when ready, adopted by consensus.
6. Using the template, the team member begins to input the data for the designated part type(s), checking drawings directly for accuracy.
7. Each team member dedicates a certain amount of time on a regular basis to data input—say, two hours a week or twenty minutes a day; a check sheet or scoreboard is maintained to keep team members on track.

Over time, this process is completed for the entire targeted series, and the iterations continue through the subsequent series on the VEP product priority list until attribute templates for all part types are entered.

Another Word to the Wise

The notion of cleaning up the parts classification system in your company may loom gargantuan on the horizon of your imagination. While this work should not be undertaken lightly, it becomes much more manageable when: (1) started early in the implementation (that is, in Stage 1), (2) performed by technically qualified employees, and (3) tackled in workable increments. The VEP software package can also be of assistance in this (see Resource Section at the back of the book for details).

Make no mistake: An information-capable parts data system is necessary and essential, even if you are not interested in VEP per se. It is a necessary and essential *good business* practice. But if you are committed to uncovering and rooting out negative variety in your company, you must have the capability to access accurate, complete, and meaningful data. Much like with our prototype company PUI, the data systems in many companies are—quite simply—a mess. Unabated, they only get worse with each passing day. Companies pay an awful price for allowing this order of inaccuracy and confusion to continue.

Moreover, should you be interested in achieving a greater degree of variety effectiveness in your organization and are unwilling to undertake this task, your success will be very limited. You are also sure to experience a great deal of frustration in any effort you make in that direction.

WHERE GROUP TECHNOLOGY FITS IN

Over the course of the development of the VEP methodology and the writing of this book, several people have asked about the link between VEP and Group Technology (GT). We want to respond to that question here in this discussion of classification systems. First, for those unfamiliar with GT, here's an overview.

Broadly speaking, Group Technology is a management system that makes parts variety visible by treating parts-related data as groups rather than as individual, isolated parts. First developed in 1948 by E. G. Brisch & Partners Limited (England), GT was widely used in the decades before JIT, SMED, and other lean production techniques to reorganize and streamline a company's manufacturing systems. It achieved and continues to achieve remarkable success.

GT's technology-based process begins with classifying parts with similar attributes and features into families or groups (hence the term "group technology"). This is followed by the weeding out of duplicate, near-duplicate, and other extraneous parts. With that as a base, the tasks are to:

1. Identify and analyze the current manufacturing processes (routing sequences) for each parts group.
2. Improve routing sequences for all part families.
3. Standardize and adopt the most effective routings.
4. Utilize these standard routings in all process planning.

VEP and GT are closely allied in several areas. Like VEP, GT recognizes the pivotal role of classification systems in the analysis needed to achieve true and substantial cost savings. Both approaches acknowledge the challenging, often unglamorous, work of making these systems capable. Like VEP, GT advocates standardization and prevention. And, like VEP, GT is software-supported.

The difference between VEP and GT lies in the scope of the endeavor. GT takes a deep dive into data systems in order to locate and minimize variation so that products can be designed and produced more efficiently and at less cost. VEP also champions those goals but widens the inquiry to include every organizational system and its role in triggering and/or preventing negative variety—in *all* its forms. VEP seeks to build variety effectiveness into every stratum of the enterprise.

In the words of W. F. Hyde of Brisch, Birn & Partners, Inc. (Fort Lauderdale): "Group Technology is VEP's best friend"—along with JIT and SMED.* You are ahead of the variety effectiveness game plan if your company is currently involved in GT. A lot of the groundwork is bound to be in place. If GT is new to you, then treat it as an option to investigate, noting that GT can represent a significant investment of time and money. While it can be a support to your VEP implementation, it is not a requirement for going forward. GT is not required for an effective VEP implementation. A sound and capable classification system is!**

---

* William F. Hyde, correspondence, August 1994.

** For more information on Group Technology, see: (1) William F. Hyde, *Improving Productivity Through Classification Coding, and Data-Base Standardization* (New York: Marcel Dekker, Inc., 1981); (2) Charles S. Snead, *Group Technology: Foundation for Competitive Manufacturing* (New York: Van Nostrand Reinhold, 1989); and (3) Gallagher and Winston Knight, *Group Technology Production Methods in Manufacturing* (Chicester, U.K.: Ellis Horwood, 1986).

WHERE TO BEGIN? SELECTING A PRODUCT STARTING POINT

The VEP preparation process (Stage 1) includes one more vital step: Determining where to begin the actual analysis.

In the United States, the culturally correct (CC), ready-to-wear, answer is: Just begin! JUST DO IT! In the best *ready, fire, aim* tradition of our American rugged individualist mentality, the only hurdle is getting started. "Do that and the details will take care of themselves," goes conventional wisdom. While VEP certainly has no quarrel with this pitch-in-and-do approach, it also takes some pains to put some structure around the decision, so that it has a chance of being a sound one. Should the three 3-View Analysis teams start with the same focus or different ones? If it's the same focus, should it be on a single product or an entire product series? Or would it be better to start analyzing several associated product lines simultaneously and set a strong pace? And whichever the case, how can the teams be confident that their efforts—whether jointly or separately—will pay off?

Determining exactly *where* the VEP analysis process should begin is the responsibility of Steering Team members. Thanks to VEP training, they know that their selection will be a single product series (or line), and it will become the launching pad for all three teams engaged in the 3-View Analysis process. It is, consequently, a pivotal decision. Their single query is: *Of all our product lines, which one will give us the most bang—the biggest return—for our analysis buck?* To answer the question, they need two things: first, a clear, systematic procedure for finding out, and second, a set of selection criteria that is valid and relevant to the organization. The VEP Steering Team at Parts Unlimited Inc. is about to encounter the need for this. Let's look in on the Steering Team, as it finds itself in the throes of the dilemma.

Steering Team Leader John Holcombe, rushing in late from another meeting, has just opened this session with a barrage of questions:

"With over 300 products and 50 product series to consider, where should we begin to look for reduction opportunities? Where should we begin our VEP analysis? Where will we get the most bang for our buck? And how do we make sure we are not just shooting from the hip? We want to make sure we're not going to waste our time and everybody else's with a long-drawn-out analysis that ends up not worth it. How do we make sure we end up looking like heroes and not like deadbeats?"

Within moments, the team begins a lively discussion of the pros and cons of starting with one product over another, then one product series over another. Thirty minutes later, Tricia MacAndrews, Chief Design Engineer, mentions that they are "getting nowhere—fast," submitting that the group is straying from the VEP method. Holcombe, coming to his senses, thanks MacAndrews and firmly suggests that the team return to the VEP approach. With a unified sigh of relief, the group focuses on step one: Develop selection criteria.

THE QUALIFYING PROCEDURE

Pulling a good starting place out of a hat for analyzing parts and products is not often the most efficient approach. Consequently, VEP provides a specific, systematic subprocedure for this. It is called "qualifying candidates." In a nutshell, it is a process for selecting and prioritizing a collection of product series from the company's product universe that are most likely to benefit from VEP analysis and the resultant reduction recommendations. They are, as a group, worth the effort, as they represent your company's most costly and complex products. At the top of that priority list is the so-called "targeted series"—the starting point for VEP's 3-View Analysis.

The VEP procedure for qualifying product candidates has three steps:

Step One: Develop assessment criteria and a weighting formula for determining which lines/series in the company's product universe will provide the biggest return for VEP reduction efforts.

Step Two: Apply these criteria and formulas, one by one, to each product series and arrive at a rank-ordered list based on the individual scores.

Step Three: Designate the single product series with the highest score as the *targeted series*, the starting point for VEP analysis.

Let's walk through the process, bearing in mind that it is a guideline—not a prescription. You may need to modify it to suit your company.

Step One: Develop Assessment Criteria and a Weighting Formula

What are the best criteria for determining the product series that will produce the biggest payoff for our VEP effort? Ask three departments, get three different answers. Engineers might want to use *level of structure complexity* and/or *ratio of dedicated-to-shared parts* as expressed in the VEP Parts Index. "That way," they say, "we'll get to improve the products that give us the biggest headaches." Marketing might well prefer to apply the *level of revenue contribution* as a key criterion; improving those products, that logic goes, will make the company's return-on-sales jump even higher. Operations would probably go with *quantity of shipped units* and/or *number of required dies and fixtures*, in keeping with its goal to make day-to-day life on the shop floor a little easier. And don't forget about the position of a product on the life-cycle continuum, another important gauge. And there are more.

The point is: All these factors are worth considering. It's the task of your Steering Team to identify as many of these as possible and then select the ones that are valid and relevant to *your* organization. Returning to the true cost discussion in Chapter 2, however, what is not tenable for

VEP purposes are criteria linked to the traditional accounting formula factors of labor + material + overhead. For one thing, they tell us nothing about the complexity of a product series.

A First-Pass Procedure, Assisted by an Optional Tool

Identifying suitable criteria is most easily effected through a procedure that begins with simple brainstorming:

Sub-step a. The team brainstorms a list of possible factors on a flip chart (no evaluation, please).

Sub-step b. Each member ranks the items on the list according to his or her own preferences.

Sub-step c. Members discuss and justify their individual preferences.

Sub-step d. Through consensus, group arrives at a joint, pared-down list of criteria.

Procedural Tool. This procedure can be facilitated by using a modified Relations Diagram as a focal point. Sub-steps *b* through *d* are essentially the same as above. Only sub-step *a* differs, and then only in form, not substance. Instead of listing the items in a row on a flip chart, the team gathers round a sheet of paper that has a circle in the center. Inside the circle is the question "What kind of product will give us the biggest bang for our VEP analysis buck?" The team members answer, marking their responses on the paper in a branching fashion around the question in the center circle (see Figure 6.12). Next, the members, continuing with sub-steps *b*, *c*, and *d*, discuss their preferences and select a final set. The Relations Diagram format can help the team arrive at more sophisticated criteria and differentiate between primary and secondary considerations in those criteria.

When the criteria are selected, you clarify each broad category and segment into subsets, as needed, and then develop a numerical scoring scale and weighting value. These help in evaluating and rating (weighting) each product series mathematically so they can be compared against each other.

FIGURE 6.12. Applying the Relations Diagram for Finding Qualifying Criteria

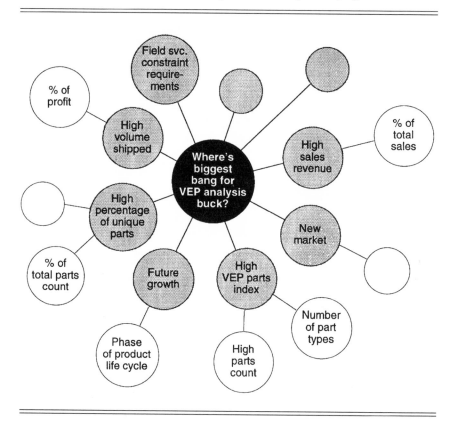

Through this process, PUI Steering Team members, for example, selected three criteria to apply to each product series: (1) Expected Growth, (2) Sales Revenue, and (3) Product Complexity which was separated further into two sub-categories:

- Dedicated Parts Index (calculate the number of dedicated parts per series)
- Ratio of Dedicated Parts to Total Parts (compute the ratio of dedicated to total parts in that series)

They then decided on the following weighting values for the four category sets above: 25%-35%-40%, respectively. Their scoring scale was:

Minor	Moderate	Major
1-2-3	4-5-6-7	8-9-10

Steps Two and Three—Apply Criteria and Formula and Designate the Analysis Priorities

When you have completed the assessment, all the company's offerings will be positioned on a summative scale or rank-order continuum, with the most qualified product series having automatically risen to the top. This series becomes the priority or targeted series and is the starting point for the VEP analysis. In Figure 6.13, you can see the partial results of PUI's qualifying process. The targeted series is Series 7.

Designating this series as the starting point is the link to the next round of VEP activity—the analysis itself. Anchored to this single product line, each of the 3-View teams begins its respective work, using the same targeted series as the jumping-off point. In this sense, the focus of the VEP implementation stays sharp and clear and prevents teams from slipping into the murkiness of too many choices, the very complexity they are attempting to unravel.

WHY BOTHER?

We strongly recommend that a company go through the qualifying process described above even if a priority product has been preselected. Yes, even if your company is pursuing the *select focus approach* to VEP (and

FIGURE 6.13. Score Sheet Based on Preset Qualifying Criteria: PUI's *Top 5 Series*

Series	Criterion 1	Criterion 2	Criterion 3	Criterion 4	Total	Notes
7*	10	8	10	8	36	Continued growth expected. High dedicated parts. High shipped units.
53	3	9	8	10	30	Moderate growth expected. High shipped units and parts.
73	6	7	7	6	26	Moderate growth expected. High dedicated parts. Reasonably high shipped units.
11	2	9	5	8	24	Tremendous revenue growth expected by 1995. Shipped units will rise rapidly in 1993–1995. Fairly high dedicated parts.
148	2	5	5	10	22	Revenue to grow very slowly. Shipped units fairly high. Total parts fairly high. Important series to process industry.

LEGEND

	Scoring Scale	
CRITERION 1 = Expected Growth	HIGH	8-9-10
CRITERION 2 = Sales Revenue	MEDIUM	4-5-6-7
CRITERION 3 = Dedicated Parts Index	LOW	1-2-3
CRITERION 4 = Ratio of Dedicated Parts to Total Parts		

* The targeted series is represented by the shaded area.

not the *deep dive*), you will benefit from systematically selecting that focus and not skipping over it and moving straight into analysis.

There are several reasons for this. First, even if you "know" which of your product lines is most qualified, going through the qualifying process will help you document your thinking and the logic by which you made your choice. Second, in doing so, you will revisit your key issues and may find you need to adjust your preset choice one way or another—only a systematic approach will allow you to do this. Finally, if you need to go to management for approval or added resources, VEP's qualifying process will help you substantiate and validate your thinking, especially in the realm of marketing and sales factors.

THE IMPORTANCE OF STAGE 1—SUMMARY

Stage 1 activities forge a strong link between information and its use in the analysis process of Stage 2, which drives future improvement. Whether you choose the deep-dive or selected-focus approach to VEP change, information is the heart of the Stage 2 analysis process. Steps taken in preparation ensure access to the vital information that the analysis process requires. Since people are the source for much of the information needed, the first preparatory step is to get people organized, on board, and ready; that means selecting, setting up, and training teams. We must also ensure that the core database on parts and products (the classification system) is accurate, relevant, complete, and accessible. During this time, the Steering Team is involved in qualifying and selecting the first focus of the inquiry that will begin in Stage 2, the series targeted for the first round of VEP analysis. All the while, and early in this first stage, the Early Victories Team begins its search for easy and often dramatic reductions in parts that show a low resistance to change; when these go, the production processes linked to them go, too. Supported and promoted by the Education and Methods Team, these early successes give the embryonic VEP implementation a needed positive publicity

FIGURE 6.14. Overview of Stage 1 of the VEP Methodology

STAGE 1— Preparing for an Effective VEP Implementation	STAGE 2— Identifying Reduction Opportunities by Applying the 6-VATs	STAGE 3— Coordinating and Prioritizing Reduction Opportunities	STAGE 4— Implementing and Sustaining the Improvement
Step 1— Select a Steering Team that then sets up the other VEP teams (Management)			
Step 2— Conduct team training & begin general awareness training (Education & Methods Team)			
Step 3— Begin to analyze and revise company policies and practices (Policy Analysis Team)			

184

Step 4—
Find and reduce parts with low-resistance to change (Early Victories Team)

Step 5—
Assess, clean up, and upgrade parts classification system (Part Type Analysis Team)

Step 6—
Target a priority product as the starting point for Stage 2 reduction analysis (Steering Team)

boost, keeping naysayers at bay and solidifying the backing that is in place within the company (see summary in Figure 6.14).

Taken in their sum, these preparatory steps go a long way to ensure that the challenging VEP analysis work that follows can provide the greatest return for the investment of time, energy, and commitment you make.

CHAPTER SEVEN

THE HEART OF VEP ANALYSIS: THE SIX TOOLS

If a hammer is your only tool, all problems begin to look like nails.

—ANONYMOUS

GET READY FOR ANALYSIS ACTION!

The task in VEP is two-fold. First, you identify and act on valid opportunities for reducing the existing pool of negative variety in your company. Then you take steps to prevent its recurrence.

In Stage 1 of the methodology, you prepared the organization for change. Teams were formed and trained, and the general work force was educated. Your existing parts classification system was purged of its deadwood and revised using the VEP attribute template to make it increasingly VEP-capable—able to support sound VEP analysis and decision making. In addition, a special ad hoc team was formed to win some early, easy victories by eliminating parts and processes with low resistance to change. And finally, your company's offerings were rationalized and rank ordered, and a priority product line was targeted for the first round of analysis.

The short of it is: You and your organization are entering Stage 2 prepared and ready for action. And the action is analysis! In Stage 2, the active search for reduction opportunities begins. The core instrument of this task is the 3-View Analysis and its three teams (Market, Product Structure, and Part Type). At the heart of that analysis is a set of six techniques known as the 6-VEP Analysis Tools*—*6-VATs*, for short.

The purpose of this chapter is to acquaint you with these six tools, primarily as they apply to parts and product structures, and give you a sense of how they can help locate and minimize negative variety. Then, in Chapter 8, we'll examine the procedures and workings of the 3-View Analysis process that the 6-VATs support.

THE 6-VATS—TOOLS OF INQUIRY

The 6-VATs are:

VAT-1   Unique Versus Shared
VAT-2   Modularity
VAT-3   Multifunctionality and Synthesis
VAT-4   Ease of Assembly
VAT-5   Range
VAT-6   Trend

All three of the 3-View teams use these tools to varying extents and in varying combination, depending on their point of inquiry. The Product Structure Analysis Team, for example, tends to make extensive use of VATs 2 through 4, while the Part Type Analysis Teams may rely more heavily on VATs 1, 5, and 6. And, where those two teams utilize the VATs in the tools' primary, engineering application, the Market Analysis Team

---

* I am indebted to Toshio Suzue and Akira Kohdate for their related discussions. See *Variety Reduction Program*.

tends to use the principles behind the VATs, rather than the engineering concepts, to clarify its central issues of customer need and markets and to diagnose clusters in the products and product lines offered by the company.

The 6-VATs also have important applications in reducing production processes and control points. In the case of the former, the inquiry starts at the parts/product level and moves, only after that analysis is complete, to the processes that support them. The reason is simple: Reducing the number of parts, simplifying product structures, and shoring up your product offerings automatically eliminates certain production processes. Let that happen organically, and you'll have less processes to deal with when you address them explicitly.*

VAT-1: UNIQUE VERSUS SHARED

The starting point in reducing negative variety is understanding where the variety is in the organization. The first of the six tools—Unique Versus Shared—is designed to do this. We apply it to get answers to a series of fundamental questions. Let's walk through these questions, focusing on parts, beginning on the model-level of the targeted series.

The first question is: Is the part under scrutiny *unique* to this model or shared with another or several other models? The next question is: If the part is shared, can it be shared more widely? That is, can it be further commonized or standardized to serve yet other product structures? If the part is unique (also known as "dedicated" or "variable"), the question is: Why is it unique? And, can we standardize the specifications sufficiently that it can be shared with at least one other model? Let's go through this again in more detail.

---

* More information on this and control point reduction is given in Chapter 9.

If the part is already shared (used in several models), we move on and apply some or all of the other five VATs to determine if it can be further commonized. If the part is dedicated or unique, we need to ascertain if the reason for this "specialness" is valid. Is it a dedicated element because of a specific customer demand? Or is it the result of an inefficiency or anomaly in the company's internal practices? In other words, we need to find out if the variation is customer-driven or internally triggered.

If the variation is verifiably customer-driven, the difference constitutes *positive* variety and is an important profit advantage. If, on the other hand, the variation is internally triggered, caused (however unintentionally) by a practice within the company, it represents *negative* variety and a suspect cost. This line of logic remains true even for product design requirements related to form, fit, or function. See Figure 7.1.

Yes, we did mean to say that: In VEP, *even* variations caused by the requirements of form, fit, and function are classified as *negative variety* if they are not specifically requested by the customer. There may be no known way around these requirements. Your product engineers may be forced to spec out the part in a way that renders it *unique* in order to fulfill the demands of the product architecture or because of production constraints. *But*, in VEP, we want to be fully aware of that. We want to understand that we are creating negative variety—and there is no way around it, at least not at the moment, given the current state of our systems. Even if we wish there were a way around it and there isn't, it still counts as variety that is internally triggered and, consequently, negative.

Unique parts in a product can constitute a significant competitive advantage when they result in product features that make the company's products distinctive in the marketplace, but variation at the parts and assembly levels is often not required or specifically desired by the customer. When that is the case, the variety is wasted. It adds complexity and no payoff. But there are other costly ramifications. Production reference points on nonstandard parts often vary and can cause wide fluctuations in production processes. When these points change from model to model, the need for special fixtures and processing escalates,

FIGURE 7.1. VAT-1: Unique Versus Shared

Definitions	1. **Shared Parts** are parts that have been sufficiently standardized or commonized so they can be used (or shared) across two, several, or many models. Also known as shared or commonized parts. 2. **Unique Parts** have not been standardized and shared either because they are linked to a special customer demand (positive) or are constrained by technological/organizational limitations or both. Certain previously unique parts, on closer look, may lend themselves to commonization.
Objectives	• To separate the constituent elements of a product into those that have been commonized or standardized and those that are unique or nonstandard. • To validate or refute an element's unique status. • To widen standardization range on current shared elements and shift over to shared as many dedicated elements as possible.
Key Questions	• What is the current level of standardization? • Could it be increased? • How valid is the part-by-part premise that customer requirements preclude commonization? • Which parts should not change from model to model and why?
Application Procedure	**Step 1.** Separate the constituent parts of a product series or family into elements that are unique (dedicated) and those that are shared (standard). **Step 2.** Widen the scope of each shared parts so more models are covered, and commonize as many currently dedicated elements as possible. **Step 3.** Develop and adhere to guidelines that promote the commonization of parts, and stipulate when parts can remain unique and variable.

as does the need for differing assembly techniques. If, on the other hand, parts are sufficiently standardized, a single standard production process can be used for multiple parts and with no added changeovers or adjustments.

Clearly, converting dedicated parts into shared parts can result in considerable cost savings related to control points as well. Since shared parts mean fewer parts, layers of transactions, such as parts re-ordering, material handling, incoming inspection, and counting, are automatically reduced every time the ratio of shared over unique parts increases.

For VAT-1 to really work its magic, all parts must be examined—on model and product series levels. No matter how low its intrinsic value, let no individual part escape scrutiny. When a so-called "unique" element is found, question its status: Does it have to remain unique? Why?

Taken as a whole, this first VAT tool (Unique Versus Shared) forces the company to assess its current level of standardization and ask: Can it be expanded?

The Limits of Sharing

VAT-1 is a key to maximizing resources and minimizing costs in product development. But there are limits to the amount of parts-sharing across product lines. Some products are specifically designed to contain one or more variable parts, expressly to make them more responsive to the marketplace; this is the part of the product that changes when, for example, mauve replaces purple as the color of the year, or ships replace alligators as insignia of distinction.

Some industries have special constraints. A supplier that globally sources truck interiors to the Big Three automakers (Ford, General Motors, and Chrysler), for example, is obliged to design products—a distinctive visor and innovative cup-holder—that make each of its customers stand out in the marketplace. Because these customers are tooth-and-nail competitors, unique distinctions between product lines must be preserved; they are not candidates for commonization.

But what about the infrastructure, the internal workings of these "unique" products? Continuing the discussion on Nissan and the variety explosion of the 1980s, we ask if a product's fasteners or hinges or O-rings must be as distinctive and exciting as the surface of the product? On the flip side, a customer's request for a special element may not necessarily preclude its being used in another product, as a crossover.

Teams are good at finding such opportunities. When the first crossover opportunity is found, it is a breakthrough. Later, it becomes a matter of routine.

The work of VAT-1 is to locate negative variation in the structure of products, the way products are segmented for market, and the specifications of the parts themselves. Teams seek to shift as many nonstandard (variable) elements to shared status—or to understand why they cannot shift them. In short, they identify and test, validate or refute, their assumptions about the variability. Doing this paves the way for applying the other five techniques in the VAT tool kit.

For a summary of VAT-1, plus a simple procedure to guide the inquiry, see Figure 7.1.

VAT-2: MODULARITY

VAT-2, the second of VEP's six analytic tools, is *Modularity*. In Modularity, the perspective shifts from individual and isolated parts to parts in groups or subassemblies. The part now takes on meaning connected with its place in a product environment. In this second VEP tool, the relationship that parts have to each other within a product (and later on, across products) takes over—how parts mate. In Figure 7.2, the four parts to the left are as they are viewed when VAT-1 is applied—distinct, separate, and isolated from each other. On the right are the same four parts, but as VAT-2 would consider them—as a unit or subassembly, that is, in relationship to each other.

VAT-2 forges the link between standardization and interchangeability by challenging us in three ways:

1. To what extent can subassemblies or given sets of parts be standardized into units or modules that can be used in several products?

FIGURE 7.2. VAT-1 and VAT-2: Two Perspectives on the Same Parts

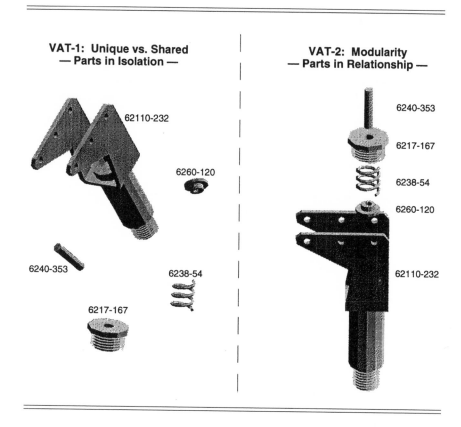

VAT-1: Unique vs. Shared
— Parts in Isolation —

62110-232

6260-120

6240-353

6238-54

6217-167

VAT-2: Modularity
— Parts in Relationship —

6240-353

6217-167

6238-54

6260-120

62110-232

2. To what extent can assorted modules be further standardized so that they are interchangeable across many products?

3. To what extent can product structures be developed so that they can accommodate standard modules—or any of an assortment of such modules?

Capitalizing on any increased levels of commonized parts resulting from VAT-1 (unique versus shared), modularity in VEP seeks to extend the concept of standardization in terms of both functions and dimensions so that parts-mating and module-mating across products are augmented. The modular approach also encourages changes in design specifications that do not necessarily require associated changes in existing product structures. New designs are achieved simply by introducing new combinations of modules. Because units are interchangeable, they can result in a wider variety of finished products merely by switching them. Combining modules in this way is a simpler and more economical means for meeting the market's demand for "new" products than is creating a product from scratch. An added benefit is that modularized units are easier to upgrade or downgrade in response to shifts in market forces. In one company, application of VAT-2, alone, resulted in a 30 percent reduction in parts. When implemented broadly, modularity can trigger powerful simplifications in a company's production systems, making it even more attractive as a cost-savings technique. See Figure 7.3.

FIGURE 7.3. VAT-2: Modularity

Definitions	**1. Modular Design.** A unit or group of standardized elements or parts that may be used within a number of different products because the unit itself is sufficiently commonized to be interchangeable across a number of products.
Objectives	• To minimize the number of required elements by combining and unitizing as many as possible into standardized components or modules that are interchangeable. • To create units of exchangeable elements (modules) in order to create wider customer choice while minimizing cross-product complexity and costs.
Key Questions	• What is the current level of modularity in products? • How can it be increased? • Can a given standard module be combined with another to create further augmented, replicated, or combined models? • Can other modules be combined or recombined so that a wider range of need or function is served?
Application Procedure	**Step 1.** Examine a model's assorted elements, looking for opportunities to combine these further into standardized units or modules. **Step 2.** Look across products for opportunities to replace highly variant subassemblies with standard modules. **Step 3.** Develop and adhere to guidelines that promote modularity in new product design.

Three Modular Styles

There are three primary ways to achieve modularity in products: (1) Amplification, (2) Replication, and (3) Combination.

Amplification. Amplification is an approach that requires a stable product base or core. Parts are then added to the base, with assorted parts resulting in assorted products. As the types of added parts vary, the variety of new products expands.

The children's toy Mr. Potato Head works on this basis. An array of plastic parts (noses, eyes, ears, hats) is added to the product core, the potato itself. The result is a host of weird-looking, impressively distinctive creatures. The same concept is used in making pizza pies. The base is the same—the crust; then all kinds of ingredients (parts) can be added, making potential combinations and the possibility of satisfying customers practically unlimited.

In another universe, the Prizm and Metro models of GM's Geo car line share an identical base—the same chassis, engine, and power train. Models diverge in terms of seats, interiors, trunk styles, dashboards, and so forth to expand the range of appeal. The same approach is popular in footwear, especially in sneakers.

Replication. The replication approach uses a series of standardized, identical modules that result in different products depending on the number of modules used.

This is exactly the way children get so many fantastic creations out of a set of plain wooden blocks or Legos®. The components are the same, but because they share common reference or mating points, they can be put together so that different end-items result. Stackable office or kitchen trays and CD racks are two other examples of replication.

Combination. The combination approach seeks to create diverse products by linking up standardized modules of varying functions.

This is similar to the way children can make a range of "things" by combining different elements in their Erector Sets—cross beams, motors, winches, buckets, corners, roofs, etc. The result is a seemingly endless stream of highly differentiated constructions, limited only by the imagination. The key again lies in the high level of standardization in mating dimensions and reference points. Modularized shelving units are a good example of the combination approach.

VAT-2: Modularity is summarized in Figure 7.3.

VAT-3: MULTIFUNCTIONALITY AND SYNTHESIS

The first two VATS are aimed primarily at minimizing the scope of variation within part types. Successful results can dramatically lower V-Costs (Variety Costs), including secondary variations in production processes, process paths, equipment, fixtures, dies, labor hours, and control points.

VAT-3: Multifunctionality and Synthesis concentrates on reducing Function Costs (F-Costs) by creating parts and units that serve multiple uses and perform multiple functions, thereby reducing the number of parts required to fulfill those functions.

Closely linked to the principles of DFM (Design for Manufacturability*), VAT-3 directs engineers to design for robustness so that a greater range of function is served through the same or fewer parts. Synthesis, the second element of the technique, focuses on finding new materials and new engineering and production technologies that allow previously separated parts to be merged or collapsed so that the same or additional functions are met through fortified and less variant specifications. The goal is product designs that keep to an absolute minimum the number of constituent parts needed to fulfill each product function.

The first step is to determine whether the part is suitable for a VAT-3

---

* We gratefully acknowledge the contribution of Dr. Geoffrey Boothroyd and Dr. Peter Dewhurst, pioneers and current-day leaders in the field of design for manufacturability and assembly (DFM and DFA).

application. To do this, think of the part in its context, as an element in the structure of the product, and answer these three questions*:

1. Does the part have to move separately from the other parts during the operation of the product?
2. Does the part have to be of a material different from the other parts?
3. Does the part have to be removed separately vis-a-vis the other parts for servicing or reassembly?

If the answer to any of these questions is "yes," the function of this part cannot be merged with that of another. If the answer to all three questions is "no," the part is a possible candidate for multifunctionality and synthesis. You are ready for the next steps:

1. Identify the product's required functions.
2. Understand how these functions are fulfilled through the constituent parts.
3. Search for ways to simplify, integrate, substitute, or optimize parts and functions.

Your solutions may take several directions. First, you may eliminate or remove extraneous specifications or surplus functions. In the case of the bracket function shown in Figure 7.4, for example, four parts and at least two kinds of material were required—a low-carbon steel bracket, stainless-steel fingers, and two fasteners. Later, the two components are combined and both fasteners eliminated.

Alternatively, you can combine or incorporate several functions into one. The design of a pressure control, for example, called for two separate parts; one part had the function of guiding the load spring that changes the range of control, and the second part was the plunger, a rod that transferred the movement from the sensor to the electrical switch. The two components

---

* These three questions were adapted for the purposes of the VEP methodology from the original DFA minimum part questions which Drs. Boothroyd and Dewhurst developed for application in simulating the assembly process.

did not move with respect to each other; they rode on top of each other. When VAT-3 was applied, it was clear that the two functions could be merged. The result was the single, multifunctional part shown in Figure 7.5.

FIGURE 7.4. Example:* Before-and-After VAT-3—Multifunctionality and Synthesis

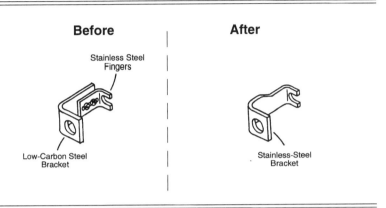

FIGURE 7.5. Example: Before-and-After VAT-3—Multifunctionality and Synthesis

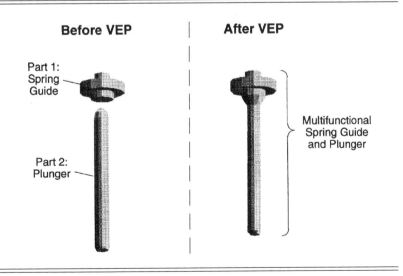

* George Boothroyd and Peter Dewhurst, *Product Design for Assembly* (Wakefield, R.I.: Boothroyd Dewhurst, Inc., 1989), pp. 2–15.

FIGURE 7.6. VAT-3: Multifunctionality and Synthesis

Definitions	1. **Multifunctionality** seeks to design for robustness, formulating product structures that include only the minimum number of elements to fulfill required functions, with each part serving a greater range of specification.
	2. **Synthesis** looks for ways to combine, integrate, or minimize such parts further by using new materials, production technologies, or structural concepts that use fewer parts to meet required functions.
Objectives	• To minimize the number of elements required to fulfill specific functions by making each element serve as many different functions as possible.
	• To create a product that provides the desired functions through a simplified structure by eliminating differing materials and making fewer materials more robust.
Key Questions	• Can a function of this product or part be merged with that of another?
	• Can the same level of capability and customer selection be maintained or expanded?
Procedure	**Step 1.** Identify specific functions of the part, components, or product.
	Step 2. **Look for ways to meet these functions through a simplified product structure, requiring fewer parts, components, or subassemblies.**
	Step 3. Look for ways to minimize the number of parts further by using different materials, production technologies, or structural concepts.
	Step 4. Develop and adhere to guidelines that promote multifunctionality and synthesis in new product design.

Applications of VAT-3 (Multifunctionality and Synthesis) have tremendous potential for reducing parts and processes. Regardless of its low intrinsic value, every single constituent product part should be queried. One "company estimated that the elimination of a single fastener would save $15,000 over the life of a point of sale terminal that had been redesigned."* A VEP team may ascertain that a part cannot be elimi-

* From private correspondence of Dr. George Boothroyd of Boothroyd Dewhurst, Inc., Wakefield R.I., July 1994.

nated because of such constraints as the unavailability of specialized equipment needed to manufacture a multifunctional part or the diseconomies of manufacture, but such constraints are discovered only *after* the tool is applied. See Figure 7.6 on the facing page for a summary of VAT-3: Multifunctionality and Synthesis.

VAT-4: EASE OF ASSEMBLY

Up until this point, the tools in the VAT kit have been aimed at reducing complexity and attendant costs through parts reduction and design simplification. In VAT-1, we standardized as many elements or parts as possible. In VAT-2, we combined standardized elements into modular configurations. In VAT-3, we integrated functions and material requirements into a multi-purpose result. Only essential parts now remain in the product. Now it is time to ensure that these are easy to assemble. This is the function of VAT-4: Ease of Assembly. Some of the important guidelines* for accomplishing this include:

1. Eliminate or simplify adjustments.
2. Minimize the use of separate connectors and fasteners (see Figure 7.4).
3. Design parts that are self-aligning and self-locating (see Figure 7.7).
4. Design parts that cannot be installed incorrectly (see Figure 7.8).
5. Ensure adequate access and unrestricted vision during assembly (see Figure 7.9).

* Adapted from material found in *Product Design for Assembly* by George Boothroyd and Peter Dewhurst. Please note: Guidelines or "rules" for assembly, as Drs. Boothroyd and Dewhurst term them, vary depending on a number of factors; for complete information, see pp. 2-12, 3-13, 4-27, and 5-23 in the above publication.

FIGURE 7.7. VAT-4: Design Parts That Are Self-Aligning and Self-Locating*

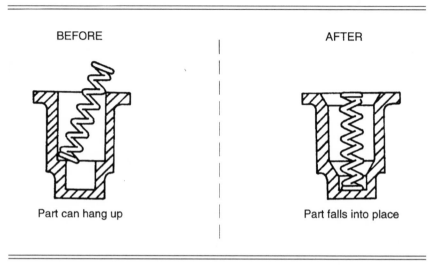

BEFORE

Part can hang up

AFTER

Part falls into place

FIGURE 7.8. VAT-4: Design Parts That Cannot Be Installed Incorrectly*

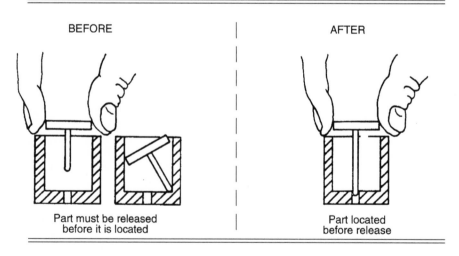

BEFORE

Part must be released
before it is located

AFTER

Part located
before release

* Examples from George Boothroyd and Peter Dewhurst, *Product Design for Assembly*, pp. 2–21.

FIGURE 7.9. VAT-4: Ensure Adequate Access and Unrestricted Vision During Assembly*

BEFORE   AFTER

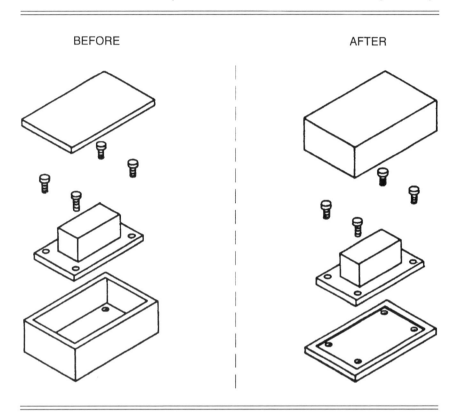

6. Ensure ease of handling of parts from bulk (avoiding parts that nest or tangle, are flexible, fragile, sticky, magnetic, abrasive, too small, too light, or too big).
7. Minimize need for reorientations during assembly; design for top-down assembly.
8. Maximize part symmetry or make parts obviously asymmetrical.

Because assembly costs are largely set in the product engineering stage, it is paramount that engineers factor in ease-of-assembly considerations from the outset of the product's design. (See Figure 7.10.)

* Ibid.

FIGURE 7.10. VAT-4: Ease of Assembly

Definitions	1. **Ease of Assembly** means that, after parts have been upgraded by applying VATs 1 through 3, we analyze all constituent parts to ensure that they are easy to assemble.
Objectives	• To make all remaining parts as easy as possible to assemble.
	• To improve costs associated with the assembly process by creating a product structure made of parts and components that are easy to handle and assemble.
Key Question	• Can part be assembled from above?
	• Can part be made to require few or no adjustments?
	• Can part be made requiring no or minimal types of fastening?
	• Can assembly motions requiring skills be minimized or eliminated?
	• Can differences between similar parts be made obvious?
Procedure	**Step 1.** Disassemble the product, part by part.
	Step 2. Reassemble the product, part by part, against VAT-4 assembly guidelines and generate alternative part concepts.
	Step 3. Develop and adhere to guidelines that promote ease of assembly in new product design.

VAT-5: RANGE

The last two techniques in the VAT tool kit—VAT-5 (Range) and VAT-6 (Trend)—take the broadest possible perspective on part values, product structures, and product lines. They look at the accumulation and pattern of variation within and across a company's entire product and parts universe. Let's learn how VEP utilizes range.

Widely used in statistics, *range* is the simplest measure of the dispersion (spread) of a group of values that share some common observable characteristic. Range is the difference between the largest and smallest of those values, including all the values along the way. In VEP, the range technique is used to identify the reach or boundary of variation relative to parts, products, and product lines.

Let's consider parts first. Companies with no unifying product development strategy often experience a mushrooming of parts specifications that parallels expanding product variety, often exacerbated (as we frequently mention) by the lack of VEP-capable classification systems. In these cases, product engineers find themselves hard-pressed to locate existing parts to carry over or to ascertain the closest part values so they might adjust the geometries of designs under development to accommodate them. As a result, new parts come flying into the system. No one notices *because no one has been designated to notice.* In short, there is nothing in the infrastructure to prevent it. As a result, the range of part values (among other things) inevitably widens; similar but not identical parts continue to accumulate, and redundancies and overlaps become numerous.

In VEP, when we apply VAT-5: Range, we begin by selecting a specific attribute variation within a specific part type. Springs, for example, share such variable attributes as *spring rate* (extent to which the spring length changes when force is applied), outer diameter (O.D.), and inner diameter (I.D.). Lead wires, as another case, share variant attributes such as gauge, material, and color. The range technique enables us to see the spread or dispersion of alterable values.

Figure 7.11 shows the dispersion of the O.D. values of PUI's 120 springs. When the Parts Type Team sees this spread, they immediately notice the dense central cluster of values and those few scattered on the edges. In an instant, team members are wondering if some of the closely clustered values can be collapsed and others extended to accommodate more variety in fewer springs, and if the outlying values are really required (customer-driven).

Their inquiring response is exactly the point of VAT-5. Observing the configuration of values in a range dispersion, especially one with high contrasts (as seen above), goads us to investigate the genesis of the variations. When we take this on, the other VATs are brought into play and applied, data point by data point; useful reduction recommendations result.

The search for reduction opportunities requires VEP teams to compile and digest a good deal of numerical information. The range technique (and trend technique which follows) allows them to present the

FIGURE 7.11. Value Range of the O.D. (Outer Diameter) of PUI's 120 Springs

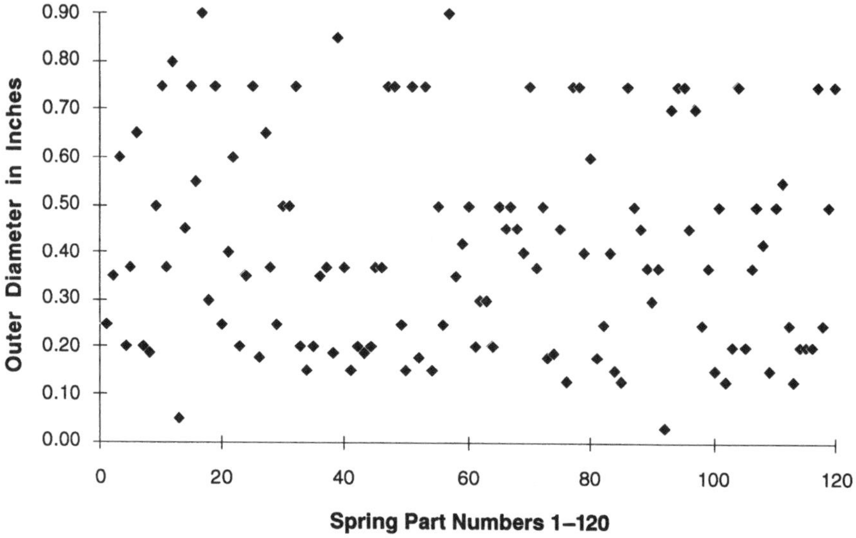

data in a usable and meaningful form so that an overall picture can be detected. Because range and trend use aggregate data, teams can construct graphs, tables, and figures that permit visualization of results and handy reference points that make the relationships between differing values more easily discerned. When product engineers can examine part types in their full value range, they discover overlaps and see opportunities, for example, to have one part replace five. Steadily, a set of convenient standard values emerges to guide the further commonization of parts. See Figure 7.12.

Other Applications of Range

While the range tool has obvious applications in part type analysis, it can also be very effective in other analytical aspects of VEP. Market analysis is a good case in point. A marketing department may trigger requests for

FIGURE 7.12. VAT-5: Range

Definition	**Range** is a mathematical measure of dispersion (or spread) that shows values that share some common observable characteristic, displaying the difference between the largest and smallest value, and the points along the way.
Objectives	• To organize attributes and other values in order to determine the degree of variation or overlap among those values. • To minimize the number of values needed to cover the range that customers require.
Key Questions	• What attribute range width is required for part(s) across all products? • Do the specifications of certain products or parts overlap or repeat? • Can certain values be merged with others so that the total number of required parts is reduced?
Procedure	**Step 1.** Compute the values range for all specifications within a given part type or product grouping. **Step 2.** Determine minimum and maximum range widths for each and identify any overlapping or extraneous values. **Step 3.** Eliminate any overlaps or extraneous values by defining a dimensional range, wide enough to encompass the required values but with minimum part numbers. **Step 4.** Develop and adhere to guidelines that support the range technique.

new products that are similar but not identical to existing ones. This may be a legitimate tactic, linked to the company's improvement-driven new product approach. But in other organizations, such requests are often not linked to a unified plan and, as a result, can introduce differentials representing negative variety. As previously discussed, such variations may masquerade as customer-driven requirements but, in reality, be internally triggered and not valid. The net effect is overlap and redundancy in market offerings. This issue rests at the core of our pondering the 3,200 different snack food products, mentioned earlier, that Borden Foods once offered.

For those motivated to look, VAT-5: Range can help companies identify the tendencies, penchants, pets, anomalies, compensating behaviors, and other biases that may exist in their decision making relative to offering product, and to product and part design. Many managers have yet to appreciate the insight and economies that can be achieved when the range of product properties and characteristics is simply exposed to the scrutiny of a team that understands the principles of variety effectiveness.

VAT-6: TREND

Just as specifications may span a range of values over time, so these same values may trace a particular pattern and direction that are observable when plotted as a group. The sixth analytical technique (VAT-6) is called Trend. Its purpose is to help us identify the pattern and direction of our design and product choices, the needs and requests of our customers, and understand the tendencies that dominate.

In marketing, for example, do most products fall into a high-profit category? Is there an emerging tendency to concentrate on low-end offerings? Is the company as a whole drifting toward commercial business and away from the individual consumer? What is the mix of commercial versus consumer over the last five years? In product design, is the number of parts per product on the rise? At what rate? At what curve? Are there discernible trends supporting more modular designs for miniaturization, or what? In parts, do the data show a growing bias for less or more durable materials? Are outer diameter specifications widening or shrinking? Do choices in switch housing incline more toward explosion-proof or fire-proof or something else?

Trend data, when correctly understood, can be a powerful tool for revealing issues related to variety effectiveness. In one company, for example, the pattern of trend data on new product offerings revealed a very positive drift (as indicated by the line that traces the center of trend data). In response, the company developed ways to affirm that direction, consolidate the bias, and strengthen the overall pattern. In another organization, where trend data on purchased parts indicated problems, teams reviewed departmental practices and took steps to arrest the drift in favor of a more advantageous core pattern.

Trend data can also provide important substantiating information. This was the case when the Part Type Team spotted an anomaly across several component groups—many new parts entering the system were getting dimensionally smaller and smaller. The team asked members of the Market Analysis Team what they could make of it. One of the explanations that team offered was that the decreasing values were linked to an increasing number of requests for miniaturization from OEM (original equipment manufacturer) customers; OEMs were reducing the size of their products, so the size of components needed to be reduced as well. The market team generated a trend chart (see Figure 7.13) that verified this for the part team.

Viewed through the lens of the trend technique, a company can gain valuable insights, for example, into both the patterns and results that

FIGURE 7.13. Trend in Requests for Miniaturization—Six-Month Intervals

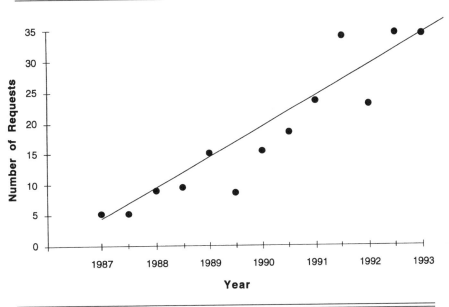

amass around corporate and departmental policies and practices. With time-based trends, it becomes easier to appreciate how negative variety has crept into the company over time and why organizational complexity is not an overnight phenomenon. Figure 7.14 summarizes VAT-6.

FIGURE 7.14. VAT-6: Trend

Definition	**Trend** is the discernible pattern and direction of a group of values, sharing one or several characteristics, when laid out in some preset order (e.g., ascending value, descending value, etc.).
Objectives	• To display and identify the drift in attribute values, specifications, and characteristics as they accumulate in other discrete segments (such as time, market segment, season) in order to determine a normalized center of such variation so that the number of parts represented therein can be minimized.
	• To determine which drifts support and which obstruct the principles of positive variety.
Key Questions	• What is the pattern of the spread of the company's design, product, and parts choices—in measurable terms?
	• What is the genesis of that pattern? What did it result from?
	• Does it support positive variety and the company's strategic direction?
	• Do we want that pattern to continue?
Procedure	**Step 1.** Study the VEP database for patterns in both the performance-related and dimensional specifications of selected products or parts.
	Step 2. Organize the values of each pattern, so that one can determine any ordering principles within it.
	Step 3. Plot these values as a numerical trend.
	Step 4. Apply a single consistent principle relative to numerical values and use this as a starting point for standardization.

SO WHAT!

Conceptually speaking, we can learn to recognize negative variety. But then what do we do about it? VEP's six analytical tools (the 6-VATs) are a set of techniques that allow us to identify the precise location of negative variety and to develop viable proposals for reducing or minimizing it. The tools do this by helping teams scrutinize the dimensional and functional values of the elements under consideration. Without these tools, the detailed differences between values and the way they are structured into products might escape detection.

The 6-VATs give us a way to search out variation, according to the specific perspective provided by each of these techniques. Each asks its own special questions. Tool by tool, these questions are:

VAT-1: Unique Versus Shared

Shared? If not, why is it different?

Must this difference remain? If so, can it be standardized enough to share it with at least one other subassembly or model?

VAT-2: Modularity

$$\triangle + \bigcirc + \square = \begin{matrix} \triangle \\ \bigcirc \\ \square \end{matrix}$$

$$\triangle + \bigcirc + \triangle = \begin{matrix} \triangle \\ \bigcirc \\ \triangledown \end{matrix}$$

Can standard portions of this product be further standardized so they can become building blocks for many other products?

VAT-3: Multifunctionality and Synthesis

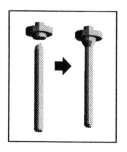

How many functions can a single part serve? Can this be extended even further by using different materials and/or technology?

VAT-4: Ease of Assembly

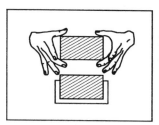

Can even more cost be designed out of this product by making it easier for its parts to be assembled?

VAT-5: Range

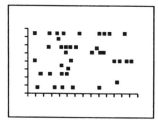

How many values support the same attribute? Can these be reduced?

VAT-6: Trend

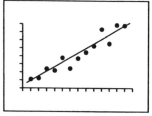

When attribute values are plotted, can a direction and pattern be observed? Do these observable patterns reveal any reduction opportunities related to variety effectiveness?

The fact is that the problem and its optimal solution are often hidden in the context of the most mundane data—the attributes themselves. Applying the 6-VATs provides a process for discovering that. When used in conjunction with the systematic processes of analysis described in the next chapter, these six techniques help teams raise and answer many important questions about why and how negative variation occurred in the first place. Resultant insights lead teams to develop specific and often creative guidelines that help the company prevent the recurrence of unwarranted variety.

CHAPTER EIGHT

VEP ANALYSIS: FINDING AND REDUCING NEGATIVE VARIETY

Which comes first, the product or the customer? The answer is, it's a bad question.

—RICHARD SCHONBERGER,
*BUILDING A CHAIN OF
CUSTOMERS*

The topic before us in this chapter is *Stage 2—Identifying Reduction Opportunities by Applying the 6 Tools*. In Chapter 6, you learned how to prepare the organization and set the stage for in-depth VEP analysis. You set up and trained teams, then upgraded your parts classification system so that it became VEP-capable. And you determined where to begin the analysis portion of the VEP methodology—you chose your *targeted product series*. In the previous chapter (7), you were introduced to VEP's six analytical tools, the 6-VATs. In this chapter you will learn about Stage 2—the analysis process itself, the work of the several analysis teams, how your new and improved classification system supports them, and how the 6-VATs apply directly to the hunt for reduction opportunities (see Figure 8.1, shaded portion).

The primary work of Stage 2 (VEP analysis) focuses on four areas of

FIGURE 8.1. Stage 2 of the VEP Methodology

STAGE 1— Preparing for an Effective VEP Implementation	STAGE 2— Identifying Reduction Opportunities by Applying the 6-VATs	STAGE 3— Coordinating and Prioritizing Reduction Opportunities	STAGE 4— Implementing and Sustaining the Improvement
Step 1— Select a Steering Team that then sets up the other VEP teams (Management)	Step 1— Begin reduction analysis of market offerings and their characteristics (Market Analysis Team)*		
Step 2— Conduct team training and begin general awareness training (Education and Methods Team)	Step 2— Begin reduction analysis of parts as they are structured into products (Product Structure Analysis Team)*		
Step 3— Begin to analyze and revise company policies and practices (Policy Analysis Team)	Step 3— Begin reduction analysis of commodities by parts type (Part Type Analysis Team)*		

Step 4—
Find and reduce parts with low-resistance to change (Early Victories Team)

Step 5—
Assess, clean up, and upgrade parts classification system (Part Type Analysis Team)

Step 6
Target a priority product as the starting point for Stage 2 reduction analysis (Steering Team)

Step 4—
Begin reduction analysis of transactions that support parts and products (Control Points Analysis Team)

Step 5**—
Begin additional analysis to reduce production processes, beyond work of 3-View teams (Production Process Analysis Team)

* One of the three 3-View Analysis teams.
** This step is optional and dependent on current levels of operational complexity.

217

inquiry: (1) market offerings, (2) product structure, (3) part types, and (4) control points. Each of these areas has its own team and a mini-procedural framework that guides it. A fifth area of analysis, the reduction of production processes, is so closely linked to the product- and part-based reduction that it is usually not necessary to engage a separate team; in companies where a distinct team is appropriate, though, one should be set up.

In this chapter, we confine our discussion to the three product-based analyses—market, product structure, and part type—known in VEP as the 3-View Analysis.

THE 3-VIEW ANALYSIS: AN OVERVIEW

The 3-View Analysis is at the analytical center of the VEP methodology. Its name derives from the multiple perspectives (or views) that VEP adopts to study and investigate a company's offerings.*

View One: Market Analysis. VEP's market analysis seeks to understand what, from the marketing perspective, makes company products different. Which specific customer requirements, niche characteristics, features, elements, or functions differentiate one product or product line from another? As these differences surface, we are set to ask the pivotal VAT-1 (Unique Versus Shared) question: Does the customer really need or want this difference? That is, is this a customer-driven or internally triggered variation? If there is no valid customer requirement, we apply the other VATs in the effort to get rid of that difference. If there is a legitimate customer expectation, we move to the next question: Is there

---

* The term "offerings" refers to both products and services. For simplicity's sake, though, we will confine our discussion to the analysis of products; services are implicitly included.

some less "unique" or differentiated way to meet this expectation? And we proceed to find out by applying the other VATs.

At the conclusion of market analysis, company catalogs may list more products, fewer products, or exactly the same number of products as before VEP. Whichever the case, customer selection is enhanced or even extended. Distinctions between products are now validated through analysis; they are clearer, cleaner, and produce more profit. Overlaps are removed, slight or nonrequired differentiations are blended, and the internal variety needed to support or make these product lines is minimized. Parts count within and across products, as evidenced by the VEP Parts Index, has been reduced.

VEP's market analysis directs us to appreciate and, where possible, improve the way in which product diversification occurs within the marketing function.

View Two: Product Structure Analysis. Product structure analysis attempts to understand and improve the way product function requirements are fulfilled through diverse parts and components so that a viable, integrated, and profitable unit called a *product* results. Similar to the market view, this analysis approach begins by identifying how products are currently configured and ends by recommending changes that streamline and strengthen this.

Using product BOMs as a base, the examination takes place on the model level, focusing on the way parts mate and components are configured, and the structural or geometric basis for differing part values. In this way, the analysis validates or refutes the architectural logic by which a company's products are developed, both as a population and in particular. The result, after an assiduous application of the 6-VATs, is a more variety-effective and a less costly line of products.

View Three: Part Type Analysis. The objective of the part type approach, VEP's third product-based analytical perspective, is to minimize the total number of different individual parts in company products, *across the board*. Here the focus is on the types of parts—called a *part type*—and the extent to which the attribute values vary within each part type. Examples of common part types include fasteners, housings, trim, handles, labels, knobs, hinges, lids, and brackets.

Part type analysis is an aggressive examination driven by a single question: Do we really need another part number? If there are 6,000 different fasteners, the question gets asked 6,000 times. If 50 percent of the housings have built-in brackets, 30 percent have no brackets, and the remaining 20 percent use 12 different kinds of brackets, we want to find out *why*. If the reasons can be found and validated by stakeholders (customers, engineers, approval agencies, etc.), the variations stay. But if there are no good reasons, they go. The same goes for those 17 different sorts of door hinges in use. The part type analysis process asks and answers these "why" questions. At its conclusion, many part numbers have been eliminated and a wider appreciation of part type economies is understood.

Why Three Views?

The multi-view approach of VEP's 3-View Analysis came out of a recognition that the triggers or causes of negative variety are multiple. They are also hard to trace. They can, however, be more easily discerned through a systematic process of inquiry that questions the basis for variation in the context of the entire product environment. Through the triple lens of this analysis, teams discover redundancy, overlaps, and other inefficiencies in the way that the company differentiates its products and parts, puts them together, and markets them. Again and again it asks: Is this a customer-driven or an internally triggered variation? This three-view approach brings the analysis down to the cellular level. Along the way, causes of negative and positive variety are tracked and a balance point struck so that *effective variety* is achieved. The prime mission of the 3-View Analysis is to find negative variety, suggest specific ways to rid the system of as much of it as possible, and devise smart and workable guidelines that prevent its recurrence.

Do We *Really* Need This Difference? In VEP analysis, the single driving question is: Do customers really need this difference? Do they really need another product series? Another ever-so-slightly-different model? Another subassembly? Another part?* Each 3-View team asks that same question from its own independent team framework of inquiry. Their respective answers expose opportunities, great and small, for reduction. Each view provides another piece of the puzzle, another way of understanding how product diversification has, over time, grown into organizational complexity and cost. Broadly speaking, the procedure followed by each team is the same:

1. Identify what is the same and what is different.
2. Identify the reason for the difference.
3. Validate or dispute each of the differences by applying the 6-VATs.
4. Where the difference is unwarranted, develop a proposal for eliminating it.

In this way, each team develops its own set of recommendations for de-complicating the system, reducing negative variety, and minimizing causes so they will not recur. Each team sends its improvement proposals separately to the Steering Team, which, in turn, assesses, coordinates, and integrates each set of proposals into an overall change schedule that reflects the best ideas across all VEP teams.** If the proposals can be implemented easily, having low resistance to change, the Steering Team expedites. If more time, patience, or research is needed, the implementation of the improvement gets slated for later in the schedule.

Let's now look at each view in greater detail.

---

* Other teams ask similarly: Do we really need another production process? Another slightly different operation? Another transaction/control point?
** See discussion on coordinating, prioritizing, and implementing the various team recommendation on pages 244–49.

VIEW ONE: MARKET ANALYSIS

Rarely, if ever, does a single-product company stay that way for very long. Today's companies are constantly adding new products—sometimes as part of a larger product diversification strategy, sometimes just to test a new market, and sometimes as a startled reaction to an unforeseen competitive threat.

The fact is, marketplace pressures do not always allow a business to develop its product lines in a wholly integrated and rational manner. Product introduction can be haphazard, and the effects can sink the enterprise. Levels of new products may overlap in capabilities and characteristics with existing products. Dozens of products may linger on beyond their productive life cycles, hanging around in the catalog, the warehouse, and on the shop floor, virtually unnoticed; when sales finally come to a complete halt, they fade into null but may never be obsoleted.

The goal of VEP's market analysis is two-fold: (1) to identify and remove redundant, declining, obsolete, or overlapping products, and (2) to identify and enhance the products which are growing. The process also generates guidelines and practices to ensure that the only products that get introduced in the future represent the *most effective* variety.

Start with Your Groundwork in Place

In many companies, this VEP team can face a heap of products across many product lines, all possible starting points, all seeming candidates for streamlining or reduction. Fortunately, VEP has already narrowed the focus by virtue of the preparatory steps in Stage 1. The analysis process will begin on the pre-designated product line called the *targeted series*. At Parts Unlimited Inc. (PUI), the targeted series turned out to be Series 7 (see PUI's "Top 20" list in Figure 8.2).

We are ready to begin—or almost. Let's check one more thing. Did

Figure 8.2. PUI'S Top 20

Series 7*	Series 33
Series 53	Series 17
Series 73	Series 137
Series 11	Series 46
Series 148	Series 28
Series 8	Series 101
Series 4	Series 1
Series 12	Series 79
Series 212	Series 85
Series 97	Series 200

* The targeted series

we standardize the nomenclature related to our product hierarchy? Perhaps you accomplished this in Stage 1, in conjunction with standardizing terminology around your parts classification system. If not, you need to do it now. What is the name given to the company's most comprehensive level of product? Is it called a *product family* or a *product series*? A *product line* or a *product group*? How is the next tier designated? Do some people call it the *series* level but others describe it as *product types*? What about the next layer? Is it referred to as the *model* or the *type* level? And the next? Neglecting to agree on a common way to describe levels of product can significantly impede the analysis work of this team. A great deal of confusion and wasted time results from not rooting out the unwarranted variety in the terms used to refer to products. Let's look at the situation at PUI.

PUI's Product Hierarchy. At Parts Unlimited Inc., the Market Analysis Team, under the leadership of Willy Sparks, sorted out PUI's various product levels into the product hierarchy shown in Figure 8.3. Here is how each level is defined:

Series. At the highest level, like-products are gathered into product groups called *Series*. These groups carry the same number designation, such as *Series 4* or *Series 7*. PUI's product series included such groups as: Explosion-proof switches, NEMA-4 controls, recorders, and

FIGURE 8.3. Terms in PUI's Product Hierarchy

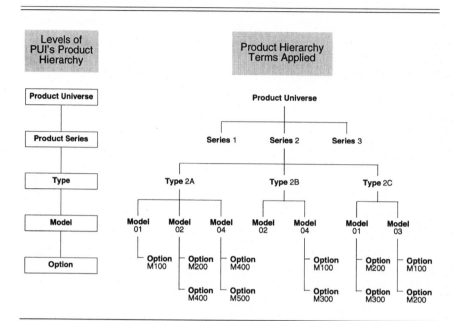

heat trace controllers. At the end of last year, 50 different product series were considered active at PUI.

Type. Within a given product series, products with similar properties are considered the same *product type* and are designated by a letter. Products with remote temperature sensing properties, for example, carry an *A* designation. *Type B* products have local temperature sensing properties, and *Type C* products control pressure. A product designated "Type 8A" is part of Series 8 and has a remote temperature sensing capability.

Model. Products at PUI with the same sensing ranges are considered the same model and are designated by a two-digit code. For example, all Model 01s have a sensing range of 20 to 200 PSI (pounds per square inch), whereas all Model 03s have a 50 to 650 degree Fahrenheit range.

Therefore, the same model can appear on one or more *Types* within one or more *Series*. For example:

Product 7A-01 = Series 7, Type A, Model 01
Product 4A-01 = Series 4, Type A, Model 01
Product 7C-01 = Series 7, Type C, Model 01

Options. At PUI, almost any type and/or model can be ordered with one or more options. Options include special enclosure coatings, optional sensor materials, custom labels, etc.

Re-Inspiring the Team

With the terminology clarified and agreed upon, PUI's Market Analysis Team is ready. To re-inspire the team and charge them up for the work ahead, Willy asks team members to choose any three series in PUI's "Top 20" list (Figure 8.2) and calculate the number of products a customer *could* order, based on the types, models, and options offered in those three series. They do this and are amazed to discover the vast number of products that customers could buy—in some cases, over 50,000—many of which have only the slightest distinctions between them (see Figure 8.4 for one such set of calculations). The team realized that, if this was

FIGURE 8.4. Example of Combination Magnitude on Three of PUI's Twenty Top Product Series

Series	Number/ Types	Number/ Models	Number/ Options	Total Possible Combinations
11	22	38	22	18,392
1	24	46	24	26,496
8	9	37	17	5,661
Total Possible Combinations Across These Three Series = 50,549				

possible considering only three series, the total number of possible combinations based on PUI's complete line of products—all 50 series— would be astronomical! The team is fired up and raring to get started.

The Market Analysis Process—Broad Strokes

Based on the priorities set in Stage 1, the team develops a series of product-attribute matrices that highlight the primary market-driven characteristics. At PUI, for example, the following was identified as primary for Series 7 (the targeted series): agency approvals, enclosure ratings, electrical ratings, and the number of control values. These were plugged into the matrix header and other product series that shared the same primary properties as Series 7 joined the matrix, listed by percentage of sales (descending order) (see partial matrix in Figure 8.5, pages 228–229).

Using this matrix, team members were able to make comparisons and search for reduction opportunities, applying the principles of the 6-VATs. They applied VAT-1 (Unique Versus Shared) to systematically question the overlaps, redundancies, and slight variations they found in many primary characteristics. They saw many chances to standardize across the various series. They also made extensive use of VAT-3 (Multifunctionality and Synthesis) as they brainstormed ways to streamline certain series or collapse one series into another. They were surprised at how easy the matrix made these applications. Its format facilitated discussion and kept brainstorming focused as they considered ways to simplify or eliminate product segments without negatively impacting customer selection. When the thinking was complete on one matrix, the team ratcheted down to the next level in the hierarchy (product type), developing a matrix on it and analyzing it. After that, the focus shifted down to the model level, and the search continued for further areas of product consolidation or differentiation that did not diminish customer selection.

Along the way, they regularly updated the VEP Parts Index, developed at the outset of the analysis to see the impact of each proposal on parts count reduction. They were also careful to check out each improvement idea with the appropriate stakeholders, as part of the validation process, before it became "official" and was submitted to the Steering

Team. After several rounds, the team submitted its first-pass reduction recommendations to the Steering Team (see Figure 8.6, page 230).

Implications of the Market Analysis Process

For companies in the habit of adding products in a less than rational manner, VEP market analysis can be an illuminating process. It is an inquiry that exposes the tangible consequences of proliferating products *without* the benefit of a proliferation strategy. In the process of finding reference points and probing for differentiation, the team gains a cross-product perspective that refutes or validates, unequivocally, the answer to the driving VEP question: "Does the customer really need this difference?" The answer is often an ever-lengthening roster of products on series, type, and model levels that represent negative variety—unwarranted, costly, and complex. When, as a result of this analysis, team members recommend combining or loping off certain products, they do so confidently, guided by the structured, systematic process of this analysis. They are assured that customer selection will not be jeopardized

Spreading Out the Reduction Net

There is another important implication of the analysis process, one that holds true for all three 3-View efforts. Looking at the proposals that PUI's Market Analysis Team submitted (Figure 8.6), you might think you see an inconsistency. Several of the product series recommended for elimination did not appear on PUI's "Top 20" list, that roster of products determined in Stage 1 to be "worth our analytical time" (see Figure 8.2, page 223). That is, Series 2, 5, 16, 31, 68, and 76 did not appear on the "Top 20" list but do appear in the recommendations above.

This is not an anomaly. The process is designed to magnetize or hook up other "items" that have characteristics in common with those of the targeted series. All VEP's analytical procedures do this. This is exactly what we see in the Marketing Analysis matrix. Anchored in the targeted series (Series 7) and its primary characteristics, the matrix

FIGURE 8.5. Series Level: Market Analysis Worksheet—Series 7 (Partial Matrix)

Series Designation	% of Sales	Market Entry Date	Agency Approvals	Enclosure Ratings	Electrical Ratings	Number of Control Values
7	12.3	8-63	UL, CSA	NEMA 4	15A- 125/250/480. Vac Res	1 or 2
12	11.9	11-81	UL, CSA, FM, ISSEP, BASEEFA, NACE	NEMA 4, 7, 9	15A- 125/250/480. Vac Res	1 or 2
33	9.0	6-84	UL, CSA	NEMA 4, 13	15A- 125/250/480. Vac Res	1, 2, or 3
4	5.5	3-57	UL Approved	None	15A- 125/250. Vac Res	1
53	3.9	10-81	UL, CSA Optional	NEMA 4	15A- 125/250/480. Vac Res	1 or 2
1	6.5	6-89	UL, CSA Optional	NEMA 1, NEMA 4, 7, 9 Optional	15A- 125/250/480. Vac Res	1 or 2
73	1.7	10-84	UL Recognized, CSA	None	15A- 125/250. Vac Res	0, 1, or 2
8	7.0	5-52	UL, CSA	NEMA 4, 4X	15A- 125/250/480. Vac Res	1
97	2.6	9-69	UL (most models), CSA Optional	NEMA 4	15A- 125/250/480. Vac Res	1

Legend: Definitions of Acronyms Found in Above Matrix

A. APPROVAL AGENCIES

1. BASEEFA = British Approval Service for Electrical Equipment and Flammable Atmosphere
2. CSA = Canadian Standards Association
3. OPTIONAL = An approval rating is not standard on this product; it may be purchased as an option.
4. FM = Factory Mutual
5. ISSEP = Institut Scientific de Service Public
6. NACE = National Association of Corrosion Engineers
7. UL = Underwriters Laboratories
8. UL APPROVED = A higher rating than UL Recognized
9. UL RECOGNIZED = A lower rating than UL Approved

B. ENCLOSURE RATINGS

1. NEMA = National Electrical Manufacturers Association
2. NEMA 4 = Weatherproof
3. NEMA 4X = Waterproof
4. NEMA 7 = Explosion Proof
5. NEMA 9 = Explosion Proof
6. NEMA 13 = Explosion Proof

C. ELECTRICAL RATINGS

1. 15A = 15 Amps
2. VAC RES = Volts Alternating Current Resistive (as compared to "Inductive"), 25, 250, or 480

D. NUMBER OF CONTROL VALUES (Number of values switch can control at once)

1. "Two control values" = switch turn-off at 15° and 45°
2. "0 control value" = value indicated but no control over it

FIGURE 8.6. Reduction Recommendations (First Pass)—PUI Market Analysis Team

Recommendations	Impact on Part Number Count	Impact on Index	Impact on Market
1. Eliminate eight different product series: Series 76 Series 16 Series 68 Series 12 Series 53 Series 5 Series 31 Series 2	Eliminate 350 part numbers	Reduce by 3182 part numbers (43 part types X 74 part numbers in the models eliminated when series are eliminated)	No discernible impact on market. PUI retains ability to meet all existing market requirements.
2. Eliminate five product types in remaining series: Type L Type S Type P Type V Type Q	Eliminate 65 part numbers	Reduce by 455 part numbers (13 part types X 35 part numbers across product types recommended for reduction)	The same, or nearly the same, functional capabilities are found in other PUI products.
3. Eliminate 16 individual models across remaining series: Model 701　　Model 153 Model 702　　Model 152 Model 703　　Model 151 Model 704　　Model 93 Model 190　　Model 92 Model 168　　Model 77 Model 167　　Model 73 Model 154　　Model 71	Eliminate 90 parts numbers	Reduce by 792 part numbers (24 part types X 33 part numbers across the models recommended for reduction)	Marketing says no ramifications; changes are "invisible" to PUI customers.
Total Part Numbers Eliminated 505	**Total Reduction of VEP Parts Index** 4,429	**Total Market Impact** PUI customer selection remains constant at lower cost and less systems complexity	

mechanism pulled in all linked series—most but not all of which were in the Top 20. As the search for overlaps and redundancies extended into the type and model levels (still anchored in Series 7), other non–Top 20 products were snared or netted. In this way, the analysis begins to touch most, if not all, of the products in the company's product universe. The analysis net spreads out, capturing all instances of negative variety in the company and holding them up to systematic scrutiny.

Now let's see the process through the lens of the next 3-View team— product structure analysis.

VIEW TWO: PRODUCT STRUCTURE ANALYSIS

A product, as VEP defines it, is *a group of elements or parts that, when fabricated and assembled, fulfill specific requirements*. Product structure analysis regards the *relationship* between a product's constituent elements as the chief determinant of negative or positive variety. This refers, variously, to: the product structure, product geometry, or product architecture—the way parts are used to form the product. In short, it examines how parts and units mate and are configured into a larger unit. The VEP goal related to this is structural simplification and equal or enhanced functionality, using fewer parts.

The process of structural analysis begins on the model level: how product functions are fulfilled through combinations of parts, components, and subassemblies. In a manner similar to market analysis, the inquiry spirals out, steadily and systematically, and through its iterations eventually encompasses virtually every company model.

Key Elements of the Analysis Procedure

The team starts, as usual, with the targeted series; that's the jumping-off point for inquiry. With this as an anchor, the team then steps through the following simple procedure:

1. Choose a priority model in the targeted series, based on an agreed-upon set of selection criteria—highest sales volume, volume shipped, and/or product complexity (as a function of the number of parts).
2. Identify where that same model is used throughout the company's product universe.
3. Generate a Bill of Material (BOM) for each model.
4. Calculate a VEP Parts Index across these models.
5. Physically gather the constituent parts (BOM) for each model.
6. Create a visual display of these BOMs, laying out the constituent parts, side by side, model by model, creating an actual "exploded" view of the products (see Figure 8.7).

Guided by a series of questions and the 6-VATs, the team focuses on the physical, visual, *real-time* examination of these parts, laid out in the above manner. (To facilitate this review and hold parts in place for extended periods, place the parts on cardboard backing and shrink-wrap them in place; this also makes it easy to carry to meetings.) Team members now look—*and they think!* As the parts are visually compared across models, important questions naturally surface, as do improvement proposals.

Let's watch the process as it unfolded with the Product Structure Analysis Team at Parts Unlimited Inc., where the focus was five Models 02s, a popular temperature-control product. The team generated BOMs (see Figure 8.8 for a partial BOM on Model 02) and developed a baseline VEP Parts Index that came in at 93,445 (see Figure 8.9 for the VEP Parts Index on a partial Model 02 BOM).

Team members then applied the 6-VATs. VAT-1 (Unique Versus Shared) helped them arrive at the fact that four of five pressure connec-

Figure 8.7. A Visual Display

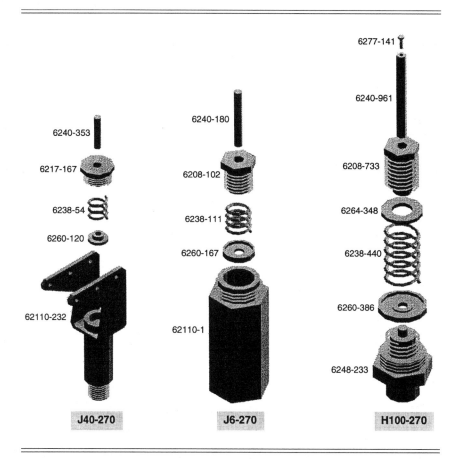

tions were *nearly* identical. Probing deeper, team members discovered that, in three cases, there was no valid customer-driven reason for the difference. Commonization became an option.

VAT-2 (Modularity) also produced strong results. Looking for options in organizing standardized parts into interchangeable units, the team discovered, for example, that standardizing the pressure connection across three of the models opened the door to a modularized pressure assembly in them as well. Doing so would also obviate the differences between Series 8 and Series 11 and eliminate the need for one of these

FIGURE 8.8. Partial BOM for One of the 02 Models

Part Number	Description
013-65	Screw 6-32 X ¼ B/H S/S
017-69	Screw 6-32 X ⅞ P/H SEMS SS
017-85	Screw 8-32 X ¼ R/H SS
52-123	Over Travel Housing
6154-1	Cover
620-25	Over Travel Button
625-24	Insulator Switch
628-56	Adjusting Screw
611-55	Computer Nameplate
621-54	Switch Bracket Assembly
627-38	Plunger Stop
623-29	Bellows Bracket Mounting
628-19	Spring
638-29	Spring
628-27	Bellows 1½ Heavy Press
626-16	Spring Guide

series entirely. The idea was tagged; John Mandella volunteered to ask the Market Analysis Team if this reduction proposal would create any customer problems. The team also saw that an identical interchangeable unit might be used in Series 17 and Series 28, if certain parts in those two series were comparably standardized; that idea got tagged, with Tricia Moodley volunteering to check in with the various other stakeholders and report back before the end of the week.

The team also found a fabulous application of VAT-3 (Multifunctionality and Synthesis). After about 15 minutes of stark silence while team members simply stared at the shrink-wrapped display board, Gerry and Danielle suddenly leapt to their feet at the same instant, pointing to the spring guide; they both saw how the functions of the spring guide and plunger for *all* five models could get collapsed into a single part (see Figure 7.5, page 199). The parts count implication of this for PUI was huge, considering that spring guides and plungers were used in practically every PUI model; the idea got tagged for review by the Parts Type Team.

FIGURE 8.9. VEP Parts Index: Partial BOM for Models 02, Series 7, 8, 11, 33, 97

Part Type	Part No.	Product 7-02	Product 8-02	Product 11-02	Product 33-02	Product 97-02	Total Part Type Occurrences
Screw	013-65	2	2				
	017-68			2	2		3
	018-85					2	
Over Travel Housing	52-108		1		1	1	
	52-123	1		1			2
Cover	6154-1	1	1	1	1	1	1
Over Travel Button	620-25	1	1	1	1	1	1
Insulator Switch	625-24	1					
	625-42		1	1	1	1	2
Adjusting Screw	628-56	1	1	1	1	1	1
Computer Nameplate	611-55	1	1	1	1	1	1
Switch Bracket Assembly	621-67		1		1		
	621-54	1				1	3
	621-90			1			
Plunger Stop	627-38	1	1	1	1	1	1
Bellows Bracket Mounting	623-29	1					
	623-27		1	1	1	1	2
Spring	628-19	1	1	1		1	
	628-29	1		1	1	1	2
Bellows	628-27	1	1				
	628-28			1	1		3
	628-31					1	
Spring Guide	626-16	1	1	1	1	1	1
Total Parts Count		**15**	**14**	**15**	**14**	**15**	**73** / **23**

VEP Parts Index = 1,679 (73 × 23)

As the team completed its first round of analysis, the VEP Parts Index had already shifted down by a factor of 12 percent—from 93,445 to 82,232. As with all VEP improvement ideas, each proposal would get *systematically* validated or invalidated against stakeholder concerns. If the idea turned out to be problematic, it was held in reserve. Validated ideas got sent to the Steering Team for review and coordination (see Figure 8.10).

Implications of Product Structure Analysis

VEP's product structure analysis obliges us to scrutinize and compare the form, fit, and function of all the parts in a given model, within and across product families. This simple but structured approach allows teams to brainstorm possibilities for eliminating negative variety, even as they are guided by a systematic application of the 6-VATs. By the time it is completed, this analysis has ensured that each part and its relationship to all other parts has been studied, probed, and understood in terms of the model's specific functionality and that of all its sister models.

This in-depth scrutiny directs a steady, uncompromising light onto the company product-differentiating tendencies and biases. It can lead to significant product simplification and a reduction in the number of differing structures across the company's product universe. The technique's extensive use of visual display (physical BOM exploded view on a model level) offers a unique window for engineers to reconsider and, to some extent, reconstruct the decision-making process by which a product was designed. Doing this can trigger valuable insights into the practices that do and don't favor positive variety. In the process, teams identify internal and external triggers of product structure complexity and ways to reduce or eliminate these causes.

We will now move on to the final of the three views—parts type analysis.

Figure 8.10. Partial List of Reduction Recommendations on Model 02 Sent by the Product Structure Analysis Team to the Steering Team

Product Structure Reduction Recommendation	Parts Impact	Supporting Data and Remarks
1. Standardize on pressure connection 5832-141 and eliminate pressure connection 5832-120.	Would eliminate total of 4 part numbers: 5832-120 assembly and 3 part numbers that make it up (5832-102, 6471-102, 6471-105).	This change would not affect model performance or specifications.
2. Standardize on higher barrier switch— 5269-618.	Would eliminate 2 insulator part numbers (6107-921 and 6107-922).	This change would increase overall switch height by $\frac{1}{16}''$. UL, CSA, and Marketing have already approved.
3. Purchase housing with brackets already in place.	Would eliminate 1 set of bracket (443-01 and 433-152) plus related spot welding processes.	Supplier would perform spot weld (piece price goes up $.04) or re-tool to make bracket part of housing (onetime charge of $2,500). Marketing sees no negative effect.
4. Add optional mounting hole locations on switch mounting bracket 8847-09.	Would eliminate 5 bracket part numbers with nonstandard mounting hole locations and all optional drilling.	Supplier says could easily make this change. Cost per piece increase would be $.07. Marketing says *no problema*.

IMPACT ON PARTS COUNT			
Reductions in Part Number Count	Total Parts Index Reduction	Reductions in Production Processes	Total Market Impact
13	954	12	No negative impact.

VIEW THREE: PARTS TYPE ANALYSIS

Where product structure analysis concentrates on the relationship between a product's diverse parts, part type analysis looks at *each* constituent part of a product—separately and in near isolation from other parts within that product. It looks at the part as a member of a group of similar but not identical parts. This group is called a *part type*, or *part commodity*.

For VEP purposes, a part type group is defined as *two or more parts that serve identical function, differing only in the specifications used to fulfill that function*. At Parts Unlimited Inc. and other switch and control manufacturers, common part types include screws, housings, brackets, springs, spring guides, O-rings, lead wires, plungers, fasteners, labels, diaphragms, and bellows—to name a few. At automotive companies, the part types list would include anything from trim, knobs, handles, hinges, mirrors, meters, visors, and windshield wipers to wheels, wheel rims, seats, engine blocks, radiator caps, and, of course, steering wheels. Computer hardware manufacturers have an ongoing need for resistors, transducers, capacitors, printed circuit boards, side panels, front panels, rollers, bases, housings, and so on and so forth—part types all.

Parts type analysis concerns itself with the number of different part numbers within each part type. Often the specifications that define parts within a part type are identical in all but one attribute, and it is not uncommon for that attribute to fluctuate widely in value within that part type. Furthermore, it is not unusual for no one to know why. Similar functions but dissimilar specifications. Why? Once again, VEP queries: Does the customer really need this difference? Is yet another part number really necessary?

Let's look in on the Part Type Analysis Team at PUI.

Part Type Analysis at PUI

Priority One. The first task of PUI's Part Type Analysis Team, set way back in Stage 1, was to clean up the company's existing parts classification system. A messy parts classification, they knew, is incapable of supporting the data queries and decision making central to the VEP method. Starting with the part types in the BOMs of the targeted series (Series 7), the team busied itself removing redundant and obsolete part numbers, creating attribute templates, and inputting specification data into those templates. They continued doing this until the system was "smart" enough (VEP-capable) to support the first cycle of part type evaluation. Although the other two teams involved in the 3-View Analysis had already begun to tackle their tasks, their work was greatly accelerated when the company's classification system reached this level of capability.

The Core Task. With an upgraded classification system up and running, PUI's Part Type Team was ready to tackle its central mandate—part type analysis and reduction. As its first step, the team generated a Parts Type list (Figure 8.11) and VEP Parts Index on Series 7 so it could identify the part type with the highest number of occurrences. That is where the analysis would begin. That part type in Series 7 turned out to be springs.

Because part type analysis, by its very nature, touches the company's entire part type universe, the team turned for help and insight to the tool that gave the widest window on the variation within part types—VAT-5: Range. In keeping with that technique, team members queried the specifications of each spring attribute captured in the spring attribute template they had previously developed, namely, spring material, rate force, outer diameter (O.D.), inner diameter (I.D.), free length, solid length, and material. The specification for each attribute was then formatted into a range dispersion.

Right off the bat, team members saw the wide range of O.D. values (heavy at the two tails), the gaps in the middle range, and the oddball single-occurrence values scattered throughout. They began to wonder

FIGURE 8.11. Part Types in Series 7 (Partial List)

Bellows	Micro-Switches
Brackets	Nameplates
Capacitors	O-Rings
Contacts	Plunger
Covers	Relays
Dials	Screws
Diaphragms	Seals
Gaskets	Spiral Pins
Housings	Spring Guides
Insulators	Springs
Knobs	Switches
Lead Wires	

why so many variations in O.D. were necessary (see Figure 8.12). Applying VAT-1 (Unique Versus Shared), the team questioned the validity of each point of variation along the range spread. They asked: (1) Is this specific variation needed? (2) If not, how might it be removed? In some cases, the team proposed reducing the range of variation by making the O.D. value more robust. In cases where the geometry of the product did not allow for that, they proposed standardizing certain values. It soon became clear that many spring part numbers could be shared within Series 7 and also across product lines. With each proposal, the team updated the VEP Parts Index and saw for themselves the potential impact of their ideas on parts count.

An application of VAT-2 (Modularity) helped the team realize that some subassemblies in Series 7 could be treated as a part type; they extended the same concept to other product lines. VAT-3 (Multifunctionality and Synthesis) led the team to consider collapsing two—even three—part types into one. In fact, the Part Type Analysis Team came up with the exact same proposal that the Product Structure Analysis Team submitted, calling for the consolidation of spring guide and plunger functions into one part (Figure 7.5, page 199).

All the VATs worked beautifully for the team. But VAT-6 (Trend) produced a special kind of magic. Using it, the team could trace the growth and overall direction of the specifications of a particular attribute.

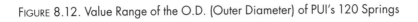

Figure 8.12. Value Range of the O.D. (Outer Diameter) of PUI's 120 Springs

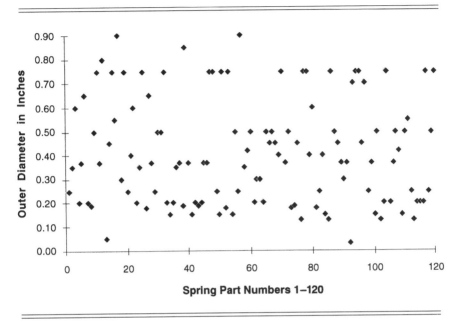

This could be done by associating one attribute with another attribute, or against a time axis. One trend query demonstrated the company's penchant for purchasing stainless steel brackets in lieu of brass in newer products, while another showed that bracket tolerances had been progressively widening over the last three years. Yet another run revealed that part specifications on original equipment manufacturer (OEM) housings had remained unchanged over the past five years in most series but were fluctuating wildly in PUI's fiber optic products. Similar to its applications in marketing, the trend technique exposed otherwise hidden and negative tendencies and bias.

Nearly every session of the Part Type Analysis Team produced a bumper crop of reduction ideas. Invariably, a good percentage of them did not pass muster when checked out with stakeholders, but enough did. Figure 8.13 shows some proposals related to screws and brackets that made it to the Steering Team for review. The team also developed some inventive proposals for preventing future proliferation. One of these,

FIGURE 8.13. Reduction Recommendations—PUI Part Type Analysis Team
Part Type/Screws, and Part Type/Brackets

Recommendations	Parts Impact	Supporting Data and Remarks
Screws 1. Eliminate all brass screws; use only stainless steel.	Total number of screws reduced by 9.	Actual cost differential is minimal, future volume of stainless steel screws will bring down piece price to within $.01 of current brass screw price.
2. Eliminate all hex-head screws; use only flathead.	Eliminates 8 more screws.	Design Engineering says no effect. Marketing advises customers willing to accept change. Manufacturing Engineering says it's acceptable to operators plus reduces number of tools required and parts locations.
3. Substitute ¼″ screw for all ⅛″ screws.	Eliminates 3 more screws.	Marketing says no market ramifications. Assembly says ¼″ screws are easier to handle.
Switch Brackets 1. Eliminate pivot parts 6332-131 and 6332-132. Standardize on using 6332-133 only.	Reduces 2 part numbers.	Engineering says 6332-133 will work on all switch brackets.
Total Part Numbers Eliminated 22	**Total Index Reduction** 3,742	**Total Market Impact** PUI customer selection remains constant at lower cost and less systems complexity.

based on an article a team member read on Nissan automobiles, was to set up "border guards," ex–VEP team members charged with blocking incursions (or parts) that would needlessly elevate the company's parts count.

IMPLICATIONS OF THE 3-VIEW ANALYSIS

We return to Nissan and the problem of its mushrooming parts inventory. The following variations in part types were tracked across a vehicle pool of 100 models:

- 1,200 different kinds of floor carpets
- 437 different kinds of dashboard meters
- 300 different kinds of ashtrays
- 110 different kinds of radiators

In 1989, one midsize Nissan sedan (the now-discontinued Laurel) alone had 62 different kinds of electrical harnesses associated with it, representing in their totality 17 yards of harness storage bins.*

Legitimately, we ask: Does this level of variation create and sustain markets—or suffocate them? Will the customer buy that difference? Nissan got part of its answer when it discovered that 50 percent of the variations that resulted in its prodigious 2,200-model range contributed only 5 percent to total sales.

While VEP's 3-View Analysis may not be able to ascertain the exact cause of variations (we know that numerous factors can contribute), it can vigorously query why these variations must remain and help to root them out. You need to see where negative variety in your company resides.

Runaway parts proliferation places huge burdens on the organization. Nowhere is this better appreciated, perhaps, than in calculating variations within each part type. But it is not just hiding in your parts type pool. It resides in a vast array of front-end and in-process decisions that

* Wall Street Journal, March 3, 1993.

cause another new product line, another new product, and another new part to enter the system. Variation and the complexity that follows in its wake are *embedded* in all company systems. Because it is "everywhere," because the problem is systemic, it can be successfully attacked only through a systematic approach. The three-prong offensive of this central analytical approach attempts to bring into balance the three often-contradicting efforts found in product marketing, product design, and product development.

HOME FREE—ALMOST

In the deep-dive VEP implementation described in these past three chapters, the most critical and challenging part of the effort is over when the VEP teams have submitted their final reduction recommendations to the Steering Team. These include improvement proposals on parts, products, and policies. With that done, you are ready to put it all together in Stages 3 and 4 (see Figure 8.14).

Stage 3: Coordinating and Prioritizing Improvement Opportunities. The next step is first to coordinate ideas and prioritize improvement proposals (Stage 3). This entails collating all reduction recommendations from the 3-View Teams; these proposals reflect their best thinking relative to negative variety in parts, products, and overall market offerings as well as to needed policy revisions and additions. Picture three streams of improvement proposals flowing into the Steering Team from three sources—the Market Analysis, Product Structure Analysis, and Part Type teams. If a separate team has been designated for process reduction, a fourth stream of recommendations will flow from it (n.b., the control points team generally works independently).

At the simplest level, these recommendations can be tracked with Post-It® notes and long pieces of brown butcher paper—in which case, it would help if the Steering Team had a room/office of its own to serve as a base camp for the duration of the project. Alternatively, the entire process of Stage 3 (and Stage 4) can be facilitated (and greatly so) through team decision-making software, your own or from the VEP software package (see the Resource Section at the back of the book). Bear both these things in mind as you read on.

Now that the Steering Team has compiled all the proposals, its task is to coordinate them into a coherent pool. This entails, among other things, consolidating the considerable number of overlaps that are bound to emerge in this dynamic and creative team process. On the surface, this may appear to be a lot of work in a short period of time. In reality, teams have been sending recommendations to the Steering Team for the duration of the implementation. What is more, all proposals are pre-qualified before they reach the Steering Team. As explained earlier in this chapter, all improvement ideas have to pass the muster of stakeholders (viz., get their approval) *before* they can be passed to the Steering Team for review.

In addition, the Steering Team encourages teams to implement certain proposals during Stage 2, many times long before Stage 3. These are the proposals characterized as having "low-resistance-to-change" among stakeholders; many times, these are also ideas that require minimal resources to implement. So simple, inexpensive changes get moved through quickly. Reminiscent of the goals of the Early Victories Team at the outset of the process, hopefully some reductions that are implemented early on will garner visibility, even a high profile, and do double service—first for their improvement impact and second for their positive promotional effect.

But some ideas need to wait for Stage 3. They need to wait, for example, because they represent a costly, even complex change, that cannot be undertaken lightly. Whether related to parts, products, or policies, some improvements require a high degree of coordination and/or multiple approvals. These are the proposals that are now prioritized and require a formal implementation calendar.

There is wisdom in this waiting, especially if teams are still working through the products and parts universe. One excellent multifunctional idea may surface in the early days of product structure analysis, just to be superseded a month later when the part types team finds an even wider application. So you go with the changes that are low-cost and can ease through the system, and exercise patience on the rest.

FIGURE 8.14. Stages 3 and 4 of the VEP Methodology

STAGE 1— Preparing for an Effective VEP Implementation	STAGE 2— Identifying Reduction Opportunities by Applying the 6-VATs	STAGE 3— Coordinating and Prioritizing Reduction Opportunities	STAGE 4— Implementing and Sustaining the Improvement
Step 1— Select a Steering Team that then sets up the other VEP teams (Management)	Step 1— Begin reduction analysis of market offerings and their characteristics (Market Analysis Team)	Step 1— Compile all Recommendations* from 3-View Analysis Teams** (Steering Team + 3-View Analysis Teams)	Step 1— Implement Approved Proposals (all teams)
Step 2— Conduct team training & begin general awareness training (Education & Methods Team)	Step 2— Begin reduction analysis of parts as they are structured into products (Product Structure Analysis Team)	Step 2— Coordinate, Consolidate, and Screen 3-View Recommendations (Steering Team + 3-View Analysis Teams)	Step 2 Set up the Preventative Monitoring Calendar and System (all teams)
Step 3— Begin to analyze and revise company policies and practices (Policy Analysis Team)	Step 3— Begin reduction analysis of commodities by parts type (Part Type Analysis Team)	Step 3— Valuate and Prioritize all Viable 3-View Proposals (Steering Team + 3-View Analysis Teams)	

Step 4—
Find and reduce parts with low-resistance to change (Early Victories Team)

Step 5—
Assess, clean up, and upgrade parts classification system (Part Type Analysis Team)

Step 6—
Target a priority product as the starting point for Stage 2 reduction analysis (Steering Team)

Step 4—
Begin reduction analysis of transactions that support parts and products (Control Points Analysis Team)

Step 5—
Begin additional analysis to reduce production processes, beyond work of 3-View teams (Production Process Analysis Team)

Step 4—
Prepare an Implementation Calendar

* These include recommendations on policy improvements. Also addressed at this time are recommendations on production process reductions, whether stemming from the 3-View teams or a separate process analysis team. (See Chapter 9 for more on process reduction.)

** The Control Point Team typically works independently, not requiring directly the organizing/coordinating function of the Steering Team. (See Chapter 9 for more on control point reduction.)

The so-called "waiting" is not time lost, however. You'd be amazed (or maybe you wouldn't) at the depth of improvement that can transpire in the values and day-to-day procedures of a work force actively engaged in VEP. Awareness of VEP principles and goals and the intention to realize them can inspire people to make simple improvements on their own, the kind that never reach any VEP team. This is especially so when coupled with concrete examples (models) close to home. Because they are changing the way they think, people will seek ways to live with that change.

We have seen this most dramatically in industrial design and product engineering functions. That staff wants to do "it" right, wants to save time and cost, and make the company money. Once their consciousness is raised about effective variety, they will find their own ways to get on with it. We have seen practices around product development aligned quietly but decidedly "overnight." The way things are done in any number of departments starts lining up with a new awareness and intention; as a result, myriad, incremental gains begin to build. These informal gains can fuel the implementation and keep the momentum going and the excitement alive even as people comply with the more formal, step-by-step procedure we call the "VEP methodology." What people may not realize is that those informal gains are also part of the method.

Stage 4: Implementing and Sustaining the Improvements. By the end of Stage 3, which might take a good month to effect, all systems are go: The proposals are on the verge of becoming a living reality in the organization.

Chances are, when the implementation calendar was developed in Stage 3, people decided on a certain improvement rhythm that would allow all that positive change to enter the company at an even and sensitive pace. A calendar was devised that allowed change to be introduced in doses that would not overload the system but would challenge the status quo. In Stage 4, that takes place.

From a certain viewpoint (viz., its impact on part values and product structures), this VEP phase resembles a massive ECN (engineering change notice) process. Truly, if mindfully done, a VEP-based approach can strengthen—or conceivably even replace—more traditional ECN procedures, especially given that all ideas are pre-qualified and represent exceptionally clear thinking.

The second key dimension in Stage 4, the final one in the VEP methodology, is that of prevention. You will remember that VEP has three main goals: (1) maximize customer selection, (2) reduce negative variety, and (3) prevent its recurrence. That means a VEP implementation cannot be considered a success *until and unless* the roots of negative variety are dug out of the organization and replaced by practices and policies that prevent it from returning. Once again, all the VEP teams are involved in this important work. Their ideas can be imaginative, as seen in the notion of "border guards" to watchdog against unwarranted addition to the parts base. And they can be practical—as in the non–CAD-driven company that decides to weed out all the deadwood in their drawing files, and remove all the now-emptied cabinets so any new drawings can't find easy places to hide. These ideas and more are identified and implemented in this stage.

And, finally, a calendar is set up that schedules a regular review of all indicators of negative variety companywide.

But we are slightly ahead of ourselves. In the next chapter, we return to Stage 2 and examine analysis and reduction efforts downstream in the area of production processes and control points.

CHAPTER NINE

REDUCING DOWNSTREAM COMPLEXITY

Unwarranted Production Processes and Control Points

Froggie *didn't* notice the water he was sitting in begin to boil. It had been such a nice warm pool for so long.

PRODUCTION PROCESSES AT PUI

In the first three months of the VEP implementation at Parts Unlimited Inc. (PUI), the Early Victories Team eliminated over 1,000 part numbers. Associated with that, team members worked with the shop floor and eliminated over 100 production processes, plus 12 dies, 15 fixtures, and two machines. The majority of these items were deadwood in the system, equipment that PUI supervisors had meant to remove ages ago but just hadn't.

In addition, the 3-View Analysis teams targeted another 65 processes for elimination. Eliminating the eight different product families, for example, that the Market Analysis Team recommended (see Figure 8.6), would wipe out a pile of ancient processes (plus dies, tooling, and fixtures) and free up an estimated 1,500 square feet of the production floor and storage space.

Five months into the implementation, the Steering Team formed a separate cross-functional team to focus exclusively on production process reduction. All the right groups were represented—Manufacturing Engineering, Marketing, Operations, Material Handling, the machine shop, stores, etc. The team's target was a 20 percent reduction from the current baseline.

First, team members went to the shop floor to learn the names of the various operations and processes. They spoke with operators, supervisors, managers, process engineers—anyone and everyone who had anything to do with shop-floor processes. They were surprised at the many different names they discovered (see Figure 9.1).

FIGURE 9.1. PUI's Tower of Babel: Various Names for Production Processes at PUI *Before* VEP

Production Process	Production Process	Production Process
1.* Mounting in Fixture	22. Drilling with Air Drill	Angles on Brackets
2. Dropping Parts into Fixture	23. Drill Press	47. Forming Corners on Metal
3. Holding Parts	24. Internal Threading	48. Gluing
4. Assembling Parts	25. Tapping	49. Bonding
5. Loading Tool	26. Threading	50. Epoxying Parts Together
6. Loading Fixture	27. External Threading	51. Super Gluing
7. Unloading Tool	28. Removing Material	52. Adding Loctite
8. Unloading Fixture	29. Punching Holes	53. Putting Insulating Material in Enclosures
9. Loading Component	30. Lathe	
10. Unloading Component	31. Turning	
11. Mating Parts	32. Milling Machine	54. Filling
12. Inserting Parts	33. Milling	55. Potting Switches
13. Adding Parts	34. Turning Down Parts	56. Mixing Potting Materials
14. Machining Processes	35. Milling Components	
15. CNC Work	36. Grinding Wheel	57. Epoxy Coating
16. Punching	37. Hand Sanding	58. Spraying Epoxy
17. Punch Press	38. Removing Material	59. Painting on Insulation Material
18. Arbor Press	39. Finishing	
19. Air Cylinder Punching	40. Sander	60. Epoxy Option
	42. Grinding Down Parts	61. Spray Paint
20. Drilling	43. Abrasive Process	62. Painting Parts
21. Drilling by Hand	44. Angling a Part	63. Changing Color of Enclosures
	45. Bending Metal	
	46. Putting Right	

* The number preceding each process represents a numerical order, not a code.

FIGURE 9.1 (continued)

Production Process	Production Process	Production Process
64. Plating	94. Removing Sharp Edges	118. Wire Cutter Machine
65. Nickle Plating		119. Hand Cutting Wire
66. Soldering	95. Tumbling Parts	120. Wire Cutters
67. Arc Welding	96. Scraping Off Rough Edges	121. Removing Wire Coating
68. Low-Temperature Joining	97. Filing Parts	122. Undressing Wire Cable
69. Resistance Welding	98. Filing Edges	
70. High-Temperature Metal Joining	99. Greasing Parts	123. Splitting Wire Cable
	100. Oiling Equipment	124. Stripping Fixture
71. Brazing	101. Oiling Component Parts	125. Burn-In Test
72. Metal Joining		126. Adding Setpoint
73. Spot Welding	102. Adding Lubricant	127. Product Calibration
74. Wave Solder Machine	103. Applying Grease or Oil	
75. Soldering PC Boards	104. Greasing Threads	128. Testing a Product
	105. Putting on Labels	129. Calibrating
76. Iron Soldering	106. Making Nameplates	130. Pressure Stand Work
77. Torch Brazing		131. QC'ing Product
78. Brown & Sharp	107. Writing Up Tags	132. Adjusting Setting
79. Putting in Rivets	108. Adding Product I.D.	133. Test and Calibration
80. Riveting		
81. Adding Fasteners	109. Stamping Part Numbers	134. Test Rig Calibration
82. Screwing	110. Coloring Coding Parts	135. Immersion Bath Procedure
83. Press-Fitting Components		
84. Pressing Dowel Pins	111. Coloring Mating Parts	136. Thermal Chamber Test
85. Knurled Pin Press Operation	112. Marking Machine	137. Vibration Check
	113. Laser Printing for Labels	138. Hose Down Test
86. Fitting Machine	114. Computerized Nameplate Machine	139. Up/Down Scale Test
87. Staking Machine		
88. Hand Staking Tool	115. Sniping Wires	140. Life Testing
89. Fastening	116. Cutting Back Wires	141. Component Calibration
90. Cleaning Parts		
91. Degreasing Parts	117. Stripping Wire Ends	142. PC Board Functional Testing
92. Wiping Off Oil		
93. Removing Excess Material		

As they made their way around the floor, team members also observed other occurrences of interest to them in light of their mandate. They saw the same part being inserted *four* completely different ways! They discovered that certain jobs were sometimes done with fixtures, sometimes not. Some assembly jobs were done by hand some of the time and by machine at others, apparently depending on the quantity ordered and the operator doing the job. No one they talked to seemed *un*comfortable with the range of differences—but no one could explain them either.

THE RISING TIDE

VEP attacks the primary causative factor of this flood of processes—the introduction of that one new part. It also minimizes proliferating processes and control points. The first three steps of Stage 2 of the VEP methodology focus simultaneously on three fronts—market, product structure, and part type (the 3-View Analysis). Steps 4 and 5 seek to reduce the aftereffects that emerge downstream (see shaded area in Figure 9.2).

The major downstream effect of negative variety on the shop floor surfaces in the form of additional production processes and a cascade of tooling, dies, and fixtures. It can also be seen in the blizzards of paperwork and computer transactions called *control points* that pile up in offices and on desks in every corner of the corporation.

Let's first examine how to reduce unwarranted production processes.

REDUCING THE NUMBER AND VARIETY OF PRODUCTION PROCESSES

VEP defines a process as *a sequence of events, steps, or activities performed in order to reach a specific outcome*—production or nonproduction related. A production-related process—such as machining—directly impacts the material state of the product as it moves from raw material to finished good. A nonproduction-related process—purchasing, scheduling, invoicing—supports the product but does not alter it (see Figure 9.3, page 258 for more examples). Our discussion will focus on the reduction of production-related processes.

In VEP, as a natural extension of the work of the 3-View Analysis teams, removing a part, product, or product group can result in the parallel elimination of some—and often many—associated production processes. This is what happened at PUI when the Market Analysis Team targeted eight different product series for elimination; that meant simultaneously eliminating more than a dozen separate production processes and scores of dies, fixtures, and tools.

Reductions in processes are further increased through the work of a *separate and distinct* VEP Production Process Analysis Team. Such a team is especially important if the company has never addressed the issues of process improvement or cell design. For organizations that have, many superfluous processes will have already been eliminated.

The Nature of the Challenge

Unwarranted variety in production processes is not so easy to spot for several reasons. First, production processes are not typically well-documented. Few companies have ever "bothered" cataloging processes, developing a database inventory on them, or monitoring the entry of new ones. In addition, as we saw in Figure 9.1, process names are not clear. These two characteristics are intimately linked.

FIGURE 9.2. Stage 2 of the Methodology: Where the Reduction of Production Processes and Control Points Fits In

STAGE 1— Preparing for an Effective VEP Implementation	STAGE 2— Identifying Reduction Opportunities by Applying the 6-VATs	STAGE 3— Coordinating and Prioritizing Reduction Opportunities	STAGE 4— Implementing and Sustaining the Improvement
Step 1— Select a Steering Team that then sets up the other VEP teams (Management)	Step 1 Begin reduction analysis of market offerings and their characteristics (Market Analysis Team)		
Step 2— Conduct team training & begin general awareness training (Education & Methods Team)	Step 2— Begin reduction analysis of parts as they are structured into products (Product Structure Analysis Team)		
Step 3— Find and reduce parts with low-resistance to change (Early Victories Team)	Step 3— Begin reduction analysis of commodities by parts type (Part Type Analysis Team)		

256

Step 4—
Assess, clean up, and upgrade parts classification system (Part Type Analysis Team)

Step 5—
Begin to analyze and revise company policies and practices (Policy Analysis Team)

Step 6—
Target priority product as the starting point for Stage 2 reduction analysis (Steering Team)

Step 4—
Begin reduction analysis of transactions that support parts and products (Control Points Analysis Team)

Step 5—
Begin additional analysis to reduce production processes, beyond work of 3-View teams (Production Process Analysis Team)*

* May be accomplished separately or included in the efforts of the 3-View Analysis teams.

FIGURE 9.3. Examples of Production and Nonproduction Processes

EXAMPLES: PRODUCTION PROCESS	EXAMPLES: NONPRODUCTION PROCESS
Stamping	Entering Orders
Cutting	Order Checking
Forming	Parts Procurement
Soldering	Proposal Writing and Bidding
De-burring	Developing Marketing Brochures
Assembly	Cleaning the Facilities
Marking	Scheduling Production
Machining	Invoicing

Let's walk through VEP's simple procedure for analyzing and reducing production processes. Step 1 is to standardize the terminology used to described those processes.

First Standardize Terminology

In some organizations, there are so many different names for a process that operators themselves get confused; it's worse for managers!

In a finishing operation, for example, the same work may be referred to as sanding, hand sanding, abrasive processing, or grinding—at other times it may be described generically as "removing material." But "removing material" may mean, in the same organization, a milling operation. In one shop, the same bending operation was variously referred to as "putting right angles on brackets," "angling a part," "bending metal," and "forming corners on metal." Is it wrong to describe the same things in different terms? Yes! When attempting, for example, to document the number and variety of production processes in order to consider how to reduce them, a torrent of terms referring to the same operation is an unnecessary burden.

Before the team can begin analysis, they must document production processes and standardize terminology. Develop a classification system. PUI developed one, step by step, in the following way. Team members wrote a Post-It® for each name on the list they complied (see Figure 9.1 for list of names before VEP), then grouped them into category sets and subsets. They then brainstormed to come up with standard names and agreed on a single appellation for each. In the end, they had distilled the original list of 142 names down to 8 broad process categories and 28 sub-processes (see Figure 9.4).

FIGURE 9.4. Active Production Processes at PUI *After* VEP

Process	Operation	Description
1.0. Assembly	1.1. Loading	Putting in/removing a component from tool or fixture
	1.2. Inserting	Putting a part in on another part(s)
2.0. Machining	2.1. Punching	Removing material using some type of press or fixture
	2.2. Drilling	Removing material via a drill or drill press
	2.3. Tapping	Removing material to create internal threading
	2.4. Turning	Any work done on a lathe
	2.5. Milling	Any work done on a milling machine
	2.6. Grinding/Sanding	Removing material by abrading or grinding
	2.7. Bending/Forming	Re-forming of a part
3.0. Gluing and Finishing	3.1. Adhesive Bonding	Gluing parts together
	3.2. Potting	Filling a cavity with insulating material
	3.3. Coating	Applying insulating coating material
	3.4. Painting	Applying paint to a part(s)
4.0. Soldering/Welding	4.1. Brazing	Metal joining, using filler metal melting above 800° F.
	4.2. Soldering	Metal joining, using filler metal melting below 800° F.

(*continued on next page*)

FIGURE 9.4. (continued)

Process	Operation	Description
	4.3. Wave Soldering	Soldering printed circuit boards, using wave soldering machine
	4.4. Resistance Welding	Metal joining, using a spot welder
	4.5. Arc Welding	Metal joining, using an arc welder
5.0. Fastening	5.1. Riveting	Installing and securing rivets
	5.2. Pressing	Assembling press-fit components by hand or by machine
	5.3. Screwing	Installing screws to secure components together
	5.4. Staking	Forming material to secure components together
6.0. Cleaning/Marking	6.1. Cleaning	Removing unwanted material by cleaning, degreasing, or wiping
	6.2. De-burring	Removing unwanted sharp edges by filing, tumbling, or scraping
	6.3. Lubricating	Applying grease, oil, or other lubricant
	6.4. Marking	Applying any type of identification to a part
7.0. Wire	7.1. Wire Cutting	Cutting wire either by machine or by hand
	7.2. Wire Stripping	Stripping wire coating off by machine or by hand
8.0. Testing	8.1. Testing	Testing, calibrating, or setting of a product

Next, the team developed a *process* attribute template for capturing the critical specifications of each of these processes. Similar to the *part* attribute template developed in Stage 1 (Chapter 6), this grid displays the characteristics to consider when cataloging and describing a given process (see Figure 9.5). The template also facilitates the entry of accurate, uniform information into the new database.

FIGURE 9.5. PUI Process Attribute Template—Welding

Process Number	Gas Flow	Weld Current	Torch Position	Tool	Part #	Material 1	Material 2
X-31	20-25 PSI	100 Amp	45°	DNV-131	Y-88-A	⅛" SS	⅛" SS
X-37	20-25 PSI	72-75 Amp	90°	DNV-137	Y-253-E	1½" SS	¼" SS

Doing this was so painless that a few members of the PUI team went on to develop a similar inventory register for tools, fixtures, and dies. With this groundwork in place, the team was equipped to begin its reduction analysis.

Begin the Analysis

Here is VEP's 6-Step Process Reduction Analysis Procedure:

1. Target a process category for analysis (for example, soldering and welding)
2. Analyze the targeted category, applying the 6-VATs
   a. Identify the functions, process specifications, and tooling requirements for this category
   b. Apply the 6-VATs and brainstorm possible reduction opportunities, querying:
      • Can this process be eliminated?
      • Can it be combined with another process?
      • Can a new process be created that eliminates this one and others?
      • Can this process be re-aligned in order to eliminate any current requirements for unique dies, tooling, or fixtures?
3. Evaluate reduction proposals systematically against stakeholder concerns, holding in reserve any proposal that does not pass this review.
4. Prioritize validated proposals according to the least/most resistance to change and least/most impact on cost.

5. Submit proposals to Steering Team for review and coordination with those of other teams.
6. Choose a new process category for reduction analysis.

All along the way, the Process Reduction Team keeps an eye out for factors that cause processes to proliferate, including those related to formal and informal policies and practices. The team submits all these to the Steering Team for review. When viable proposals are implemented and the number of processes decreases, the team continues to monitor the shop floor for any signs of unwarranted process proliferation.

REDUCING THE NUMBER AND VARIETY OF CONTROL POINTS

A control point is *any activity or transaction—paper, electronic, or otherwise—that supports the design, procurement, sorting, retrieval, inspection, production, or cataloging of parts and products.*

Proliferating paperwork and computer transactions are a bane of corporate existence. Companies rarely, if ever, identify or track them in a systematic or comprehensive manner. Yet control points consume enormous amounts of an organization's resources—both time and money. And it all starts innocently enough, with the introduction of a part.

Let's walk through this progression metaphorically from the control point perspective. Imagine a part as a seed. Even before the part is "planted" in a product, it has begun to sprout control points. See Figure 9.6. Although we would like to think of each part residing in its own uncluttered little burrow, reality soon makes itself known. The longer the part is "alive," the more control points associated with that part multiply. Joined by other parts and their related control points, the organizations turns into a veritable jungle of complexity. See Figure 9.7, page 264. The

FIGURE 9.6. A Part in the Process of Sprouting Control Points

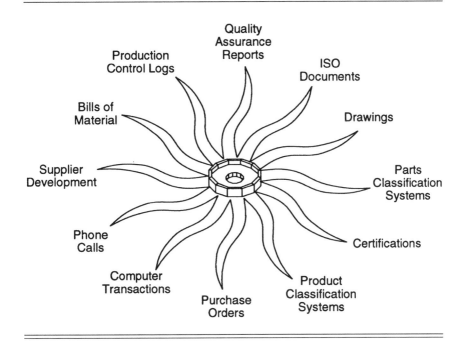

congestion spreads slowly and surely, covering the entire enterprise. The more the company struggles to free itself from complexity's grip, the more it becomes entangled.

Control points adhere to parts, but they are not always easy to detect. Twenty-six control points, for example, are required for PUI's electronic subassembly XJ-889, composed of just three purchased parts and seven made parts (see Figure 9.8, page 265). This number does not break out detailed computer transactions.

If the number of control points reaches 26 for a single subassembly, that number becomes exponential for an entire parts inventory. But let's look deeper into the nature of the control point challenge. Here's part of the scenario at PUI.

FIGURE 9.7 Control Points, or *Guess Who's Coming to Dinner?*

We would like to think of each part as residing in its own uncluttered burrow...

Part Ⓐ	Part Ⓑ	Part Ⓒ	Part Ⓓ	Part Ⓔ
Part Ⓕ	Part Ⓖ	Part Ⓗ	Part Ⓘ	Part Ⓙ

...but from its outset, each part begins to sprout control points.

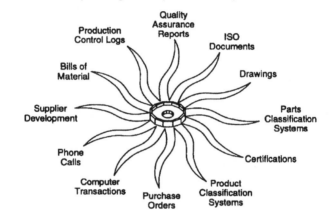

As parts and their control points multiply, the jungle of complexity spreads.

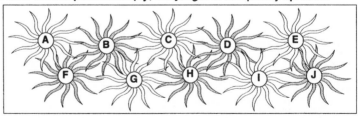

FIGURE 9.8. Some of the Control Points Associated With Sub Assembly XJ-889

Purchased Parts	Made Parts
Drawings	Drawings
Purchase Orders	Production Orders
Certificate of compliance	Manufacturing Procedures
Receiving Paperwork Creation	Inspection and Testing
Receiving Transactions	Parts and Fixture Retrieval
Inspection	Computerized Scheduling Transactions
Expediting	Receipt Transactions to Stock
Product Master File Coding	Inventorying
Unpacking	Routings
Paying Suppliers and Freight Bills	Product Master File Coding
Order Status Reports	Moving, Storing
Shortage Reports	Shortage Reports
Packaging to Avoid Damage	Packaging to Avoid Damage

Control Points at Parts Unlimited Inc.

Procedures—Documented and Undocumented

At PUI, the number and types of work procedures vary widely from department to department. Since the company decided to seek ISO registration a short time ago, a huge documentation challenge in itself, everyone handling paperwork braced for the mountain of effort they knew would be required to document these procedures.

In Operations, for example, VP Wardwell holds her direct reports responsible for documenting required procedures, but she also knows that, at this point, no *one* has clarity about which procedures should or should not be documented. She recently remarked: "Quite honestly, we do a lot of things without formal written procedures—even though we know the same procedure should be followed each and every time we do something, like building a product, placing a purchase order, or 100 percent testing an outgoing order. I think the sheer variety of control activities performed by Operations has a good deal to do with why we do a poor job of creating and maintaining work procedures. Everything seems to be an exception."

Drawings—Standardizing and Maintaining

The number of drawings at PUI and the amount of maintenance associated with them is a significant problem. But no one knows *how* significant since the true cost of a drawing has never been determined, except perhaps in the payroll figures of the Drafting Department.

One cost indicator is lead time in the Drafting Department, which is now measured in weeks, not days, and is a source of frustration for that department as well as for those it supports. There are many days when Drafting Manager Art Brennan wonders how many other, more productive things he and his staff could do if the sheer number of drawings was reduced. And how often has he discovered staff working on drawings that should have been obsoleted six months ago? And how many drawings are there on duplicate parts? According to Brennan, the answer to both questions is: "A lot!"

Forms—Number, Variety, and Overlap

Every PUI department uses dozens of forms in the course of a normal business day and many more at the end of the month. Most forms are designed by individual departments because, managers point out, they have "special" needs. Consequently, offices are awash in purchase orders, logs, fax transmittal sheets, etc., that are all slightly (but, according to each department, importantly) different. In response to a recent customer product query, a customer service person griped: "Should I send the ECN, SRO, or MCN form or all of the above to get this looked at by Engineering?!?"

The Control Points Reduction Team and Its Tasks

The Control Points Reduction Team gets formed early in a VEP implementation. Because control points are found everywhere in the corporation, the team includes representatives from all departments—Purchasing, Systems, Drafting, Engineering, Materials, Finance, Quality Assurance/Control, Marketing, and Customer Service. Their mandate is to:

- Classify and analyze control points by department and company-wide, applying the 6-VATs, and identify viable opportunities to reduce them.
- Recommend revisions in policies and practices to better regulate and minimize the addition of control points in the future.

As you may have already anticipated, the team begins by developing a classification system for control points, if one does not currently exist. This, of course, requires that:

- The terminology related to control points (names of forms, transactions, etc.) be simplified and standardized.
- All control points be identified and cataloged.

To do this, the team selects a reduction focus; in all likelihood, it will begin with forms and reports (order entry, credit applications, accounts receivable activity report, accounts payable activity report, deposit slips, etc.). Next, with the help of their departmental colleagues, individual team members compile hard copies of all forms used in their respective departments and determine how often each form is used (daily, weekly, monthly, quarterly, annually). The forms are then grouped into categories, according to underlying commonalities, and a label is found for each group—reports, fax forms, order forms, accounting documents, etc.

The next step is to put all such forms into a master binder by category and to develop a master list for the department. This master list is put into a matrix, showing each form and its usage frequency, so that an index can be calculated. This index, a quantification of the relationship of form type and use, is exactly parallel to the VEP Parts Index used in the 3-View Analysis process (see Figure 9.9). The result (number of forms times frequency) represents the indexed figure.

The team is now ready to reconvene, with each department bringing its binder and index to the meeting so that a company-wide binder and index can be developed.

Using the company-wide index and hard-copy master as baselines, the team now begins the analysis process. The aim is to find ways of simplifying, combining, or eliminating forms, applying the 6-VATs; the first three tools (Unique Versus Shared, Modularity, and Multifunctionality and Synthesis) will prove most helpful, with the last three (Ease of Assembly, Range, and Trend) having more limited applicability.* Some checklist questions are:

- Can this form be eliminated?
- Can this form be combined with another existing form?
- Can a new form be created that eliminates this form and even other forms?
- Can this form be revised so that it eliminates the need for another form?
- Can the information on this form be communicated or retained in another way?

Interface with Steering Team

While the Control Points Reduction Team keeps the Steering Team closely informed of its progress, it is more autonomous than other VEP teams since there is little interface with parts per se. Decisions, therefore, can be made there by consensus, linking directly back to the departments as necessary. The team is also empowered to effect most of

* See Chapter 6 for a review of these.

FIGURE 9.9. Control Point Index—Forms

A	B Name of Form	C Reference #	D Day 252	E Week 52	F Month 12	G Quarter 4	H 6 Mos 2	I Year 1	J Occurrences
1	5-Days-in-Receiving Report			1					52
2	A/P Aging Report				1				12
3	A20		6*						1512
4	Account Summary by Cost Center			1					52
5	A/R Activity Report		1						252
6	A/R Aged Trial Balance Detail		1						252
7	Application for Credit			1					52
8	Authorization for Payment			4					208
9	Back-Order Stock Ship List								756
10	Bank Change/Info on Address								52
11	Bank Deposit Receipt		1						252
12	Bank Deposit Ticket		1						252
13	Buy-Part P.O.			1					52
14	Canadian Pick List		3						252
15	Cash Deposit Report				1				12
16	Cash Receipts		1						252
17	Cash Receipts Final Register		1						252
18	Certification Approval Notice					4			16
	Different Forms	10	5	2	1	0	0	18	5,044

VEP Index for this page of control points = 90,792 (18 different forms × 5,044 total occurrences)

* Any number over 1 in columns D through I indicates the number of copies distributed of this form.

269

its improvement and reduction proposals without Steering Team approval.

Similar to the other teams, the control points group is on the constant lookout for internal and external causes of control point proliferation and ways to eliminate these causes. Once all remaining control points are validated and put on a master list, team members regularly monitor that list for any signs of unneeded proliferation. Gatekeeping functions can be set up in each department to monitor this activity.

Some Actual Results

Members of the Control Points Reduction Team in one company were very proud of their results. Having identified 226 forms, they eliminated 52 within the first 90 days of activity. Six months later only four new forms had been added. More impressively, this reduction reduced the Forms Index by nearly 20,000. Control points reduction in the Drafting Department was also dramatic. Seventy-two cabinet drawers of drawings were whittled down to 16—an 80 percent reduction (see Figure 9.10).

FIGURE 9.10. Some Actual Results

Control Point	Before	After	Added Since
Actual Number of Forms	226	52	4
Forms Index	62,449	43,025	548
Actual Drawings	72 cabinet drawers	16 cabinet drawers	1 cabinet drawer

SUMMARY: DOWNSTREAM IS WHERE THE SILT PILES UP

The part is an almost-invisible obstruction in the flow as products make their way to the end-user. But look downstream from that part for further evidence of its impact. There you see a silt pile-up in the form of excessive production processes and control points that builds a dam in the flow that can slow it down to a trickle. Look there, too, for another gauge of your progress in regulating mushrooming parts. As unwarranted parts, products, and production processes are removed, the flow gains speed, getting more rapid still with the elimination of unneeded control points.

The success of your efforts to curb and minimize processes and control points gets reflected in a new sense of spaciousness and ease in the company's internal systems. The infrastructure regains some breathing room and, as a result, the flow accelerates.

PART THREE

The Bottom Line

CHAPTER TEN

DESIGNING FOR THE BOTTOM LINE

Many companies pay for their products twice—once in the development phase and again in the level of complexity they add to their systems.

COMPLEX SYSTEMS

Organizations are complex organisms in which a great many independent elements interact in a great many ways. During the course of a single workday, literally thousands of individual acts and discrete transactions transpire in support of the company. These transactions can either weave a rich and successful tapestry of collective effort or a strangling web of complicated minutiae and organizational congestion. Because they are also dynamic, organizations can dance along the edge that separates the collective from the complicated—for a while.

VISION OF VARIETY EFFECTIVENESS

Organizations are also flexible and adaptive. They learn. They learn, for example, to cope with the stress that enters with the introduction of each new part, nudging their internal complexity quotients, however

275

fractionally, just that much higher. Corporate structures can absorb huge amounts of complicating stress, but just as stress in the body can lead to actual physical complaints—headaches, ulcers, heart disease—sooner or later, the burden on a company's infrastructure exhibits itself as assorted and costly problems—long lead times, defects, rework, scrap, a tangle of processes, miscommunication, schedule changes, delays, searching, waiting, etc. At a given point, the system reaches overload and goes tilt. Stress factors and their compensating responses have become entrenched and the company enters an organizational gridlock that becomes chronic, and profits erode.

We think organizational gridlock and profit erosion are high prices to pay for product diversification. From VEP's perspective, the culprit is not the diversifying products. The culprit is unwarranted variation and the complication it can generate. Even when your hot-selling products reach the end of their productive life and are retired, even when parts are obsoleted and removed, the complexity that surrounded these remains— a tight web of cause and effect that has taken on a life of its own. This web does not come unraveled by itself. It must be *systematically* dismantled, strand by strand.

Smart, simple design means getting smart about getting simple. The payoffs can be remarkable. Imagine that the principles and methods of variety effectiveness discussed in this book are in practice in your company. Imagine your parts levels at 30 percent to 40 percent less than those of your competitors—even while you turn out one great new hot-selling product after another. Imagine a development process that is so robust and fluid that product lead time becomes a genuine commercial advantage. And imagine an internal system so process- and support-lean that your employees, increasingly, have the time and the spaciousness to add real value to their work. This is the vision of VEP: Variety Effectiveness Process.

This vision is what many companies are in the process of realizing. Nissan sales peaked in 1985. After that, company profits began a downward slide that didn't hit bottom until 1991. Nissan knew it was in trouble and looked inward (instead of outward). The nub of the issue was ineffective variety, coupled with an untenable cost structure (as discussed in

Chapters 2 and 3). Nissan struck back, triggering an internal revolution that has not been without pain. It's goal: get simpler. And it did. From using over 6,000 fasteners across 100 different vehicles, for example, Nissan now requires 1,000. In another case, model types of its popular Laurel car were slashed from 23 to 10 and floor carpet options from seven to two; and only 10 types of steering wheels are now offered for that model, down from 87! The direct cost savings of these and other reductions triggered during this period of reform are significant. But the indirect cost savings throughout the company in terms of support functions and organization complexity are inestimable. Nissan has become a force to be reckoned with, and its customers are in full support. Witness Nissan's introduction in May 1994 in the United States of its made-in-Japan Maxima at a base sticker price of $2,500 less than the previous version— an astounding corporate feat not just in terms of comebacks but in the face of an appreciating Japanese yen.

Hewlett-Packard is another company that has profited from de-complicating its products and its organization. HP Loveland (Colorado) designs, manufactures, and markets a variety of electronic products for use in the test and measurement market. Its digital multimeter product line, which ranges in price from several hundred to several thousand dollars, represents a $300 million segment of a $5 billion market which, since the de-escalation of military spending, is characterized by slow growth and increased global competition. In 1990, the Loveland division set its sights on delivering a multimeter (model 34401A) with a performance comparable to that of instruments costing $3,000 to $5,000 *but* at a $1,000 price. And, by late 1991, it did! Using assorted but *linked* development tools (QFD, DFM, DFA, activity-based costing, concurrent engineering), the team designed a product with: (1) reduced assembly time—from 20 to 6 minutes; (2) reduced number of hand-assembled parts; (3) reduced overall parts count; (4) reduced number of screw part types—from 25 to 2; (5) reduced number of required screws—from 27 to 11; (6) all screws the same size; (7) an innovative terminal block that snaps into place; (8) auto-calibration instead of manual-calibration; and, (9) nearly $200 in reduced direct cost. The product's simplified and reliable design, which was a finalist for the 1994 APEX Product

Development Excellence Award,* also had a sizeable impact on downstream processes, as evidenced by sharply reduced floor space requirements and inventory levels that dropped from the 60 to 75 days typical for such instruments to 2 to 4 days for the 34401A. And 15 months after production release, not a single ECN on this product was written to insure product shipment. Three years later (as of the writing of this book), the 34401A still sells for under $1,000.**

Chrysler's story is also sparkling. On the brink of insolvency a bare two years before, Chrysler earned more than Ford and GM combined in 1993. With operating profits of about $2 billion, it also topped all nine Japanese automakers. Not only is Chrysler turning out terrifically successful automobiles, it is changing the way vehicles are made. In 1989, it launched platform teams and has consistently bested its development time and budget targets since. About the same time, Chrysler ramped up standardization efforts, simultaneously cutting the number of options it offered; the net effect was a reduction in special order delivery time from 70 to 33 days. And customer selection never suffered. Costs are down, margins are up and so is Chrysler's popularity. It's designing smart—with the customer *and* the corporation in mind.

United Electric Controls Company (UE), the company where variety effectiveness and the VEP methodology were developed, tells of similar (as well as other orders of) success. First, armed with a clearer understanding of true costs, UE is marketing *existing* products more aggressively *before* taking steps to broaden its line. Products once thought "too costly" have achieved a resurgence in volume, increasing economies of scale, and better utilizing available production resources. Secondly,

---

* APEX: American Product Excellence is an annual product development award. The APEX award comes later in the life of new products, with criteria related to sales, quality track record, and profitability, in addition to those related to design and performance. For more information, contact award sponsor: Management Roundtable, Boston, MA 02215, telephone 1-800-338-2223.

** Special thanks to Mark D. Balley, Product Marketing Engineer at HP Loveland, for materials and clarification on the 34401A multimeter. For further details on the 34401A project, see Robert A. Williams, *Concurrent Engineering Delivers on its Promises: Hewlett-Packard's 34401A Multimeter,* in *Successful Implementation of Concurrent Engineering Products and Processes,* edited by Sammy G. Shine (New York: Van Nostrand Reinhold, 1994).

new product development now focuses more clearly on *new* products rather than revised versions of older products. Prior to VEP, engineering resources were frequently tied up developing product extensions which ultimately cannibalized existing sales while, at the same time, increasing variety of parts. Products developed at UE today typically fill a new niche rather than overlapping current sales. Scarce engineering resources are deployed with a greater assurance of return. Finally, attempts to manage costs on new and existing products have proved more fruitful since the advent of VEP. Consideration of true costs has led to more robust designs with fewer parts and processes. Emphasis on achieving economies of scale (which recognize Variety Costs) have improved inventory turns and gross profit. Products developed since the introduction of VEP have 20 percent to 60 percent fewer parts that older products. Prior to VEP, conventional wisdom equated variety with customer selection. Today, UE employees realize that through proper management of variety, the selection of end products and services to the customer can be greater than ever, while the base of component parts and processes is continually reduced.

VARIETY EFFECTIVENESS—WHY IT IS RIGHT FOR YOU

VEP is not a hard sell for companies for whom proliferating products and part inventories have become a burning issue. Resources are tight and launch activity is high. To them it makes sense. No company wants to "re-invent the wheel"—the latch, knob, cover, screw, switch assembly, face plate, or engine. They know that anytime they avoid re-invention, un-utilized resources can be harnessed for other gains, and the results go straight to the bottom line.

In fact, many companies are engaged in some facet of the VEP process. Some are upgrading their classification systems and part type analysis through Group Technology. Others are simplifying their product structures and facilitating assembly operations through value analysis/value engineering and/or through Design for Manufacturability and Design for Assembly. Still others are engaged in cutting their parts inventory and reducing their processes through cell design and one-piece flow. And many businesses are minimizing control points through paperwork simplification.

A UNIFIED FIELD

Many companies are doing many things to improve their products. But few are tying all these together into a single unifying strategy such as VEP. Because these efforts are not united, their full value and benefit may elude the enterprise. Furthermore, some companies inadvertently exacerbate the situation by applying excellent improvement techniques but in an isolated manner. An already-mentioned case in point is fragmented use of value analysis/value engineering for reducing Functional Costs on individual products while unintentionally triggering variety across the product universe.

Any effort done in isolation cannot maximize its potential value to the organization. The reverse is more often the case and its price is often exorbitant and needless cost. Nick Vanderstoop, synchronous administrator for the Canadian division of one of the world's largest automakers, discovered a 40 percent redundancy across 240 development projects. Though the duplication was quickly curtailed once discovered, Vanderstoop was moved to observe: "Products, parts, projects! They sprout in a corporation like fins on a leviathan. Some of them propel you forward, but lots of them paddle in the opposite direction—backwards. When you get too many going backwards, the company is heading for a dead-end and, most of the time, doesn't know why. It's just too darn big to keep track of everything that's happening on its huge body." Without a unified approach, efforts may "create" improvement but it is not integrated.

A similiar need for unity recently surfaced in the engineering department of a wildly successful electronics company on the West Coast. For over a decade, this company, with over sixty thousand employees and billions of dollars in annual sales, has been cashing in on huge cost savings by simplifying its product structures through DFMA technologies. Its leading-edge products continue to win customers and awards. But a company Engineering VP recently confided that, despite an outstanding product track record, the company still lacks an overall and unifying approach to product expansion. There is no formal, behavior-based system that ensures that the company's sizeable DFMA investment is maximized. The VP commented on the situation, beginning with the matter of carrying over/sharing parts:

"Whether parts get carried over still depends on who's the engineer or what the preferences of the team are. It's never a matter of routine. We just don't have any formal practices in place to get us to do it. And we also haven't learned how to leverage off someone else's work in a systematic, disciplined way. Not yet, anyway.

"This is an engineering-driven company. Creativity is in our blood. Plus we're really de-centralized. Everyone likes to do their own thing. That's what they are used to. Yes, we're heavy into DFMA and it's working great, but there really isn't anything right now to prod us to look at the issue of variety from a wider perspective than just the product sitting in front of us."

We wonder what other opportunities this flourishing company may be missing, or not maximizing, and what the genuine profit potential of the organization is.

Indeed, we know of many organizations that have not yet learned to leverage off the good efforts they are making. The policy and marketing arenas are particularly neglected. It is equally rare to see specific improvement practices linked up and integrated, so that the enterprise moves from strength to strength. Without a unified and systematic approach, companies can miss what they have nearly in their grasp—the payoff.

Designing *for* the bottom line is what it is all about—designing products and designing the organization for the payoff, maximum profitability. This unity of design requires a level of integration that allows all facets of the organization to work together, in harmony and mutual support. The tangible result is more productivity and more profit. But the intangible effects are as powerful—more sense, more flow, more ease—in short, a smart, involved, and spirited enterprise.

More and more companies are beginning to view themselves holistically—as a unity of effort—and not merely as a container for the disparate functions called departments. They know that it is not enough to be linked together by demand. Because organizations are dynamic systems, improvement techniques must be connected to the larger issues of the organization as an aggregate.

MAKING THE CHANGE: HIGH-LEVEL IMPLEMENTATION ISSUES

It has probably not been too many days since you heard about some great new method that will work miracles in your company *if*—you are cautioned—if it is implemented "accordingly to plan." That usually means someone else's plan. We present no such caution about VEP. If you think VEP is a question of *all the way* or no way, you are wrong. The day of the one-size-fits-all improvement strategy is gone. You probably already tried that with SPC, JIT, Baldrige, or some other system. Sometimes, the soup got spoiled.

The reality is that most "new" improvement strategies are waiting to get implemented in companies that are already *over*-implemented. Many of these companies have become the "lean organizations of the 90s"—and proud of it! But that's the point: How can a lean organization absorb yet another system, no matter how "right" it is? How can a maxxed-out staff implement yet more improvement? What does a company do when it is so lean that it can't absorb the very solution it knows it desperately needs?

In the discussion that follows, we want to present you with some things to consider as you think about what to "do" about variety effectiveness and the promise of a VEP implementation.

Maximize Your Selection

VEP is about maximizing customer selection. In keeping with that, we say to you: Customize VEP to your own purpose and intention. If you are interested in a *deep-dive* implementation of VEP, know that it could take six to ten months or more, depending on your organization's maturity, size, culture, level of internal complication, *and* classification system. In deep-dive, you work to simultaneously build the understanding and practice of variety effectiveness throughout the company. During the implementation, VEP teams actively attack negative variety even as they structure in a new awareness and new ways of thinking; values and practices get internalized.

The *select* approach, on the other hand, can be very selective. It may mean concentrating on a single product line. Or, it may mean simply conducting a series of VEP Awareness Sessions to do just that—raise the awareness of effective variety across the organization. This can be a very effective starting point. Initiate awareness, then let it trickle down into improvement efforts that people and their departments can do on their own. Gradually, awareness gains strength, and cross-functional activity begins to surface up from that grass root activity.

Gauge Your Absorbency Levels

Whether you go deep-dive or select, one of your keys to success is in first recognizing that people and organizations can absorb only as much as they can absorb. This is a crucial understanding. So you need to determine your absorbency level and that of your group or company *before* you commit to an implementation level. In the here-and-now, what level of improvement can your group actually handle? Leave the home-run scenarios at the door. Stay rooted in your *actual* reality—your reality now.

Culture Is Not the Enemy: Behavior Is

Someone once said, "It's a mistake to ignore culture, but it's a worse mistake to make it the principal target of change."

A company's culture does not necessarily have to change in order for change to happen. What needs to change is people's awareness and their understanding. Out of that emerges new behaviors—behaviors that make sense and are tied to things that really matter. Improvement springs out of that, and the culture shifts in response.

In presenting the principles of variety effectiveness and VEP in this book, we hope to provide you with a template—a template for change. We are not out to change your culture. We are out to create a shift in thinking, in awareness, and in understanding. We believe that, out of this, changes in behaviors and practices will follow. You and your company will shift, naturally, into more practices that advance effective variety in your organization as understanding increases.

Most companies drawn to VEP are in their second or third generation of improvement and looking for the next stretch goal. They have done quality. They have done teams. They have an organizing strategy. For their next step, they want a process that is sufficiently congruent with existing programs to make an extension into it natural and logical. They can afford to be aggressive—they have the infrastructure. They have no intention of dropping their current efforts but look, instead, to weave the new into the existing, build on the strengths of both, and keep the improvement momentum going. Their culture is doing just fine.

It's Work!

This is another cut on the previous discussion on determining the "right size" for your VEP implementation and "customizing your selection."

You'll remember that VEP's deep-dive implementation has two distinct components. First, clean up the past: Set up viable classification systems; review and revise your policies and formal and informal practices; get rid of the unwarranted variety in parts, products, production and nonproduction processes, and control points that exist right now in the organization; root out the internal triggers of negative variety, strengthen the causes of positive variety, and determine the balance point called "effective variety" that is valid for your company.

Second, prevent: Monitor the master lists; assign border guards to gatekeep new part variations, processes, and control points. This phase is easier when and if the cleanup is already done. But you can start with prevention first. Certainly, if anything gives a company pause before committing to VEP comprehensively, it is the cleanup phase and the level of time and people resources it can require. So, unless you are aiming for comprehensiveness, it can make sense to start out building prevention practices.

Then again, if yours is a naturally hardworking company, driven by the puritan ethic and with a habit of rising to a challenge, you may be ready to take the deep-dive and "go for it." VEP will work you hard, but the methodology will keep you focused and keep the momentum building, one reduction after another. Plugged into VEP's systematic approach, you and your company will experience great satisfaction in the near term— and huge cost savings and dramatic jumps in profit margins later on.

The willingness to "go for it"—VEP—is as much a decision as a state of readiness. The best way for VEP to happen is for the top people in the company to publicly state, "We're gonna do this!"—and stay visible. High-profile commitment gets and keeps others on board. If your company's thought-leaders and visionaries have accepted the need for the kind of change VEP is designed to create, you are on your way! And if you happen to be a leader in your company, remember to turn over authority to the teams when you turn over responsibility.

If, on the other hand, managers hesitate in the face of "all that work," or don't "see" parts variation as a problem, but you do, start with a small pilot on a closely defined line of products. Let VEP work its magic within those constraints. Adopting a *slow-and-grow* approach can help you build your credibility and support; with those, you are in a better position to extend your effort into the next and wider cycle.

Improvement Fatigue

Certain organizations will not be able to connect with the VEP challenge. In some cases this will be due to a lack of corporate will. While the company may, on some level, know that the only way to rid the system of complexity, congestion, and unwarranted cost is through deep VEP cleaning, clarification, and reduction, management may simply *not* want to make that level of effort. There are often valid reasons for this. After years of effort and commitment to quality and productivity improvement, the company may be suffering from improvement fatigue. JIT, TQM, *poka-yoke*, SMED, Malcolm Baldrige Quality Award, cell design, kaizen, teams, ISO certification—the list of improvement interventions grows longer every year. While the vast majority of such methods are good and many are excellent, the notion of "yet another improvement program" can be overwhelming.

Low Key = High Effect

In more cases than not, it is not advisable to introduce exciting new improvement methods like VEP with too much fanfare. Big programs that make big promises sometimes result in big disappointments. After the initial buy-in and groundwork are in place, do a low-key launch. Begin by building a common awareness. Introduce employees to VEP principles, concepts, and models of "variety effectiveness." Make sure to conduct awareness sessions for as many functions as possible, especially for operations where you can get a big boost from the hourly personnel who have to deal with the day-to-day effects of unwarranted parts variation in the form of congestion, frustration, searching, mistakes, changes, and delays.

Your Choice

Whichever genre of company yours falls closest to, understand that VEP, in its most comprehensive form, stretches across a broad spectrum of effort. Reaping its sizeable and dramatic cost benefits will take work, whether your company is 5, 10 or 60 years old. Give pause before embracing this "latest" best and consider what your company really needs at this time. Can you afford another improvement initiative at this time? Have you digested and integrated the last one? Are people stretched beyond caring? What are your options for getting started without upsetting the status quo or constraining your production schedule?

We do not advocate attacking organizational complexity through another complex solution. If you are drawn to VEP, consider the principles and issues raised in this book and enter the process where it will best serve your own company's purposes.

ONE MORE TIME: WHY VEP?

The ecology of the marketplace is marked by explosive global rivalry, rapid breakthroughs in product technology, wide fluctuations in raw material prices, and design-to-price competition. The goal isn't just to sell more product. The goal is to make more profit, too. But total value and total cost are often at loggerheads.

This paradox cannot be resolved by stemming the flow of new products. This not only does *not* solve the problem but will likely sink the enterprise. The only solution is to understand and eliminate the true causes of cost and maximize true value for the customer. You begin by dismantling the layers of complication that cover and choke the infrastructure.

VEP is not just the latest corporate recovery program, promising to make your company the biggest and brightest. VEP is an improvement approach that systematically addresses long-hidden sources of corporate dis-ease—cost, complexity, and congestion. This dis-ease enters the company system much further upstream than anyone ever before suspected. It enters at the point of product conception and infects one process after another as it moves through the organization on its way to the end-user. No one is safe. No departmental function escapes.

The real goal of VEP and this book, *Smart, Simple Design*, is to create a shared understanding of the problem and its solutions. VEP is too important a technology for companies to ignore because of battle fatigue. The fact that ineffective variety is not only *not* inevitable but avoidable means that organizations must systematically head off the negative aftermath of new product introduction *before* it takes root. Companies need an approach that will help control and then reduce their parts inventory and dismantle existing complexity from the inside, and they need to do this even while they initiate new practices and policies that prevent negative variety from recurring. When you've done this, your company is positioned to grab genuine competitive advantage. Then you are truly designing products for the bottom line.

GLOSSARY

Activity-Based Costing (ABC): A system of cost accounting that aligns closely with the objectives and activities of lean production, providing information about total cost and the actual consumption of company resources linked to so-called product "cost-drivers" (e.g., number of purchase orders, customer orders, engineering change notices (ECNs), material moves, machine setups, tools issued to shop floor, product insertions, manual soldering tasks, products shipped); can provide a picture of product costs radically different from data generated by GAAP/traditional accounting systems.

Attribute: Any property, quality, value, or characteristic of a part, service, or activity.

BOM (Bill of Material): A list of the constituent parts of a product or assembly.

CADCAM (computer-aided-design/computer-aided manufacturing): A software-driven system that integrates computers into the entire production cycle, from design to fabrication.

Cell Design: A system of shop-floor layout that groups a number of different machines together (in a center or cell), enabling all production tasks to be completed with practically no movement of materials, people, or tooling.

CIM (Computer Integrated Manufacturing): A software-driven manufacturing system in which all processes are integrated and controlled by computer, enabling all personnel—product designers and engineers, planners, schedulers, shop-floor foremen, and accounting—connected with the process to use the same data.

Control Costs (C-Costs): One of VEP's three categories of True Cost; refers to costs associated with task and information transactions that support the other two VEP cost categories—Variety Costs and Function Costs; includes costs associated with drafting, ordering, buying, inspecting, transporting, storing, and machine and facility maintenance; roughly equivalent to indirect costs or overhead in scope and variety.

Control Point: Any transaction—paper, electronic, or otherwise— which supports the design, procurement, sorting, retrieval, handling, production, assembly, or inspection of parts (including both non-production and production functions).

Deep-Dive Approach: In VEP, a comprehensive, company-wide approach to achieving variety effectiveness in an organization; supported by a full complement of VEP teams, with immediate and measurable results within 30 to 90 days, and more widespread improvements over a period of 5 to 12 months; compare with the *Select Approach*.

DFM (Design for Manufacturability): A software-driven system that assists companies so that they can design, manufacture, and assemble their products in the least time and at the least cost.

Disinflation: A macro-economic phenomenon that is characterized by rising customer demand and falling product prices; the opposite of inflation (rising consumer demand *and* rising prices); to combat disinflation, companies launch aggressive cost-cutting because they can no longer achieve profit margins by raising prices.

Ease of Assembly (VAT-4): One of VEP's six analytical techniques; seeks to ensure that all constituent parts which have been upgraded through the other five VATs (VEP analytical tools) are also easy to assemble.

Economic Order Quantity (EOQ): A type of fixed order quantity used when making or purchasing items; reflects the minimum amount of items that need to be produced to absorb acquisition and carrying costs.

Effective Variety (also Variety Effectiveness): The extent to which the variety represented in new products builds profits. Effective variety is the balance point between customer-driven (positive) variety and internally triggered (negative) variety; as the company rids itself of the negative causes of variety, this point of balance shifts increasingly in favor of the positive. Effective variety means achieving customer-driven variety at the *least* cost.

Fail-Safe/*Poka-Yoke* Device: A physical device (mechanical, electronic, or otherwise) used to 100 percent inspect a part or product at, or near, the source of its fabrication and/or assembly in order to reduce or eliminate the possibility of a defect, or of an error that may lead to a defect.

Function Costs (F-Costs): One of VEP's three cost categories; refers to costs that are generated as the company furnishes a product with its required functions through parts specifications, values, and dimensions. F-Costs are triggered in the product development process.

GAAP (Generally Accepted Accounting Principles): The traditional approach to cost accounting, codified in the 1930s, and still widely in use today; tends to mask complexity and ballooning parts inventories.

GAAP Definition of Profit: The difference between product price and product cost.

GAAP Definition of Product Cost: Material costs + labor costs + overhead costs.

Industrial Designer (a.k.a. Stylist): Person responsible for conceptualizing and pre-inventing all aspects of a new product—its function, geometry, style, and visual impact; primary focus is realizing the needs of the customer in product form.

Ineffective Variety: The condition that arises in an organization when negative variety outweighs positive variety; signifies that efforts to rid the company of negative (internally triggered) variety can be strengthened; even when strengthened, some degree of ineffective variety may continue to exist temporarily due to momentary technological or budgetary constraints.

Internally Triggered Variety: Negative variety; variety that results from policies, practices, or requirements internal to the organization and *not* from the customer; is the opposite of customer-driven (positive) variety.

Kanban: A visual pull system for parts usage, used to create and ensure minimum levels of WIP and inventory; a supporting methodology, used in conjunction with JIT, cells, and lean production.

Labor Cost: A GAAP term referring to company expenditures incurred in providing the manpower, mechanization, and automation required to convert a parts list (BOM) into the desired level of product; in GAAP, a direct cost.

Least Cost Sum: The total cost figure that represents the least amount of company resources needed to achieve a specific outcome, such as a new product.

Material Cost: A GAAP term referring to the purchase price of each component part or raw material that a product requires, as listed on the Bill of Material (BOM) of that product; in GAAP, a direct cost.

Modularity (VAT-2): One of VEP's six analytical techniques; seeks to combine multiple parts into single units or sub-assemblies that are interchangeable within and across product lines, thereby decreasing total cost and increasing the possibility of creating new products by using already existing units or modules.

MRP (Material Resource Planning): A software-driven method for planning, scheduling, and forecasting all the resources needed in the manufacturing process.

Multifunctionality and Synthesis (VAT-3): One of VEP's six analytical techniques; *Multifunctionality* seeks robust design, formulating product structures that include only the minimum number of parts needed to fulfill required functions, with each part serving as wide a range of functions as possible; *Synthesis* seeks to extend product robustness by using new materials, production technologies, or structural concepts that allow previously separated parts to be merged, collapsed, or eliminated.

Negative Variety: Internally triggered variety; any variation that is not in direct response to a customer demand, request, or interest, that is not customer-driven; adds cost, not value; results in escalating organizational complexity and parts inventories.

New England Farmhouse Effect: A VEP analogy to express the similarity between the unplanned and haphazard expansion of a company's product offerings and the way a farmhouse tends to spread—in any shape and direction, as needed at the time.

Non-Value-Adding Activity (NVA): Waste; usually divided into seven categories (Seven Deadly Wastes) of non-value-adding activities: (1) making defects, (2) overproducing, (3) overprocessing, (4) material handling, (5) motion, (6) delays, and (7) making inventory. Also includes opportunity loss.

Overhead Cost: A GAAP term referring to a group of expenditures that are allocated across all products on a formulaic basis; an indirect cost; includes depreciation on equipment, heat, light, power, taxes, research and development costs, maintenance costs as well as salaries and wages for operations-support personnel and fringe benefits for direct labor and operations-support personnel.

Part: One of the discrete, constituent elements into which a product can be physically separated.

Parts Attribute Template: In VEP, a grid for capturing the characteristics (attributes) of a part which engineers have identified as primary and necessary for making sound VEP-based decisions when developing new products; such templates are developed for each part in the company's part universe; used by the VEP Part Type Analysis Team in developing a VEP-capable parts classification system.

Positive Variety: Variation that is customer-driven and, as such, directly linked to a verifiable customer interest or demand; adds value and increases sales but does not add unwarranted costs.

Process: A sequence of tasks, steps, or operations that are performed in order to produce a specific production or non-production outcome.

Product: A group of elements or parts that, when fabricated or assembled, becomes a unit of function that fulfills pre-planned customer requirements.

Product Engineer: Person responsible for realizing the form, fit, and function of the product concept that the industrial designer creates; specifies a product's geometry (geometric functionality) within given budgetary constraints.

Quality Function Deployment (QFD): A method for developing a product plan that objectively and systematically translates customer demands into specific design targets, product functions, and quality and cost criteria so that the resultant product not only satisfies the user but is profitable for the company.

Quantity-on-Hand (QOH): The exact quantity of material or parts that is currently in-house, available for use, and not otherwise scheduled.

Quick Changeover (QCO): The process by which machine tooling for making one product is removed at the end of a production run and replaced with tooling for a new product; QCOs allow companies to produce in smaller batches than required by an EOQ (economic order quantity) approach; QCO time target = nine minutes or less; a.k.a. SMED (Single-Minute-Exchange-of-Dies).

Range (VAT-5): One of VEP's six analytical techniques; a statistical measure of dispersion (spread) of a group of values that share some common observable characteristic that shows the difference between the largest and smallest of those values and includes all the values along the way; used in VEP to identify and minimize redundancies and overlaps (or near overlaps) in variations in parts, products, product lines, and processes.

Select Approach: In VEP, a tactical (or limited) implementation approach to achieving variety effectiveness; typically involves a task force of experts that analyses single product lines for reduction; usually requires two to six months to complete; compare with the *Deep-Dive Approach*.

6-VATS: The six VEP analytical techniques (VATs) used by VEP analysis teams; VAT-1/Unique versus Shared; VAT-2/Modularity; VAT-3/Multifunctionality and Synthesis; VAT-4/Ease of Assembly; VAT-5/Range; and VAT-6 Trend (see individual listings for definitions).

Statistical Process Control (SPC): A method for gauging the likelihood that the output from a process will fall within acceptable limits; well-known SPC tools include checksheet, cause-and-effect diagram, bar graphs, scatter diagram, and other assorted graphing techniques.

3-View Analysis: VEP's central analytical process for streamlining the company's product line, simplifying product structures, and minimizing part counts; analysis work is divided between three VEP teams: View 1/Market Analysis, View 2/Product Structure Analysis, and View 3/Part Type Analysis.

Total Cost (according to VEP): Variety Costs + Function Costs + Control Costs.

Trend (VAT-6): One of VEP's six analytical techniques; seeks to identify the pattern and direction of a group of values that share some or several characteristics, laid out in some pre-set order (e.g., ascending value, descending value, etc.); used in ascertaining design, usage, customer, and/or other biases or tendencies in the product development arena.

Tri-Cost/True-Cost Model: VEP's perspective on product and total cost that differentiates between costs incurred by the company: (1) to achieve product function (Functional Costs or F-Costs), (2) to offer/make multiple products (Variety Costs or V-Costs), and (3) to support products, parts, and production and non-production processes (Control Costs or C-Costs).

True Cost: A VEP reference model that differentiates three categories of cost: Function Costs (F-Costs), Variety Costs (V-Costs), and Control Costs (C-Costs) in order to: (1) clarify the levels of organizational complexity brought about by negative variety, and (2) identify opportunities to reduce or dismantle that complexity; aligns more closely to the authentic causes of large part inventories than more traditional cost models found in GAAP; does not (and does not attempt to) provide an exact dollar reckoning of each cost per product.

Unique Versus Shared (VAT-1): One of VEP's six analytical techniques; seeks to identify those parts which are dedicated or unique (a.k.a. variable) and those which are shared or commonized (a.k.a. standardized, carried-over); seeks to minimize the number of unique parts and increase the number of shared or standardized parts.

Value-Adding Activity (VA): Activities that change/transform/convert company resources into a product or service—into something of value that the customer is willing to pay for.

Variety Costs (V-Costs): One of VEP's three cost categories; refers to costs that are triggered when a product line expands or diversifies, even if only one attribute of a single part changes; V-Costs can be customer-driven or internally triggered.

Variety Effectiveness (also Effective Variety): The extent to which the variety represented in new products builds profits; effective variety is the balance point between customer-driven (positive) variety and internally triggered (negative) variety; as the company rids itself of the negative causes of variety, this point of balance shifts increasingly in favor of the positive; variety effectiveness means customer-driven variety at the *least* cost.

VEP-Capable Classification System: A company database that houses information on parts and products that is accurate, relevant, complete, and accessible and that supports design and marketing decision making based on VEP goals and principles.

VEP: Variety Effectiveness Process®: A systematic, team-based methodology directed at maintaining or increasing customer selection while reducing negative variety in parts, processes, and control points and preventing its recurrence. VEP's goal is to lower costs dramatically and de-complicate systems while maximizing a company's ability to respond to the demands of the market.

VEP Parts Index: A matrix of information that delineates: (1) all part numbers by part type in the associated bills of material for a given model or product population, (2) the number of times each part number occurs across that population, and (3) the result of *multiplying* the total number of occurrences *times* the total number of parts in that population. This index model is based on a definition of variety as *the total quantity of parts handled.*

Work-in-Process (WIP): All the materials, parts, and subassemblies that exist on the plant floor between the release of raw material and finished-goods inventory.

X-Type Company: A company that practices effective variety, as evidenced by steadily rising sales, coupled with parallel decreases in costs and part counts.

Y-Type Company: A company that does not practice variety effectiveness, as evidenced by escalating part counts and part inventories— even in the face of increasing sales.

VEP RESOURCES

VEP CONSULTING AND TRAINING SERVICES

Smart, Simple Design is written to alert companies to the link between variety effectiveness and increased profitability. If you are considering VEP for your organization, Quality Methods International Inc. (QMI/Boston, MA) offers VEP seminars, training courses, and on-site consulting to support your implementation. For more information, please contact QMI:

> Dr. G. D. Galsworth
> Quality Methods International Inc.
> Post Office Box 1031
> Cambridge, Massachusetts 02140
> Phone   617-489-9909
> Fax   617-489-6276

VEP SOFTWARE

In conjunction with QMI, International TechneGroup Incorporated (Milford, OH) has developed a VEP software package, utilizing standard, off-the-shelf PC-based products to support the VEP process, including: voice of the customer technology; data analysis for capturing and evaluating product, part, and process data; product analyzers for bills of material;

attribute template technology for parts standardization; team management support for planning and organizing the project; decision support for itemizing, evaluating, and coordinating team proposals, and for selecting and scheduling the implementation of approved proposals; and a report writer for sharing updates, time lines, and results. Other PC-based software tools (with network capability) can also be included to meet any special company or team requirements. For more information, contact:

R. Scott Leckie
International TechneGroup Incorporated
5303 DuPont Circle
Milford, Ohio 45150
Phone   513-576-3900
Fax   513-576-3994
Internet rel@iti-oh.com

INDEX

ABOUT THE AUTHOR

Gwendolyn D. Galsworth is founder and president of Quality Methods International Inc. (QMI), a consulting and training firm based in Massachusetts that specializes in systematic improvement approaches, including the visual workplace, variety effectiveness, strategic matrix policy deployment (*hoshin kanri*), and team problem solving.

Previous to forming QMI, Dr. Galsworth was Director of Business Development at Productivity Inc. and principal developer of such core Japanese-based methods as visual control systems and the 5-Ss, zero defects through *poka-yoke*/failsafe systems, and *CEDAC®* (cause and effect diagram with addition of cards). She was also instrumental in adapting *TPM* (*Total Productivity Maintenance*), *SMED* (single minute exchange of dies), and *TEIAN* (Japanese suggestion approach) for western audiences.

With over a dozen years in the field, Dr. Galsworth has assisted companies, large and small, to accelerate their rate of improvement and become superior competitors. These clients include Alcoa Aluminum/Australia, Continental Can, Crompton Greaves/India, Culinar Foods/Canada, Furon Company, General Motors/Canada, Hamilton Standard, Honeywell, ITT/Aerospace, Motorola, Marada Industries, Packard Electric, Pratt & Whitney, Prince Corporation, Simpson Timber, TVS Sundaram Clayton/India, and United Electric Controls Company.

A two-term Malcolm Baldrige examiner, Dr. Galsworth is an expert in Total Quality Management/TQM and frequent speaker on quality and productivity improvement. She periodically leads study missions to some of Japan's finest production facilities.